Prescribing and Mental Health Nursing

D1513367

Counselling and Mental Health

Prescribing and Mental Health Nursing

by

Austyn Snowden

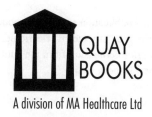

QUAY
BOOKS

A division of MA Healthcare Ltd

Quay Books Division, MA Healthcare Ltd, St Jude's Church, Dulwich Road,
London SE24 0PB

British Library Cataloguing-in-Publication Data
A catalogue record is available for this book

© MA Healthcare Limited 2008
ISBN-10: 1-85642-363-8
ISBN-13: 978-1-85642-363-2

Printed by Ashford Colour Press, Gosport, Hants

Contents

Preface

The growth of mental health nursing scholarship emanating from mental health nurses has been one of the most remarkable developments in mental health care research in the past few decades. The current position contrasts strongly with that which existed less than half a century ago when 'mental nursing', as it was then called, was deemed to have no intellectual basis and to be carried out by people who were fit to do no more than blindly obey orders and adhere to rigid routines. The skills of mental nursing were largely transferred from one generation to the next through an oral culture, and little was written down. Those who taught mental nursing had no specialist knowledge, but were either general nurses or psychiatrists who imparted what they wanted nurses to know and do, as opposed to how nurses might respond to the identified needs of people with mental health problems. Their focus was predominantly on mental illness, on symptoms and aetiology, while little or nothing was taught about how to manage it or, indeed, to prevent it from occurring in the first place, or recurring after an initial episode.

It is not a question of blaming these early teachers and nurses, but rather of recognising where we were in order to assess our progress since. In my long years associated with varying aspects of mental health nursing, I have always been impressed by the brightness, sensitivity and compassion of mental health nurses and, if given the opportunity, I believe that they are capable of doing far more than the 'system' and the culture of mental health services often allows them to do. In fact, the quantity and quality of scholarship in recent years coming from mental health nurses is nothing short of astounding. This encompasses research, literature, service development and policy making. While managers at different levels assume responsibility for directing health care services, it falls to nurses to deliver the bulk of mental health services in the UK and elsewhere. Far away from policy making, nurses have to make difficult decisions, take responsibility for the service and endeavour to provide care for people in an effective and tailored way.

Despite the growth of other mental health professional groups, and of the diversification of services in recent years, nurses remain the backbone of mental health service delivery, and were it not for them, patients and clients today would be receiving a much poorer service. Long ago, astute observers of mental health care such as Alexander Walk and Professor Michael Shepherd, eminent psychiatrists, pointed out that it was usually the case that 'progressive' policies were written by senior psychiatrists and civil servants, but implemented by nurses (Nolan, 1993). It is now becoming clear that the structure and culture of organisations have historically been responsible for repressing the potential that exists within nursing. Mental health services have been bedevilled by rigid professional boundaries and professional territorialism, by unbreakable managerial hierarchies and a defensive culture that resisted any attempts to contest the status quo.

In *Modernising Nursing Careers* (Department of Health, 2006), the Chief Nursing Officer for England pointed out that a prerequisite for the modernisation of the NHS was the modernisation of the nursing profession. It is now obvious that service users are capable of doing more for themselves than was ever imagined in the past, and so are mental health nurses. Restraining the potential of health care providers by role specifications and titles is a sure means of limiting service provision, while supporting them to do more than was once expected of them liberates them and enhances the services they provide.

I am convinced that one of the most imaginative developments in recent years has been the introduction of non-doctor prescribing. This has opened the way for the creation of new and expanded services, to faster access to health care, and to combining assessment with information provision, health promotion and assisting people to make healthy choices about the ways in which they live their lives. For mental health nurse prescribing to have the impact of which it is capable, we require nurses who are strategic thinkers, enthusiastic teachers, knowledgeable about the context in which services are provided, and analytical thinkers, able to determine what makes medication beneficial for service users and their carers. Various books have emerged over the past few years to address these issues, but I believe that Austyn Snowden's makes a significant contribution, particularly in putting prescribing into a much wider context than has previously been explored. In this one book, he manages to address the history of mental health care medication, the evolution of mental health nursing, the types of conditions for which medication is used and the circumstances under which people taking medication can do so safely.

I know that readers will enjoy this book. They will appreciate the breadth of the author's scholarship and will be impressed by the analysis he undertakes in every chapter. He notes that among the many criticisms which have been levelled at nurse prescribing, attacks on the quality of training and education have been persistent. As was the case in the past when nurses with no experience of mental health care delivered training to people destined to work with mentally ill patients, so today, many lecturers who teach on prescribing courses are far removed from practice; some have no experience of mental health care, while others focus solely on theory and skills. Mental health nurses have complained about a lack of 'big picture' literature about nurse prescribing. The publication of this book should help them. They now have a text that recognises that there is an ongoing and certainly unresolved debate about the appropriate role of medication in mental health care, and which looks at issues surrounding the treatment of schizophrenia and bipolar disorders, depression and anxiety and many of the common mental health problems presenting in various services today. The author draws on a variety of sources, including the research literature and his personal experience.

I commend this book to all concerned with the improvement of mental health services, and particularly to those concerned with medication. Each chapter contains a wealth of information. Taken as a whole, the book provides a rich critical enquiry into prescribing practice. I would urge all course tutors to make it required reading on their courses. It should also be available within practice settings for staff to access; and users and carers who are invited to contribute to service development and evaluation should also be able to see it.

Finally, I salute the new generation of mental health nurse researchers and writers and I am absolutely confident that they will take the delivery of mental health services to new heights.

References

Department of Health (2006) *Modernising Nursing Careers – Setting the Direction.* London: Stationery Office (Gateway Ref 6950)

Nolan P (1993) *A History of Mental Health Nursing.* London: Chapman & Hall

Peter Nolan
Professor of Mental Health Nursing,
Staffordshire University

Acknowledgements

First of all thanks to Maria Anguita and Jessica Anderson, my editors, for commissioning this work in the first place and all their subsequent support. Thank you to all my colleagues who read and commented on earlier drafts of this book. Particular thanks go to Dr Alan Hughes who bravely read the whole thing. Dr Gary Boyd and Andrew Mackenzie pointed out some early errors in pharmacology for which I am very grateful. The expert educational views of Anita Neilsen and Ellen McCormick were highly valued as were those of Boyd Thomson, Dave Deady, Dr Jean Rankin, Jane Camp, Trish MacBride and Jai Seebaluck.

A special mention is reserved for Frank Newsum who painstakingly provided expert guidance on style, grammar and structure. Finally I would like to thank Professor Peter Nolan for taking such an interest and for writing the preface to the book. I am very proud to be associated with all these people. I retain sole responsibility for any errors which may remain, and all opinions expressed are my own.

Overview

Mental health nursing has not yet found the best way to engage with the expansion in prescribing rights. Despite being legally able to prescribe since 2003 very few mental health nurses have undergone training to do so. Many of those who have trained are not prescribing. Reasons for this are unclear, but one factor is undoubtedly the lack of a coherent lead on the subject. There is disagreement over whether or not prescribing fits with the current concept of mental health nursing. The 2006 national reviews of mental health nursing in both Scotland (Scottish Executive, 2006) and England (Department of Health, 2006) were ambivalent about prescribing in mental health nursing. They instead advocated the more traditional role of the mental health nurse as therapist and partner on an individual journey of recovery. While clearly expressing the zeitgeist this perspective does not leave much room for interventions which do not immediately appear to align with current concepts of recovery.

Yet while mental health nurses worry about whether and how to put prescribing into practice other nurses are just getting on with it. There is evidence that this is because other nurses feel positive regarding the impact of prescribing on practice whereas mental health nurses do not (Snowden, 2007). One of the more practical reasons for this may be that it is more complex to prescribe psychotropics than antibiotics or laxatives, for example. If this is true it may underpin the finding that mental health nurses do not feel the current independent prescribing course prepares them to prescribe psychotropics (Bradley et al, 2008). Should they therefore be administering them? This hints at a deeper disquiet with mental health nurses and medication management, supported by studies indicating inappropriate use (Baker et al, 2007) and inadequate knowledge (Davies et al, 2007) of administering PRN (*pro re nata*: 'as required') psychotropic medication.

So on the one hand prescribing seems to be philosophically incongruent with person-centred recovery models, and on the other hand psychotropic medication is very difficult to understand. It is no wonder then that many mental health nurses do not want to prescribe, and employers are reluctant to support those that do.

In order to explore and address this topic this book combines a historical and a practical approach. The first section unravels the origins of the current prescribing climate by looking in depth at current theories of psychotropic drugs, prescribing legislation and mental health nursing history. Combining these stories reveals a clear rationale as to why mental health nurses should therefore learn to prescribe. At the very least they should be familiar with the content of this book if they are to administer medication safely. Ninety-one percent of mental health inpatients take two or more drugs (Healthcare Commission, 2007) so disengagement from drug treatment is not an option.

The second section looks at practical prescribing considerations in mental health nursing by breaking prescribing decisions down into key questions. For example, how do you arrive at a diagnosis? When would you not prescribe an antidepressant? What is the worst that can happen if you do? Why? Highest quality evidence is provided throughout to illuminate these discussions.

References

Baker JA, Lovell K, Haris N (2007) Mental health professionals' psychotropic *pro re nata* (prn) medication practices in acute inpatient mental health care: A qualitative study *Gen Hosp Psychiatry* **29**: 163–8

Bradley E, Wain P, Nolan P (2008) Putting mental health nurse prescribing into practice. *Nurse Prescribing* **6**(1): 15–21

Davies SJC, Lennard MS, Ghahramani P, Pratt P, Robertson A, Potokar J (2007) PRN prescribing in psychiatric inpatients – potential for pharmacokinetic drug interactions. *J Psychopharmacol* **21**(2): 153–60

Department of Health (2006) *From Values to Action. The Chief Nursing Officer's Review of Mental Health Nursing*. Available from: http://www.dh.gov.uk/en/Publicationsandstatistics/Publications/PublicationsPolicyAndGuidance/DH_4133839 [Accessed 7 June 2007]

Healthcare Commission (2007) *Talking About Medicines: The Management of Medicines in Trusts Providing Mental Health Services*. London: Commission for Healthcare Audit and Inspection

Scottish Executive (2006) *Rights Relationships and Recovery*. Available from: http://www.scotland.gov.uk/Resource/Doc/112046/0027278.pdf [Accessed 14 December 2006]

Snowden A (2007) Is mental health nurse prescribing qualitatively different? *Nurse Prescribing* **5**(5): 66–73

Chapter summary

Section 1 sets the scene on how and why mental health nurses are now able to prescribe. This is achieved through integration of the histories of psychiatric medication development, mental health nursing and medication management. These areas are all covered in great depth elsewhere, and the purpose is not to go over the same ground, but rather to integrate these histories in a manner relevant to prescribing in mental health nursing. That is, the role of prescriber is best understood within context. Understanding what can be prescribed and what it is likely to do is simple on one level. Understanding the broader implications of prescribing decisions involves a deeper engagement with a wide range of different agendas. This is particularly relevant to the mental health nurse, who more than any other nurse practises in a complex world of competing philosophies.

Section 1 is split into three chapters as illustrated in *Figure 1*. The first chapter focuses on the biology of mental illness and the development of psychopharmacology, concluding with contemporary thinking about likely future developments. By illustrating the discovery of clinical application of psychotropic therapeutic agents some of the mystery will be removed from these substances. The element of luck and the role of empiricism emerge as major themes in this story.

The second chapter focuses on the history of mental health nursing. It starts by examining historic attitudes to the concept of madness and care of people suffering mental ill-health, before addressing some larger social factors which saw mental health nursing evolve from the 'basket man' to its modern form. The chapter notes that society has always sought to segregate deviation from the cultural norm, and always required people to police it. Mental health nurses have increasingly professionalised this role but remain public servants first and foremost. They have a long history of pragmatism as a result and are therefore comfortable with complex and competing agendas. In short, they have always been therapists and custodians. The latest manifestations of the mental health acts in both Scotland and England perpetuate this duality with the extension of authority to treat and detain sitting alongside the principle of offering care within 'least restrictive options'. I remember while a staff nurse in 1988 asking a person to return to an acute ward voluntarily or I would have to detain him under the mental health act of the time. This is pragmatism in action, which turns out to be a major theme of this story.

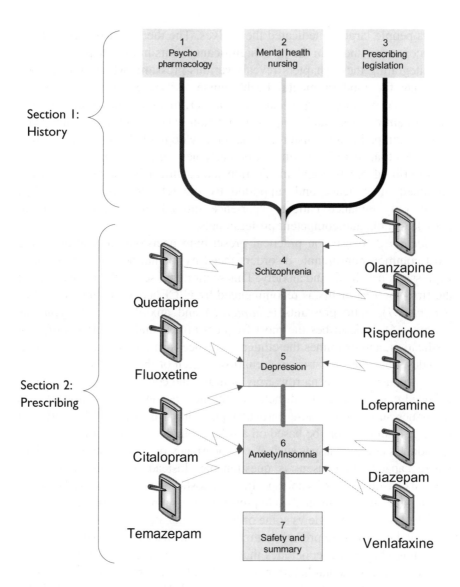

Figure 1. Overview of structure.

The third chapter looks at the history of prescribing and administering medication, beginning with the period when self-prescription of patent medicines was the norm through to medical domination as a consequence of opium regulation. This gives a background to understanding current legal, professional and ethical decisions and why these are now being made by nurses and other health professionals. A striking element of this story is that it is only since 1941 that the medical profession has controlled the prescription of drugs, following the legal creation of prescription only medications. Prior to this people largely medicated themselves. The themes of power, politics and economics underpin the most significant events in this chapter.

Integrating these chapters reveals various pressures which have helped to create the modern mental health nurse: a 'value for money', semi-professional working as advocate and partner, therapist and jailer, with the skills to aid recovery and the power to detain, who has now been handed a prescription pad to administer treatment many do not believe in. The section concludes that there is nothing particularly new in these dynamic tensions. If prescribing practice and medication management is demonstrably safe, grounded in evidence and supported by the relevant organisation, then it can only enhance patient experience through interaction with more knowledgeable and competent professionals.

Section 2 focuses on practical prescribing decisions in relation to the most common non-organic disorders faced by mental health professionals: depression, psychosis and anxiety. This section focuses on the prescribing of the first-line treatments as recommended by NICE, covering antipsychotics (*Chapter 4*), antidepressants (*Chapter 5*) and anxiolytics and hypnotics (*Chapter 6*). It describes the most frequent effects and side effects of each medication, and examines the clinical evidence for their claimed efficacy. It also describes the 'worst case' scenarios of each of these drugs.

By focusing on this narrow array of drugs and conditions in some detail it is hoped that this section will help practitioners become more confident with the issues surrounding these particular prescribing decisions. More difficult decisions can therefore be based on a solid grounding. That is, the book does not address complex issues such as polypharmacy or prescribing in situations where capacity to consent is questionable. Instead it discusses in detail general consultation skills and specific diagnostics within each area. These are transferable skills requisite to safe prescribing in more complex areas.

The last chapter reviews some of the latest debate and emerging research on mental health nurse prescribing in light of the discussions contained in the preceding chapters. It concludes that nurse prescribing will not be a career choice for every mental health nurse, and that there are many good reasons for this, from the practical to the philosophical. However, it also concludes that some patients will clearly benefit from the initiative as some already have, and outright rejection of the initiative is akin to putting a finger in the dyke. Non-medical prescribing is cheap, safe and effective and so politically, clinically and economically it is unstoppable.

As the book is initially taking a broad historical approach the terms insanity, madness, mental illness, lunacy and mental health problems all broadly refer to the same concept. This is to contextualise each discussion and use the terminology of the time. It is not meant to cause offence.

Dedication

For Mags and Molly with love

Section 1

A history in three parts

CHAPTER I

Psychopharmacology

This chapter discusses the emergence of psychopharmacology as a significant factor in the treatment of mental illness. Its role in enhancing the credibility of psychiatry and by association mental health nursing is discussed in *Chapter 3*. The focus here is specifically on the development of psychotropic substances and the associated quest of how to explain their observable actions. This has not been a smooth process and biological models of mental illness are still rejected completely by some thinkers. So before current biological models are discussed in any detail it is important to discuss why this is so.

Biological models of mental illness

Prescribing medication involves impacting on biology. That is, there is a biological change in the recipient which results in a change of state. It does not necessarily follow that there is a biological foundation of mental illness. It has been argued that mental illness is instead a construct of Western medicine designed to pathologise any behaviour considered abnormal. The concept of mental illness is just a metaphor for moral conflict (Szasz, 1961), a strategy for coping in a mad world (Porter, 2002) or a justification of medical power (Foucault, 1965). Administering medication is therefore ethically questionable. To support these perspectives critics point out that the American *Diagnostic and Statistical Manual* (the DSM) is developed by consensus as opposed to biology. That is, illnesses are not objectively measurable entities like stroke or cellulitis but creations of psychiatry. One result of this is that specific diagnoses can have entirely different causes. Each cause requires different treatment and thus the DSM does not indicate what treatment is necessary.

These arguments generally precede criticism of the expanding volume of psychiatric disorders. The DSM has grown from 134 pages in DSM-II to 934 pages in the latest revision, DSM-IV-TR. DSM-V is scheduled for 2011 (Moon, 2004), and consultation is well under way. The consensus required for inclusion of a particular disorder ultimately rests with a few individuals, who have attempted to include some contentious categories of mental illness in the past. For example the provisional category of masochistic personality disorder was omitted altogether in 1985 because of protests by feminist academics, although the watered down compromise category of self-defeating personality disorder made it into the appendix of DSM- III (Kutchins and Kirk, 1997). Some clinicians continue to use its criteria. Self-defeating personality disorder sought to define a pervasive pattern of self-defeating behaviour which resulted in the sufferer becoming attracted to doomed relationships and avoiding positive situations. The reason the category caused such furore was that opponents believed the category not only scientifically invalid, but sexist and dangerous. They feared it would be used as a justification for abusive behaviour (of men) by pathologising the victim. The feminists countered by introducing for consideration the category of delusional dominating personality disorder, a category which sought to pathologise the controlling and grandiose behaviour of its (male) sufferers. They believed this category demonstrated the invalidity of self-defeating personality disorder by holding a mirror up to its creators.

The most regularly cited example used to expose the politics of this classification system is homosexuality. Homosexuality was defined as a mental disease by the American Psychiatric Association until 1975, when it was removed by postal vote. Homosexuals effectively became powerful enough to lobby the 'disease' out of the manual. If mental illness were really an illness in the biological sense then the idea of deleting homosexuality or anything else from the categories of illness by having a vote would be absurd (Stevens, 1999). The inference is therefore that the current contents of the DSM may be seen as equally unsound at some future point, when society as a whole views the world differently. So why not view it as unsound now? The logical conclusion of this argument is that mental illness is not an illness. It is merely a question of values, of right and wrong, of appropriate versus inappropriate, and who holds the casting vote on these issues. This argument is generally taken to be a clear demonstration of the frailty of psychiatry's scientific aspirations. Statements such as the following subsequently follow in order to decry biological conceptions of mental health problems:

> *Contrary to what is often claimed, no biochemical, anatomical, or functional signs have been found that reliably distinguish the brains of mental patients.*
>
> Valenstein (1998: 125)

> *There is no evidence that any psychiatric or psychological disorder is caused by a biochemical imbalance.*
>
> Breggin (2000: 139)

These statements appear to lend support to the modern face of 'antipsychiatry'. They are written by people in pursuit of genuine clinical progress. However it is important to note they do not deny the existence of mental illness. Rather they say that the biological mechanisms underpinning it are poorly understood. This is different from saying they do not exist. If that were the case then cancer would not exist either, given its aetiology is also incompletely understood. Although the existence of mental illness is often contrasted with medical diagnoses to make the point that psychiatric diagnoses are less clear, the fact is that many apparently well-accepted medical diagnoses are also regularly revised. The definition of myocardial infarction is constantly under revision (Boersma et al, 2003). Incomplete understanding does not prevent attempts to alleviate suffering. Alleviating suffering is a primary goal of medicine (and psychiatry) and this process is as scientific as aetiology. No one would argue against alleviating physical pain in cancer and therefore the question of both its existence and purpose is not subject to moral scrutiny. However, consider depression. Should the fact that the biology of depression is unclear and actions of antidepressants poorly understood prevent people with depression from receiving the best possible medical attention?

Few would argue with this, yet some do, and this is the grey area of practice in which mental health nurses find themselves. This grey area has become a breeding ground for competing theories of mental distress, many of them initially plausible. For example some theorists suggest depression is an ancient adaptive response to adverse conditions (Stevens and Price, 2000). They suggest that if an individual is unsuccessful in a particular battle low mood reinforces a feeling of loss thereby preventing more serious damage occurring to the individual by trying again. On the face of it this appears to be a perfectly reasonable theory. Losing triggers a period of deep reflection in which the loser adapts, readjusts and creates new strategies. In other words, depression is natural. It is society that has changed leaving ancient responses inappropriate in modern times. Apparently an individual is much more likely to face losing situations on a regular basis today (Stevens and Price, 2000) and consequently has a greater chance of being depressed. So even if it is accepted that depression exists as a concept then medical intervention is still not required as the reaction is perfectly normal. Society needs to change to stop making us all feel depressed.

Evolutionary theories explaining mental illness are popular at present despite, or probably because they are impossible to test. That is, there are no available ancestors in which to demonstrate these hypothesised responses, nor any comparable ancient society in which to test them. The fact that untestable ideas like these can gain credence adds weight to the argument that nobody really understands depression but it does not mean each theory is worthy of equal consideration. Few dispute the existence of gravity for example, and therefore untestable contrary theories are sparse. However, this is because the theory of gravity is testable. If a theory of depression is to be meaningful then it also needs to be testable. That is, it is impossible to condemn or defend any construct in relation to untestable theories (Popper, 1959). For the purpose of further discussion it will be assumed that mental health distress exists within an individual and that this appears to have a biological component as both these factors can be demonstrated. A further assumption is that this may be treatable, although not necessarily via pharmacological means. A final assumption is that this should be treated if possible. This assumption is missing in some of the purist antipsychiatry philosophy. The next section therefore examines the evidence that has been gathered regarding the psychopharmacology of mental illness.

Psychopharmacology of mental illness

Here is a brief summary of psychiatry before chlorpromazine. Prior to the 1950s knowledge of the brain and its mode of action was limited. Drugs had little effect other than knocking people out, and therapeutic interventions were based primarily on psychosurgery or Freudian principles of psychotherapy. For example, barbiturates were given to highly disturbed patients with often fatal consequences. Even when administered safely relief was only temporary and often led to addiction. Over 40 000 lobotomies were performed in the USA, predominantly in the early 1950s. Dr Walter Freeman, part surgeon part showman performed over 3000 of them, and despite some partial successes did irreparable damage in many cases. President Kennedy's sister for example was permanently disabled as a result of Dr Freeman's procedure. In contrast to this anatomical approach psychiatry was broadly concerned with the inner workings of the mind and as a whole was equally as disinterested in pharmacology. This is the commonly held and often quoted view, and is only partially true.

For example, drugs had played a much bigger and more effective role than is generally acknowledged, and it is important to put later discoveries into context. People largely self-medicated for minor ailments including those that today would be considered within the realm of mental health care, e.g. 'nerves'. Understanding of how these remedies worked was limited relative to today, but congruent with the understanding of the time. Paul Ehrlich was the first scientist to coin the term 'receptor' to refer to a specific target for a chemical within the body, and proposed the receptor theory of drug action. He was also one of the first to discover a substance that selectively killed disease micro-organisms, winning the Nobel Prize for Physiology and Medicine in 1908. His drug, Salvarsan (also known as 606, as it was the 606th derivative of atoxyl to be tested), effectively cured the previously untreatable syphilis.

The safer antibiotics replaced this arsenic derivative in the 1940s, but Salvarsan is widely credited with initiating the era of chemotherapy, which subsumes the notion of targets for drugs. Ehrlich worked systematically with a team of researchers in search of what he called 'magic bullets' by testing the properties of hundreds of different analogues of atoxyl. This notion of the magic bullet has persisted and largely underpins current cultural knowledge of how drugs work. Consider advertisements for pain killers which 'target pain right where it hurts'. Researchers still look for magic bullets today, but thousands of times faster than Ehrlich due to computer-assisted technology. The principle is the same though. That is, they still start their search by testing as many potentially therapeutic chemicals as possible.

The early part of the 20th century was a period of great invention and progress in medicine, but psychiatry was not at the forefront. Gerhard Domagk discovered that the red dye Prontosil was active against streptococcal infections in 1932, and won the Nobel Prize for ushering in the era of sulphonamides. His daughter was his first patient, cured of septicaemia, which would have been otherwise fatal. Fleming, Florey and Chain more famously won the prize in 1945 for penicillin. Selman Waksman coined the word antibiotic and discovered streptomycin, which was the first agent effective against tuberculosis. This won him the Nobel Prize in 1952. Compare this with psychiatry. Three years earlier Moniz had been given the prize for discovering the therapeutic effect of lobotomy. It is easy to assume that psychiatry was going in a more anatomical than pharmacological direction in comparing these snapshots. However, although it is fair to say that psychiatrists did not achieve the breakthroughs their medical colleagues celebrated in the first part of the 20th century, they were not entirely without success.

For example, in the 19th century uric acid was thought to be a cause of a number of disorders including mood disorders later classified as manic depressive (Healy, 2002: 22). The theory was that mania may be a form of gout, hence the 19th century term 'gouty mania' (Reines, 1991). Given that lithium dissolves urates and urates are a product of uric acid the Danish neurologist Lange tried lithium with manic patients and found it to have a prophylactic effect. He treated hundreds of patients with a degree of success, as did William Hammond in New York. However, around 1900 the uric acid hypothesis was found to be completely wrong. Lithium treatment disappeared with it, having to be reinvented 50 years later fortuitously by Cade. In other words understanding why something works appears to be as important as the fact that it does work for people to maintain faith in it. The why in present understanding of psychopharmacology is largely provided by neuroscience, and will be discussed in detail shortly. First let me just give a quick example of why I think that if something works then that should still be the most important aspect of treatment (as long as it is safe), and this is where nurses have as big a role as anybody.

I was a staff nurse in 1989 in Bridlington, East Yorkshire taking part in treating a lady with sleep therapy. The lady was in her 60s, she was very well liked and a well-known patient to the services through multiple admissions. She generally presented with a degree of anxiety, then described as 'agitated depression'. On this particular admission her agitation was intractable, and she was in a constant state of motion and deep distress. Over a period of months she had failed to respond to any medication and subsequently failed to respond to ECT (eletroconvulsive therapy). She slept for minutes if at all and was highly distressed 24 hours a day. It was decided to try sleep therapy, a relic of much earlier times (Laborit et al, 1952).

Sleep therapy involved administering barbiturates regularly to maintain her in a coma-like state for a period of five days and nights. My job as night duty staff nurse was to check her vital signs every hour and to rouse her for her six hourly doses of barbiturates. I remember feeling that we were trying something unusual and desperate. Nevertheless, this lady's distress warranted desperate intervention, and I greatly admire the consultant who prescribed it. All I wanted was for it to work, and perhaps this would be a better story if it had. Four nights into the treatment I was checking her at 4 a.m., and as I took her blood pressure she opened an eye and looked at me. I said 'hello' and asked how she felt. She seemed to think about it for an eternity and finally said 'tense'. I have honestly never seen anybody less tense in my life, but knew there and then that this was not going to work, as her subjective experience of distress had not changed.

Although it did not work immediately she apparently spontaneously remitted a few weeks later and went home. Subsequent admissions revealed that she was very unhappy in her abusive marriage and could not express this at the time. I often wonder what would have happened had she been able to do so, and how and if we could have facilitated this. The point is, we did our best at the time, and we ended up attempting a treatment which would have been a staple of the treatment armoury 100 years ago. We did this not just because we wanted it to work but because we knew in some instances it did, despite not knowing why. All treatments are given based on a probability of them working. Chlorpromazine effectively sidelined a lot of pharmacological treatments in its wake, but to write them off would be to misrepresent the history. Insulin coma therapy (ICT) was used for 20 years before chlorpromazine eliminated it, and the science underpinning ICT was astute and empirical.

For example Healy (2002: 54) cites two studies which claim equal therapeutic efficacy for insulin coma therapy, barbiturate sleep therapy and chlorpromazine. He goes on to attribute some of this to a possible placebo effect, citing the excellent morale of the staff administering these sophisticated treatments. Nevertheless, he makes the over-riding point that the science for these treatments was sound. There is clearly an element of luck and teamwork in any discovery. Many investigators in the basic disciplines of chemistry, biochemistry, physiology, pharmacology, psychology, and toxicology as well as clinicians dealing with patients have all had a part to play in both discovering the remarkable therapeutic effects and the basic mechanisms of these psychoactive treatments.

Progress has largely been driven by astute clinical observation across disciplines rather than deductive biological understanding. This comes later and is integral to successful drug development, as is marketing it in the right place. That is, if the theory or even popularity underpinning the efficacy of a drug is shown to be false or weak the treatment is likely to be withdrawn whether it is effective or not. This is pertinent to the rise and fall of valium, which will be discussed in *Chapter 6*. It is also apparent that therapeutic effects may not always be immediately obvious. For example the therapeutic potential of chlorpromazine was at first misunderstood. It was initially marketed as an anti-emetic, as Smith Kline and French did not want to market a psychiatric drug (Domino, 1999).

Typical antipsychotics

Although pro-vivisectionists claim otherwise (Reines, 1991) Henri Laborit is widely credited with first noting the potentially psychotherapeutic effects of chlorpromazine. Laborit was a surgeon attempting to improve the care of his patients by experimenting with an antihistamine sent to him by Charpentier in 1952. Laborit wanted a pre-anaesthetic to counter the shock some of his patients suffered, and Charpentier knew his new antihistamine had central nervous system depressant effects as a result of animal tests. (This is why pro-vivisectionists believe they were first to discover chlorpromazine and in a sense they were.) He had earlier synthesised promethazine and was attempting to improve on its sedative properties with this new derivative. However, when Laborit administered Charpentier's new drug he noted an unusual calm about his patients. This is where Laborit's skills of observation were key. His patients became oblivious to their surroundings in a state Laborit referred to as 'euphoric quietude' (Swazey, 1974). He eventually persuaded his psychiatrist colleagues to try the drug in their more disturbed patients and they discovered remarkable effects. Much of this work is credited to Deniker and Delay (Turner, 2007), who published the first clinical trial. However a great deal of the observations underpinning these trials were undertaken by nurses, none of whom are credited. For example, it was nurses who discovered chlorpromazine was effective without 'hibernation' treatment, a process where the patient was simultaneously cooled down as this was supposed to aid recovery.

Previously catatonic or acutely deluded patients regained an immediate sense of relief from their highly distressing symptoms. More significantly the effects seemed to persist and improve with continued use as opposed to the short-term sedating properties noted in previous antihistamines. Chlorpromazine was subsequently prescribed for over 100 million people (Wikipedia, 2006). Chlorpromazine's trade name is Largactil, which stands for 'large number of actions'. Despite its widespread use in treating a range of mental disorders from the early 1950s its effectiveness in schizophrenia was not scientifically established until 1964. Given that it was clearly effective in relieving a variety of distressing symptoms this logically suggested an underlying biology of mental illness. That is, if symptoms can improve when treated chemically then those chemicals must be working on something.

The dopaminergic theory of schizophrenia was the first biochemical theory to emerge as a result of the side effects noted with high doses of chlorpromazine. The resultant movement disorder mimicked Parkinson's disease to a large degree. Parkinson's disease was known to be the result of dopamine depletion in one of the dopaminergic pathways in the brain linking the striatum and substantia nigra. It was thus hypothesised that schizophrenia may be due to an overabundance of dopamine in the brain.

This hypothesis was given further credence through studies with reserpine. Reserpine was used for hypertension in the 1950s, and had been a traditional Indian remedy for anxiety in its natural form, *Rauwolfia serpentine*, or snakeroot. Reserpine was also effective in relieving symptoms of schizophrenia, and also mimicked Parkinson's disease in higher doses. Arvid Carlsson discovered that chlorpromazine and reserpine both affect dopamine function, but in different ways. He noted that reserpine reduces the overall amount of dopamine in the brain and chlorpromazine blocks its action at receptors. Carlsson won the Nobel Prize in 2000. It is also interesting to note that chlorpromazine causes hypotension, which is considered to be a side effect as opposed to a therapeutic effect, yet is predictable given the original therapeutic function of reserpine. Noting of 'side effects' will be returned to later in the discussion on yellow card reporting, as new therapeutic uses for existing drugs have been discovered in this manner, like Viagra for instance. These 'discoveries' are of course often based upon a redefinition of what is therapeutic and what is defined as a side effect. The dopamine theory was a major leap in the understanding and particularly the treatment of mental illness. Drug manufacturers began urgently developing and testing other antihistamines and their derivatives. Other neurotransmitters (*Box 1.1*) also became the objects of intense investigation. Research on psychiatric medication has since been linked mainly with serotonin, acetylcholine, norepinephrine, glutamate and

---

Box 1.1. Neurotransmitters

Neurotransmitters are the chemicals which modulate messages between neurons and another cell, exerting their effect both pre- and post-synaptically. Each synapse is made up of two nerve cells separated by the synaptic cleft. Neurotransmitters are released into the cleft following activation (action potential) of the first neuron. The neurotransmitter then diffuses into the synaptic cleft where it binds (or not) to receptors on the post-synaptic neuron. These receptors (protein molecules) are specifically activated by a particular neurotransmitter. They either fit or do not fit. The next nerve is either more likely, as likely or less likely to fire as a result.

That is, although some receptors have intrinsic activity, most unbound synaptic receptors do nothing. Activated synaptic receptors send signals to the next neuron which modulates the possibility of it firing as a consequence. The sum of these trillions of signals creates one explanation of experience.

---

gamma-aminobutyric acid (GABA) as well as dopamine. Combinations of these neurotransmitters are most likely to be involved.

It is increasingly clear how difficult it is to understand any part of the system without understanding the rest. This is why clinical trials are important. Understanding that dopamine is implicated in hypotension, Parkinson's disease and schizophrenia adds to the evidence base and improves the aim of targeted treatment but it only begins to explain the whole process.

For example, dopamine synapses are normally clustered together in the substantia nigra, frontal cortex, limbic system and basal ganglia. Blockage of dopamine at various specific areas causes different effects. Blocking dopamine in the frontal cortex and limbic system seems to be best at relieving psychotic symptoms. This does not mean the same as suggesting that it is directly this action that relieves the abnormal thinking of people with psychosis. If this were the case then chlorpromazine would work immediately, yet it takes a few weeks to reduce delusions and hallucinations. This clearly suggests another mechanism at work. The link between dopamine and psychosis is far from clear.

Atypical antipsychotics

The first clue to a deeper understanding came from clinical studies with clozapine, which had been manufactured in the 1960s by Sandoz as part of the rush to cash in on the success of chlorpromazine. Clozapine appeared to be more selective in its action on dopamine receptors. Its unique properties became apparent as a result of its withdrawal from the market. Clozapine was just as effective at alleviating positive psychotic symptoms and appeared effective in some of the negative ones as well, but it caused agranulocytosis, which left people vulnerable to life-threatening infections as a consequence. Sandoz voluntarily removed it from the market. However, in attempting to re-establish therapeutic regimes for those no longer prescribed clozapine it became apparent that there were some individuals who only responded therapeutically to clozapine. Their misfortune raised the possibility that there may be other 'treatment resistant' people for whom clozapine may work, if the agranulocytosis could be controlled or monitored. Kane et al (1988) demonstrated this to be the case and clozapine was remarketed to those willing to have their blood monitored regularly. Agranulocytosis occurs in about 1% of individuals in the first six months, reducing to 0.1% thereafter. Clozapine was popular because it appeared to be more effective at targeting the negative symptoms associated with schizophrenia. That is, it appeared to help with apathy and social withdrawal. Also, parkinsonian symptoms were markedly reduced. So, although clozapine clearly affects the dopamine system in some way it seems relatively more effective in the regions which appear to control thought and emotion as opposed to movement. This reduced the possibility of it causing tardive dyskinesia, a highly unpleasant side effect of the neuroleptics. A weekly blood test was seen as an acceptable trade off to reduce the risk of this intractable and embarrassing movement disorder. There is more about this in *Chapter 4.*

Clozapine was the first 'atypical' antipsychotic, a category of drug mainly defined by the relative absence of these movement disorders. The obvious next step became a search for an equivalent which does not require a weekly blood test. This meant answering some of the questions which clozapine had raised, most notably in relation to the understanding of the role of dopamine. Did clozapine affect one particular part of the dopamine system and not another? If so, how?

In the 1980s it was found that there were five different receptors for dopamine: D1 to D5. Drugs which targeted multiple receptors are now known as 'dirty drugs'. For example, chlorpromazine targets all D receptors to a degree along with some serotonergic, histaminergic and cholinergic receptors, as well as inhibiting reuptake of dopamine into the presynaptic neuron. What had once been its biggest selling point now became Largactil's major flaw. Far from winning the Nobel Prize like Carlsson, many early pioneers of chlorpromazine were effectively hounded out of their jobs in the 1960s as part of the antipsychiatry backlash. More of this in *Chapter 2.*

The notion of clozapine as a 'clean drug' would be misleading though. Although it binds more specifically to D4 receptors than the others, it also binds non-selectively to D1 and D2 receptors and also to some serotonergic, adrenergic, histaminergic and cholinergic receptors. Nevertheless, it was seen as relatively cleaner, as it exerted its action mainly at D4 and some serotonergic receptors. This provided the impetus for drug companies to target interventions at a similar spectrum of receptors to attempt replication of the beneficial effects of clozapine, but without the agranulocytosis.

Risperidone was the first successful drug to market in this class. Janssen's patent ran out in December 2007, so generic versions will arrive shortly making the treatment significantly cheaper. It is not completely free of side effects though and can cause nausea, anxiety, insomnia and weight gain. It has also been implicated in increased risk of stroke. Like the older (typical) antipsychotics parkinsonian symptoms and tardive dyskinesia remain a risk, although not as great a risk. It also causes diabetes in some instances. Olanzapine followed, which is structurally very similar to clozapine, but with more affinity for serotonergic as opposed to D2 receptors. It also causes weight gain and increased risk of diabetes. Parkinsonism persists, but to a lesser degree. Quetiapine also targeted specific dopamine and serotonergic receptors, but claims to have lowered the risk of parkinsonian symptoms further. All the drugs may still cause neuroleptic malignant syndrome, a potentially life-threatening neurological disorder. Comparable data with the typicals are not yet available, but trends appear to suggest a lower risk.

Atypical atypicals

Currently under review are the 'atypical atypicals'. Amisulpride for example allegedly exerts its effect by acting solely on D2/D3 receptors, suggesting that action is not required at serotonergic receptors for 'atypicality' (Lewis, 2002). Amisulpride has been used in France for the last 15 years and studies support a modestly superior side effect profile with similar therapeutic efficacy. Aripiprazole is different again in that it exerts its effect through partial agonism at the D2 receptor. The idea is that dopaminergic activity can be modulated if it is high or low thus approaching the problem as one of restoring balance.

However, these drugs are all more or less the same in their mode of attack, and as already discussed this mode is improperly understood. As a further complication receptors for other transmitters have also been implicated in psychosis. For example, the NMDA (N-methyl-D-aspartic acid) receptor is a glutamate receptor. Diminishing the effects of glutamate by blocking NMDA receptors with phencyclidine (PCP – 'angel dust') can generate the whole range of psychotic symptoms, positive and negative. So is glutamate deficiency the core neurochemical process in psychosis (Moghaddam, 2005)? This is difficult to test as a global increase in glutamate can lead to excitotoxicity and cell death. Snyder and Ferris (2000) came up with a safer method of approaching the hypothesis by focusing on the co-agonists glycine and D-serine. These amino acids can both safely augment the response of NMDA receptors to glutamate.

Snyder and Ferris found glycine and D-serine untherapeutic when given alone, but when given in conjunction with other antipsychotics D-serine produced additional improvement in psychotic symptoms. D-serine is now seen as a key regulator of NMDA receptor activity and may be the main physiological ligand at the coagonist site (Wolosker, 2006). (A ligand bound to a receptor alters the shape of the receptor, which in turn alters its function.) Like many studies in molecular biology, even when a hypothesis is accepted further unexpected information is often generated. This does not necessarily clear the picture. As Snyder and Ferris commented, 'The diversity of novel neurotransmitters and venues of their activity afford multiple opportunities for therapeutic intervention.' This is a positive spin given that this approach appears to be becoming increasingly complex. D-serine is one of 100 neurotransmitters currently under investigation.

One natural consequence of the discovery of novel neurotransmitters has been to cast doubt on the definition and function of existing neurotransmitters. The purpose of Snyder and Ferris' article is to suggest a new definition of neurotransmitter. This is currently under debate, but to return to the observation which generated this study in the first place it remains evident that PCP can, better than any other drug, most closely induce the whole spectrum of symptoms most commonly attributed to the label of schizophrenia. What is known is that PCP blocks the action of glutamate at the NMDA receptor. That we are unable to understand the biology of this process is frustrating. It is also illogical to infer that because schizophrenic symptoms can be chemically induced there must be a neurochemical cause to the disorder (Shean, 2004). It is another piece of the jigsaw however.

Meanwhile, further clues to the process underpinning therapeutic effects of psychotropics are seen in the mechanism of mood stabilisers such as lithium and valproate. They do not actually have any direct effect on neurotransmission. In other words, if there is an underlying process it may have nothing to do with neurotransmitters directly, however they are defined. Rediscovered through a similar process of highly skilled empiricism and good fortune (Cade, 1949) these drugs exert their influence directly on the internal nerve cell machinery to influence the activities of several critical proteins. These structural changes are thought to be responsible for the eventual stabilisation of mood. Again the 'therapeutic lag' from drug administration to effect is two to four weeks. The fact that there is a therapeutic event led investigators to look more closely at these second messengers (*Figure 1.1*), as this could explain the time differential between

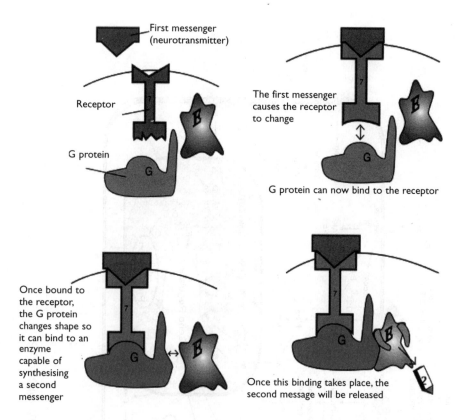

First messenger (neurotransmitter)

Receptor

G protein

The first messenger causes the receptor to change

G protein can now bind to the receptor

Once bound to the receptor, the G protein changes shape so it can bind to an enzyme capable of synthesising a second messenger

Once this binding takes place, the second message will be released

Figure 1.1. How neurotransmitters activate second messenger systems (from Stahl's Essential Psychopharmacology, 3rd edition, Cambridge University Press, 2008, copyright Neuroscience Education Institute).

neurological and therapeutic effect across a range of drugs exhibiting this therapeutic lag.

Second messengers are molecules that (often) relay signals received on the surface of the cell to the target molecule within the nucleus. The neurotransmitter binds to a membrane-spanning receptor protein molecule which then exposes a binding site inside the cell. The internal molecules which bind to it are called G proteins because they are either GDP (guanosine diphosphate) or GTP (guanosine triphosphate). When one of these G proteins binds to the receptor on the inner membrane of the cell it becomes able to exchange a GDP molecule on its alpha subunit for a GTP molecule.

Once this exchange takes place, a subunit of the GTP becomes free to move along the inner membrane and contacts another membrane-bound protein – the primary effector. This primary effector then creates a signal that can diffuse within the cell. This signal is the secondary messenger. The secondary messenger may then activate a secondary effector whose effects

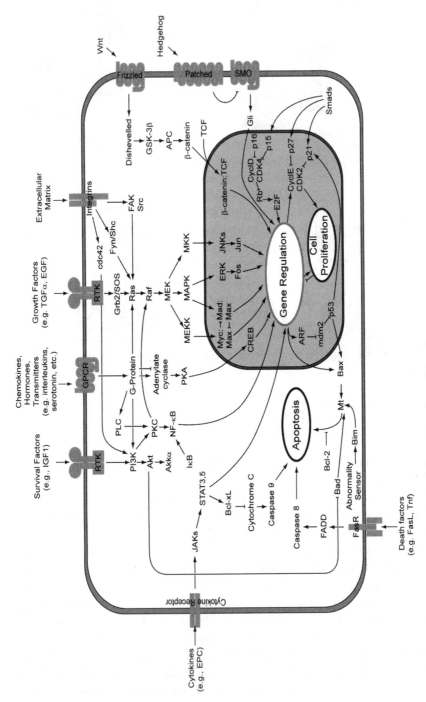

Figure 1.2. Multiple pathways within the cell. From: http://en.wikipedia.org.

depend on the particular secondary messenger system. Taken as a whole they are part of a signal transduction cascade of intracellular events.

Not all receptors are G protein coupled. For example the NMDA receptors are ligand gated ion channels as noted by Wolosker (2006) above. There are also several different secondary messenger systems. However even though the substances involved and effects are different they all are quite similar in overall mechanism. For example they can amplify the strength of a signal. Lithium is thought to exert its effect through the second messenger inositol 1,4,5-trisphosphate (Dixon and Hokin, 1994), whereas the effects of valproate appear to be largely dependent on other protein kinase isoforms (Brunello and Tascedda, 2003). This leads to speculation that despite their similar therapeutic efficacy their physiological action may be explained at a deeper level still.

Genetics

One explanation is the effect of this biochemical cascade to open or close ion channels and change the overall sensitivity of the receptor. The cascade can also permeate the nucleus thereby directly affecting genes. Genetic expression may be refined as a result leading to phenotypic alterations such as structural changes in the cells. This may be responsible for therapeutic effects of psychotropics. Affecting nucleus activity via genetic modifications is a complex process (*Figure 1.2*) and it can take days for changes to be fully operationalised. This offers a good explanation for the therapeutic lag across a range of drugs however. Also, the duration of effect can last weeks (Keltner and Gorman 2007), and take a similar time to 'wear off'.

Figure 1.2 is included not to describe each potential interaction but to show some of the intracellular genetic, molecular and chemical activity occurring within a cell at any time. Shalizi (2007) believes a reductionist perspective is consequently beyond comprehension. The brain has 100 million cells making trillions of connections which further influence the activity of each cell. Even if it was possible to understand this the brain subsequently does not function in isolation. It is further connected via the spinal cord to the rest of the body and beyond, which influences and is influenced by the brain. However to remain at the micro level please visit http://www.studiodaily.com/main/searchlist/6850. html for a remarkable animation on a small portion of what happens within a cell. These are all potential targets for action, but currently raise more questions than they answer.

For example, are these apparently different cellular pathways segregated in some way? Do they use the same chemicals, and if so how do they then express a specific event? Why do the messages not get crossed? Is there really any more to be gained from inferring regulatory networks based on input/output data from such a complex and clearly interconnected system? Are neural networks a better model? These questions are beyond the scope of this book, and most of them currently end up as philosophical issues. However, a biological endpoint of a lot of these cascades is gene regulation, hence the logic of searching there for further information. Coupled with computer enhanced imaging techniques, improved data analysis and experimental methodologies the role of genes needs to be further explored before the deterministic model is rejected out of hand.

From a technical point of view for example zebrafish have replaced mice in many genetic studies on vertebrates. This is because they are easier to observe throughout the life cycle including embryonic phases and have a simpler genetic structure. Muscular dystrophy, still the most commonly inherited birth defect, has been successfully mapped and genetically created in zebrafish (Steffen et al, 2007). It has subsequently been 'knocked out' of these fish. The connection is that if there is a genetic composition to psychosis as there appears to be in muscular dystrophy then it can be altered via a similar process. Unfortunately this is difficult to test, but not impossible, hence the logic in attempting to do so. It is falsifiable (Popper, 1959), albeit with great difficulty at present, and success has been sporadic so far.

Epigenetics

Crow (2007) compared recent meta-analyses of genome scans including large scale twin studies ($N > 300$) related to schizophrenia, bipolar and schizoaffective disorder. He concluded that these meta-analyses failed to find replicable support for any of the candidate genes thought to underpin development of psychotic symptoms. This has consistently been the case since Sherrington et al (1988) first claimed to have identified a genetic susceptibility to schizophrenia. Their results were not replicable, and subsequent claims have also failed to replicate. Crow thinks that failure to find a link could be because instead of the proposed DNA sequence variation laying in accumulation of small effects across multiple genes (as is the standard psychiatric geneticist view) instead it lies in epigenetics. That is, instead of being a consequence of hard wired positional differences it is due to heritable changes in gene function that occur without a change in the sequence of DNA. If this is true then correlations would be invisible to the traditional genetic linkage approach to investigation. The relevant variation may lie in modification of the components of the chromosome as opposed to alteration in the DNA itself.

This provides an alternative explanation for the less than 100% manifestation of schizophrenia in identical twins. Prevalence is generally around 50% in identical twins and 12–15% in dyzygotic twins. Although generally interpreted as being a factor of environmental differences, another explanation points to a more random and non-deterministic hypothesis (Crow, 2007: 17). Crow believes the variation associated with psychosis is linked to language development. The appeal of this lies in the clear central dysfunction of language processing evidenced in psychosis. His well-supported view is that language emerged 100000 years ago as a direct genetic consequence of humans separating from pre-hominid species 6 million years ago. Interindividual variation is epigenetic however. So while genes determine overall development, epigenetics provides a theory to describe modifications that account for diversity in cells carrying identical DNA sequences (Petronis et al, 2000). This theory fits well with the observation that people respond differently to the same drug. Further understanding of this process could lead to more individual tailored drug regimes based on individual epigenetics. This is discussed in more detail in *Chapter 4* with Bray et al's (2008) claim that epigenetics may lie at the heart of idiosyncratic reactions to antipsychotics.

However, genetic investigation is far from exhausted, and the complexity of the problem does not rule out the more traditional view of multiple small effects. Going back a step further still, in direct contrast to Valenstein's (1998) and Breggin's (2000) view that there is no difference between biochemistry, function or anatomy of mentally ill and 'normal' subjects, several studies refute this. Some support directly the criteria developed by the DSM. As far back as 1988 John et al demonstrated that data derived from quantitative electroencephalography (EEG) were strongly correlated with DSM diagnoses. Although it is fair to say that genotypes are currently unable to inform prognosis, treatment or prevention, genetic research supports the biological reality of psychoses as well as the clinical. This view is supported by positron emission tomography (PET) scan results (Potkin et al, 2002; Turner et al, 2006) which are becoming more powerful, specific and detailed. Drug development is shifting into this area as a result.

The search for better drugs is driven by commercial as well as scientific agendas, hence the 'me too' rush in the 1950s and 1960s which followed the discovery of chlorpromazine. However, this 'better mousetrap' approach is reasonable in itself and has generated some excellent results.

Antidepressants

A fortuitous consequence of this search for better drugs was the discovery of the first tricyclic antidepressant (TCA) imipramine. Kuhn (1957) was expecting to discover antipsychotic effects as imipramine is a cogener of chlorpromazine and very similar in structure. His patients did not become less psychotic though. Some even became more agitated, but those patients who were also depressed improved in mood, leading Kuhn to hypothesise that imipramine could be an antidepressant. This was supported in subsequent trials.

Even more fortunate was the discovery of the first monoamine oxidase inhibitor (MAOI), iproniazid, which was being tested as an antibiotic in patients with tuberculosis. Again this was ineffective in its tested purpose but a number of patients reported feeling much brighter and more energised, and in some cases euphoric. This clinical effect was noted by Kline (1958) and investigated further, resulting in iproniazid being marketed as an antidepressant. Other MAOIs followed.

Like the early antipsychotics the fact that TCAs influenced neurotransmitters, in this case increasing serotonin, dopamine and norepinephrine levels at synapses, suggested similar biochemical imbalance theories. Depression was thought to be caused by a shortage of these neurotransmitters. The problem was that these theories were all too simplistic. For example, as already discussed above, if it was just a matter of changing levels of these chemicals in the brain then why did the therapeutic benefit lag behind this demonstrable increase? Dopamine certainly appears to be a factor (Malhi and Berk, 2007) but it generally takes antidepressants in the region of three weeks to begin to lift mood in depressed individuals. Also, in around 50% or people they do not work at all.

The search for a better antidepressant progressed without answers to these questions and stemmed mainly from the side effect profiles of the TCAs and the MAOIs. They cause constipation, dry mouth, blurred vision and heart irregularities. Tyramine has to be avoided with MAOIs which poses dietary restrictions including avoidance of some cheeses and chianti wine. On top of that these drugs can be lethal in overdose, which was highly undesirable in an obviously risky population. A study of suicides in older adults found that 95% of successful attempts in the late 1990s used TCAs (Shah et al, 2001).

Selective serotonin reuptake inhibitors (SSRIs)

Arvid Carlsson was at the forefront of this search for a better antidepressant as well. Again he started with an antihistamine and tested it for efficacy among an array of psychiatric symptoms. Carlsson discovered that brompheniramine blocked reuptake of norepinephrine and serotonin, as imipramine had. When Carlsson and colleagues tested a derivative of this they found it only blocked reuptake of serotonin, yet retained its antidepressant properties. In 1982 this was marketed by Astra as Zelmid. Unfortunately, several patients developed the acute autoimmune neuropathic Guillain Barre syndrome, an ascending paralysis of the legs that spreads to the upper limbs and the face. Zelmid also had a range of peculiar hypersensitivity reactions, and it was banned worldwide.

Meanwhile, Eli Lilly had been testing derivatives of diphenhydramine (an active ingredient of the popular antihistamine Benadryl). One of these derivatives was found to be a potent inhibitor of serotonin reuptake and a weaker inhibitor of norepinephrine reuptake (Wong et al, 1995). Fluoxetine was discovered in 1975. However, Wong's discovery was not immediately apparent. Had it not been for Zelmid and its recipients' misfortune, fluoxetine (Lilly 110140 or Prozac) may well have gone unnoticed.

Like the antipsychotics the successful development of new antidepressants came about despite an incomplete knowledge of their mechanisms of action. Serotonin and norepinephrine have wide and diverse effects throughout the brain. Because these actions are so diverse it is very surprising that antidepressants have anything like a therapeutic effect at all, instead of simply disrupting many complex and misunderstood systems. Also like the antipsychotics, the main therapeutic effect also takes weeks to emerge despite immediate biochemical effects. This again suggests some sort of cascade reaction in which the initial reaction is just a stage, and again second messengers and their subsequent pathways are currently being studied. Some of the latest theories involve the role of the P11 protein which seems to augment the effect of serotonin in mice models (Rosack, 2006).

Anxiolytics

Altogether more straightforward at first sight are the benzodiazepines, as they appear to exert their therapeutic effect as a direct consequence of first messenger activity. They offer fast relief from anxiety by potentiating the GABA (gamma-aminobutyric acid) system. They cause the receptor to become more responsive to endogenous GABA which has an almost immediate therapeutic effect. When GABA receptors are activated, chloride channels that span these receptors open allowing chloride to flow in and increase the negative charge of the intracellular space. This has the effect of slowing the rate of apparently overactive neurons which provides relief from the symptoms of anxiety.

However, they cause sedation, wear off quickly, do not have any long-term effects (presumably because of their lack of action on second messengers) and cause rebound anxiety, tolerance and hence dependence. Research is currently under way to try to separate out the sedative aspects from the anxiolytic aspects of benzodiazepines with some success. An irony of this is that the Z drugs currently in favour for sedating without anxiolysis (Zopiclone, Zimovane) were products of this search. That is, they were found in a search to find exactly the opposite.

Part of the difficulty is due to the nature of the GABA receptor. The GABA receptor is actually a misnomer as there are potentially thousands of differently configured GABA receptors. They are all made up of different combinations of component proteins. GABA-A is the receptor affected by benzodiazepines. Four alpha proteins bind benzodiazepines in this receptor and therefore these alpha proteins became the focus of study. McKernan et al (2000) followed up Rudolph et al's (1999) findings by demonstrating that sedative and anxiolytic properties could be separated by blocking the GABA-A alpha-1 type receptor in mice. The mice were just as fearless as other mice given diazepam but not sedated like their counterparts. In other words, it looked as if the alpha-1 receptor was responsible for sedation.

Through a series of deductive experiments knocking out one protein at a time and observing the effects the current thinking is that the alpha-2 protein is the most likely target for the anxiety reducing effects of the benzodiazepines. Merck, Rocher and Pfizer are currently testing candidate drugs in humans, in what could be a massive market. However, an underlying presumption is that it is the sedation which causes the benzodiazepines' abuse potential. That may turn out not to be the case even if these designer benzodiazepines do what their researchers expect them to do. There is also conflicting evidence developing implicating the anxiolytic roles of other alpha proteins, especially alpha-3 (Morris et al, 2006).

Summary

Developments in the 1950s and 1960s led to great expectations within the psychiatric community that the underlying pathology of psychiatric conditions would soon be mapped. Unfortunately this optimism was premature, and no more effective treatments have been developed since. SSRIs and the selective norepinephrine reuptake inhibitors (SNRIs) have been developed rationally as a result of these advances but are no more effective than the TCAs. The fact that they are less lethal makes them preferable as a first line treatment (NICE, 2004). The same can be said of the atypical antipsychotics as compared to the original phenothiazines. Nothing has improved on diazepam as an anxiolytic despite the effort.

One obvious explanation is the sheer complexity of the science. What was once thought to be an imbalance of dopamine has turned into a study of epigenetics underpinning trillions of chemical interactions. Another more cynical explanation is a financial one. The drug companies have become extremely sophisticated at marketing. Why would they spend billions searching for alternatives when they already hold recipes for another generation of look-alikes which they can market at great profit? Some go as far as to suggest that these companies dictate current definitions of mental disorder and that the tail wags the dog (Healy, 2002). This leads us back in a circle to Kutchins and Kirk's (1997) previous point that there are no biological models of mental illness. It is all culture bound.

For example in 1962 regulatory requirements made the marketing of tonics more difficult in the USA. Prior to this what are now considered as antidepressants were marketed as tonics for 'nerves' and fatigue. In order to continue selling these chemicals the market had to be reframed. When amitriptyline was launched in 1961 it was accompanied by 50000 copies of the book *Recognising the Depressed Patient* commissioned by Merck, and amitriptyline, like the book, quickly became a best seller. Couple this with the apparently addictive nature of the anxiolytics in 1970s and the concept of depression provided a treatable and marketable underlying rationale for these conditions previously labelled anxiolysis and nervousness. These arguments are powerful. However, although it is important to engage with this debate the major problems facing nurses and patients are usually a lot less esoteric. That is, nurses will be looking to their armoury to help the distressed individual in front of them to the best of their ability. That armoury now includes prescribing.

Further reading

Healy D (2002) *The Creation of Psychopharmacology*. Cambridge, MA: Harvard University Press'
  This book is about 'drugs, insanity and society and about how changes in the relationship between them cause changes in the way we experience ourselves'. The *Creation of Psychopharmacology* is the forerunner to Healy's more polemic *Let Them Eat Prozac* and a follow up to *The Antidepressant Era*. The focus of this book is on the story of the emergence of antipsychotic medication and the subsequent evolution of Ehrlich's concept of the 'magic bullet'. Healy also puts forward a convincing critique of the randomised controlled trial as the gold standard of treatment efficacy.

Noble D (2006) *The Music of Life: Biology beyond the Genome*. Oxford: Oxford University Press
  This is an alternative perspective for those interested in epigenetics and beyond. Noble argues that the study of the genome is limited in its explanatory power. That is, the microscopic rarely bears straightforward correlation with the observable from a systems perspective. Noble rejects the reductionist approach in favour of a very eloquently developed analogy with music. Although this metaphor has been used before (for example by Wittgenstein) what makes this book special is that Noble's arguments are grounded in an expert knowledge of reductionism as specifically applied to biology.

References

Boersma E, Mercado N, Poldermans D, Gardien M, Vos J, Simmons ML (2003) Acute myocardial infarction. *Lancet* **361**: 847–58

Bray J, Clarke C, Brennen G, Muncey T (in press) Should we be 'pushing meds'? The implications of pharmacogenomics. *J Psych Ment Health Nursing*

Breggin P (2000) *Reclaiming Our Children*. Cambridge, Massachusetts: Perseus Books

Brunello N, Tascedda F (2003) Cellular mechanisms and second messengers: Relevance to the psychopharmacology of bipolar disorders. *Int J Neuropsychopharmacol* **6**: 181–9

Cade J (1949) Lithium salts in the treatment of psychotic excitement. *Med J Australia* **36**: 349

Crow TJ (2007) How and why genetic linkage has not solved the problem of psychosis: Review and hypothesis. *Amer J Psychiatry* **164**(1): 13–22

Dixon JF, Hokin LE (1994) Lithium stimulates accumulation of second-messenger inositol 1,4,5-trisphosphate and other inositol phosphates in mouse pancreatic minilobules without inositol supplementation. *Biochem J* **304**(Pt 1): 251–8

Domino EF (1999) History of modern psychopharmacology: A personal view with an emphasis on antidepressants. *Psychosom Med* **61**: 591–8

Foucault M (1965) *Madness and Civilisation: A History of Insanity in the Age of Reason*. New York, Random House

Healy D (2002) *The Creation of Psychopharmacology*. Cambridge, MA, Harvard University Press

John ER, Prichep LS, Friedman J, Easton P (1988). Neurometrics: Computerassisted differential diagnosis of brain dysfunctions. *Science* **293**:162–9

Kane J, Honigfeld G, Singer J, Meltzer H, and Cloraril Collaborative Study Group (1988) Clozapine for the treatment resistant schizophrenic. *Arch Gen Psychiatry* **45**: 789–96

Keltner NL, Gorman AG (2007) Second messengers. *Perspectives in Psychiatric Care* **43**(1): 60–4

Kline NS (1958) Clinical experience with iproniazid (Marsilid). *J Clin Exp Psychopathol* **19**(Suppl 1): 72–8

Kuhn R (1957) Uber die behandlung depressiver zustande mit einemiminodibenzylderivat *Schweiz Med Wochenschn* **87**: 1135–40

Kutchins H, Kirk H (1997) *Making us Crazy. DSM: The Psychiatric Bible and the Creation of Mental Disorders*. New York, Simon and Shuster

Laborit H, Huguenard P, Alluaume R (1952) Un nouveau stabilisateur vegetatif (le 4560 RP). *Presse Med* **60**:206–8

Lewis AL (2002) Atypical antipsychotic medications and the treatment of schizophrenia (Editorial). *Am J Psychiatry* **159**:177–9

Malhi GS, Berk M (2007) Does dopamine dysfunction drive depression? *Acta Psychiatrica Scandinavica* **115**(S433): 116–20

McKernan RM, Rosahl TW, Reynolds DS, Sur C, Wafford KA, Attack JR, Farrar, S, Myers J, Cook G, Ferris P, Garrett L, Bristow G, Marshall A, Macaulay N, Brown N, Howell O, Moore KW, Carling RW, Street LJ, Castro JL, Ragan CI, Dawson GR, Whiting PJ (2000) Sedative but not anxiolytic properties of benzodiazepines are mediated by the GABA-A receptor alpha-1 type. *Nature Neurosci* **3**(6): 587–92

Moghaddam B (2005) *Current hypotheses.* Available from: http://www.schizophreniaforum. org/for/curr/Moghaddam/default.asp [Accessed 1 August 2007]

Moon KF (2004) *The History of Psychiatric Classification: From Ancient Egypt to Modern America.* Available from: http://kadi.myweb.uga.edu/index.html [Accessed 30 November 2006]

Morris HV, Dawson GR, Reynolds DS, Atack JR, Stevens DN (2006) Both α2 and α3 GABA-A receptor subtypes mediate the anxiolytic properties of benzodiazepine site ligands in the conditioned emotional response paradigm. *Eur J Neurosci* **23**: 495–504

NICE (2004) *Depression: Management of depression in primary and secondary care. NICE Guideline 23.* Available from: http://www.nice.org.uk/pdf/CG023quickrefguide.pdf [Accessed 6 June 2007]

Petronis A, Gottesman II, Crow TJ, DeLisi LE, Klar AJ, Macciardi F, McInnis MG, McMahon FJ, Paterson AD, Skuse D, Sutherland GR (2000) Psychiatric epigenetics: A new focus for the new century. *Molecular Psychiatry* **5**(4): 342–6

Popper K (1959) *The Logic of Scientific Discovery.* New York, Basic Books

Porter R (2002) *Madness: A Brief History.* Oxford, Oxford University Press

Potkin, SG, Alva G, Keator D, Carreon D, Wu JC, Fleming K, Fallon JH (2002) A PET study of the pathophysiology of negative symptoms in schizophrenia. *Am J Psychiatry* **159**: 227–37

Reines BP (1991) On the locus of medical discovery. *J Med Philosophy* **16**(21): 183–209

Rosack J (2006) Protein discovery may lead to new psychiatric drugs. *Psychiatric News* **41**(3): 18

Shalizi C (2007) *Signal Transduction, Control of Metabolism, and Gene Regulation.* Available from: http://cscs.umich.edu/~crshalizi/notebooks/signal-transduction.html [Accessed 21 May 2007]

Rudolph U, Crestani F, Benke D, Brunig I, Benson JA, Fritschy JM, Martin JR, Bleuthmann H, Mohler H (1999) Benzodiazepine actions mediated by specific gamma aminobutyric acid-A receptor subtypes. *Nature* **401**: 796–800

Shah R, Uren Z, Baker A, Majeed A (2001) Deaths from antidepressants in England and Wales 1993–1997: Analysis of a new national database. *Psychol Med* **31**: 1203–10

Shean GD (2004) *What is Schizophrenia and How Can We Fix It?* Oxford, University Press America

Sherrington R, Brynjolffson J, Petursson H, Potter M, Dudleston K, Barraclough B, Wasmuth J, Dobbs M, Curling H (1988) Localization of a susceptibility locus for schizophrenia on chromosome. *Nature* **336**: 164–7

Snyder SH, Ferris CD (2000) Novel neurotransmitters and their neuropsychiatric relevance *Am J Psychiatry* **157**: 1738–51

Stahl S (2006) *Essential Psychopharmacology. The Prescriber's Guide: Antidepressants.* Cambridge, Cambridge University Press

Steffen LS, Guyon JR, Vogel ED, Beltre R, Pusack T, Zon LI, Kunkel M (2006) Zebrafish orthologs of human muscular dystrophy genes. *BMC Genomics* **8**: 79

Stevens LS (1999) *Does Mental Illness Exist?* Available from: http://www.antipsychiatry. org/exist.htm [Accessed 30 November 2006]

Stevens A, Price J (2000) *Evolutionary Psychiatry: A New Beginning.* London, Routledge

Swazey J (1974) *Chlorpromazine in Psychiatry: A Study in Therapeutic Intervention.*

Cambridge, MIT Press

Szasz T (1961) *The Myth of Mental Illness*. New York, Hoeber–Harper. Revised edition 1974, Harper and Row

Turner T (2007) "Unlocking psychosis". *Brit J Med* **334**(Suppl): S7

Turner JA, Smyth P, Macciardi F, Fallon JH, Kennedy JL, Potkin SG (2006) Imaging phenotypes and genotypes in schizophrenia. *Neuroscience* **4**: 1

Valenstein ES (1998) *Blaming the Brain: The Truth About Drugs and Mental Health*. New York, The Free Press

Wikipedia (2006) *Chlorpromazine*. Available from: http://en.wikipedia.org/wiki/Chlorpromazine [Accessed 15 December 2006]

Wolosker H (2006) D-Serine Regulation of NMDA Receptor Activity. *Sci STKE* **10**: 41

Wong DT, Bymaster FP, Engleman EE (1995) Prozac (fluoxetine, Lilly 110140), the first selective serotonin uptake inhibitor and an antidepressant drug. Twenty years since its first publication. *Life Sci* **57**, 411–41

CHAPTER 2

The history of mental health nursing

The history of mental health nursing is closely linked with the history of nursing and the history of psychiatry. More importantly, it is linked with the history of mental health and the way society views it. This is where the chapter begins. As with the previous chapter this history is written in greater depth elsewhere, and recommended reading is suggested at the end of the chapter for some excellent, varying and detailed accounts. The purpose here is to link some of the major milestones specific to mental health nursing with the factors raised in *Chapters 1* and *3* in order to understand mental health nurse prescribing within its much broader historical context. This provides insight into how and why mental health nurses became able to prescribe mind altering drugs to people in their care, and to discuss whether or not they should. This knowledge allows a deeper and more focused engagement both in the practicalities of prescribing and in the wider debate on mental health. The timeline (*Figure 2.1*) illustrates the factors discussed in detail in this chapter.

The social construction of mental illness

There has always been a social component to mental illness. It could not exist otherwise. Abnormal can only ever be defined in relation to a description of normal. The story of mental health nursing is to some extent the story of policing this concept. We look back with horror at some of the so called treatments which were forced on those we would now attempt partnership with, and feel morally superior as a consequence. But this is a mistake. Certainly history is full of appalling stories of barbaric treatment of the 'insane'. However the simple dichotomy of contrasting behaviour now with an incomplete image of both the past and present provides moral security but excludes deeper engagement. It is therefore worth exploring this history in greater depth in order to gain a more balanced view of our current understanding. Debate then becomes more informed in relation to whether nursing actions, attitudes and behaviour have evolved, and if so, how. This is particularly relevant in the light of recent nursing texts which seek to define the 'core' of nursing (Barker, 2006). In illuminating historical themes

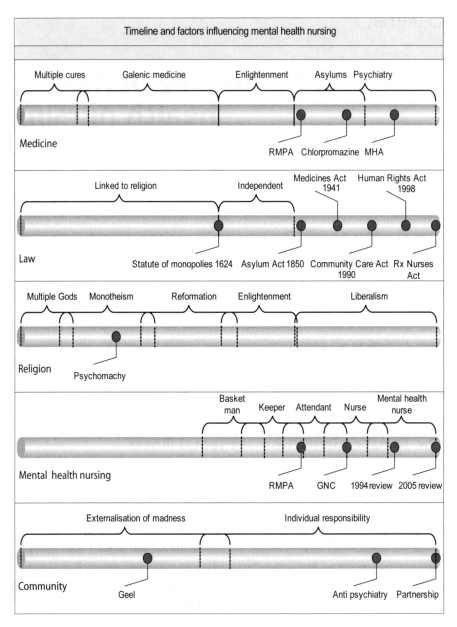

Figure 2.1.Timeline.

it should be possible to draw conclusions on what, if anything, this core of mental health nursing has been. Themes will therefore be highlighted as they arise, and discussed as a whole in the conclusion. Prescribing decisions can then be understood in relation to a clearly defined mental health nurse.

In ancient history (10000 years ago) it would seem that as now mental illness existed in the form of behaviours which did not conform to the social norm. Treatment involved a variety of shamans, witch doctors and ritual appeals to the gods. There was no distinction between magic, medicine and religion. Archaeologists have found trepanned skulls dating back to 5000BC which probably indicate that the individual was thought to be possessed by spirits and that the holes would let them out. As far as conceptual understanding goes, the Egyptians appear to have equated everything to the Nile. What they did to their bodies in times of distress replicated actions they observed to be effective on the Nile and its environment. For example, channelling and scraping relieved congestion and encouraged flow. The notion of bile originates here according to Ramsamy (2001), representing both the mud of the river bed and the substance that needed to be removed from the body in times of human madness.

By 2850BC there is evidence of carefully worded malpractice laws in Egypt, suggestive of more modern notions of equity and respect. Treatment was based on sleep or occupational therapy. Success was attributed to the gods, as the modern concept of self was absent. That is, there is a school of thought which equates gods in ancient time with current understandings of feelings (Blackmore, 2005). Distress was felt but not owned by the individual. The notion of inner conflict with a conscious operator is relatively new. For example, around 800BC Homer's odyssey is characterised by its lack of inner sentiment. Emphasis is on adventure and drama around action and metaphors. Heroes have great virtue and morals are taught but they are reinforced by fear of the gods, not self-reflection.

Madness has often been viewed as a punishment meted out by a god. Hindus have a specific demon responsible for seizures, as did the Babylonians, Assyrians and Mesopotamians. This ancient history is thus notable for its common externalisation of madness. It is not until the 4th or 5th century BC that the idea of the inner psyche and its consequences emerge. That is, there is seen to be a relationship between reason, morality, individual action and consequence without reference to external forces as the creation of these conflicts. The ensuing turmoil is represented in the plays of Aeschylus, Euripides and most notably Sophocles. These tragedies often show madness being self-inflicted, or certainly a consequence of conscious inner conflict. Freud named the Oedipus complex after one of Sophocles' plays.

The distinction between physical and mental health has a similarly lengthy history. In 2000BC in Mesopotamia a distinction was clearly made between mental and physical health. Physicians treated the physically unwell and priests drove out demons of the mentally unwell. The priests studied the dreams of their clients and used techniques similar to psychotherapy to treat them. All diseases had their own demon and each priest his own god. This may possibly have been the first classification system of mental illness. In general, disease was seen as a punishment from the gods, and this theory has not been entirely eliminated. Jesus performed exorcisms (Wikipedia, 2007) and it is still a recognised albeit rare practice of Catholicism, Eastern orthodox and some Protestant churches. Annelise Michel underwent the last known infamous exorcism in 1976. However it is fair to say that someone claiming possession today is much more likely to be advised to see a psychiatrist than an exorcist, even by an evangelical priest.

It is easy to see these ideas as unsound in relation to current thought, but it is illogical to infer superior morality based upon decontextualised historical events. Consider Socrates and morality. Socrates is widely acknowledged as seeking truth, knowledge and justice. His quest was for an honest investigation of anything and everything. A great deal of what is now considered to be moral can be directly attributed to Plato's writings about Socrates. Socrates is therefore considered a moral man. He died for his moral beliefs. However Socrates, in describing his ideal society, also suggested that the 'offspring of the inferior...or deformed... will be put away in some mysterious, unknown place, as they should be'. (Plato 1901: Para 460c). He goes on to describe a form of selective breeding, ensuring only the fittest be allowed to survive. This would be considered morally repugnant by most people who would air a view publicly now.

The point is we live in an age where such suggestions remind us of Nazism, ethnic cleansing and genocide. It is difficult to suggest that anybody may be inferior to anybody else without generating moral indignation. This is because morality is socially constructed and contextual. The European Convention of Human Rights 1950 emerged as a direct consequence to the opposition of Nazism. Yet rights are neither logical or finite. People were probably no less moral in Socrates' or Annelise Michel's day, but it is easy to judge them as such without a contextual understanding. Hunter and Macalpine (1970) argued that 'lack of appreciation of the past tends to foster overevaluation of modern achievements and the assumption...that what is present is good and what is past is bad'.

The evidence shows that compassion has always existed and has always been valued. For example in Roman times Tullius Cicero was a great promoter of Greek thought to the Latin world. He gave a very detailed presentation of the Stoic philosophy of mind and of mental disorder in his Tusculan Disputations (46BC) (Nordenfelt, 1997). From this he developed a structured clinical interview to systematically elicit the state of mind of the mentally ill. A compassionate and civilised approach to mental illness resulted. Seranus, a Roman teacher and physician, believed healing lay within the caring relationship (Nolan, 1990a), and it is this caring relationship which has been formalised in the role of the mental health nurse.

Identification of madness and religion

Religion plays a major role in the history of mental health. The Celtic church had a big influence on early treatment of mental distress in the UK. Its approach was spiritual and promoted social integration. Each monastery had monks known as 'soul friends' who had a special interest in mental health. Some allowed 'penitents' (the profoundly disturbed) to live with them and participate in daily and spiritual life (Clarke, 1975). There is evidence that the Celtic monks used Cicero's interview format.

In early medieval times pilgrimages gained in popularity as Cicero's influence waned. Individuals suffering mental ill-health would travel with a companion to various shrines, springs and wells. Inability to recover was blamed on the traveller or companion lacking in faith. As in the early civilisations above, externalisation of madness appears to predominate here as well. These beliefs were powerful, and many of the Victorian asylums were built at or near sites of former shrines (Foucault, 1965). The power of faith and its healing potential is an enduring theme.

Christianity in particular has always denied that reason counted for a great deal. Most important were sin, faith, divine will and love. While it could be argued that the pre-medieval period focused predominantly on action based on the more positive aspects of Christianity, the narrative of sin often drove the medieval era. Caelius Aurelianus, one of the greatest Greco Roman physicians and last medical writer of the Roman Empire is credited with repopularising the thought that devils existed in the guise of male or female human beings. Their primary task was subsequently to deceive the opposite sex. The murder of thousands of the allegedly insane was justified as ridding these people of the evil souls and devils that possessed them.

The underlying premise was that the Holy Ghost and the devil battle for individual souls. This is called psychomachy (Baldick, 1990). That is, instead of having different gods (polytheism) responsible for different ailments and cures there were only two, with one god (monotheism). So as a method of conceptualising madness psychomachy can be seen as a replacement for the multiple gods and devils in ancient times. Believers attributed their distress to diabolical possession or a lost soul (Porter, 2002). The fact that this struggle is internal and hence not necessarily supernatural says more about the relative power of rationality, science and religion at any time in history than it does about whether these representations are right or wrong. This is important because morality is linked to power (Nietszche, 1895; Foucault, 1965; Paley, 2002) in that it is defined in relation to the prevailing society.

Community care

Western society was deeply religious until the 18th century. It is a mistake to think of mental illness as being defined in terms of witchcraft, heresy and possession however. There is evidence of a much broader tolerance going back centuries and back to Egyptian times as discussed above. There are few details but various records point to an asylum existing exclusively for people suffering with mental illness in Mets in northern France as far back as 1100 (Roberts, 1981). Of more significance due to its survival into the present is the community formed over 700 years ago in Geel, Belgium.

Geel's history begins in the 6th century. Goldstein and Godemont (2003) recount the story of Dymphna. In the 6th century Dymphna ran away from her father, the Irish King Damon. This is because her father was overcome with grief having lost his wife. He wanted his daughter to replace her, apparently having failed otherwise in his search for a new wife. When he tracked Dymphna down to St Maartens church she refused his advances and was beheaded along with her elderly protector and priest Gerebernus. Dymphna became legendary for not giving in to her father's madness. Whether true or not, the site of her martyrdom became a focus of pilgrimage and a symbol of hope, being increasingly associated with apparently miraculous cures for mental illness. In 1247 she was canonised as the patron saint of the mentally ill and a larger church was built. Treatment for pilgrims consisted of a nine-day stay at the church. Due to its success queues formed. People waiting for treatment were housed by members of the local village at the request of the church canons, and many pilgrims stayed on if the treatment had been unsuccessful. These arrangements were informal at first, with oversight by the local canons. People were accepted by the village in any state of distress.

It would be a misrepresentation to hold this up as a perfect model of community care. When Esquirol visited in 1821 he was unimpressed by the inequity within the community and worried about the care of the most vulnerable, suggesting that the Belgian Government build an asylum instead. When people first hear of Geel they often imagine an ideal. Yet the reality is that it has not been replicated anywhere in Europe and is often referred to by the surrounding community as the 'city of fools' (Goldstein and Godemont, 2003: 449), suggesting stigma has simply been geographically displaced a little further than usual. The community is diminishing but not disappearing. The 'foster families' have no formal training in psychiatry and use practical solutions to integrate their 'boarders'. They do not diagnose or treat. What Geel still does very successfully is accept and acknowledge the needs of the boarders and then respond to those needs pragmatically. Boarders are not just members of a family but members of a wider community, a community that protects rather than fears the mentally ill.

Similar attitudes underpinned many developments around 1400. In 1409 a monk named Joffre founded an asylum at Valencia out of pity for the lunatics he saw bullied by crowds of people. Further asylums were founded in Saragossa in 1425, Seville in 1435, Valladolid in 1436, and in Toledo before the end of the century. St Mary of Bethlem (Bedlam) started admitting psychiatric patients in 1403, and further asylums were built in Europe throughout the 15th century.

Religiosity

In the early middle ages there was no organised strand of medieval medicine. Instead people relied on folk medicine, prayer, astrology, spells, mysticism, or on an established physician if they could afford it. A distinctive feature of the era was the variety of healers. There were no definitive boundaries between any of these or any consensus as to standards of practice. Many practitioners were part-timers. Classic texts like Galen were not deviated from in any way. As Christianity grew in power tension developed between the church and folk medicine due to the mystical and magical nature of the latter.

The underlying principle of medieval medicine was the theory of humours, a theory of balance developed by the Greeks, or possibly the Egyptians according to Ramsamy (2001). The balance of humours in humans could be achieved by diet, medicines, and by blood-letting, using leeches. Mental health problems like others were seen in terms of imbalance. Words such as sanguine, phlegmatic and melancholic are still used to describe personalities and originated from the names of the humours thought to physically dominate such features.

A great proportion of hospitals in medieval Europe were directly affiliated with monasteries or other religious institutions. The term hospital encompassed hostels for a wide range of need, including homes for the blind, lame, elderly, and mentally ill. These hospitals developed therapeutic and spiritual treatments. Women served as nurses caring for the physical needs of patients. Patients were also supposed to help each other through prayer and calm, perhaps benefiting as much from this as from any physical treatment offered. This raises comparisons with modern therapeutic communities. Some hospitals had as few as 10 beds.

However, during the middle ages church and state were united as never before. Popes, kings and bishops were the ruling elite, and together maintained social order. To question the state was to question the church and vice versa. Hundreds of thousands of witches and heretics (mainly women) were killed during the late 16th and early 17th century (Porter, 2002: 25). The church did not kill or even spill blood directly. It used other barbarous tortures and the secular arm carried out executions. This is relevant to the history of mental health nursing because it was physicians who led the counter-revolution of reason, thus gaining significant power for themselves. That is, they reframed this quite clearly misguided attempt at social control by pathologising the zealots. They pointed out the similarities between this religious fringe and the lunatics they sought to persecute. Some likened 'zeal' to epilepsy for instance, and 'enthusiasm' became likened with psychopathy. The underpinning rationale was easy to attack because as a method of social control it had not worked. Further evidence emerged with the plague. The church taught that God sometimes sent illness as a punishment. In these cases repentance could lead to a recovery. Yet the plague killed as many clerics as sinners.

Especially after 1650 'possession' was seen more and more as individual sickness, and this pathologising of religious madness itself led some Enlightenment thinkers to pathologise religiosity in general. This has remained an enduring theme, and the church has had to contend with some hostility towards its internal logic ever since. For example Freud saw God as an illusion, 100 years before Richard Dawkins saw him as a delusion. Nietzsche (1895) was particularly disparaging about religion, viewing it as a slave morality, artificially elevating qualities such as compassion and caring to compensate for a lack of power. This is an unpopular view, which assumes everybody has 'will to power', which is not at all obvious. However medicine had not only re-established balance, but also asserted itself as the rational option. This began the current understanding of mental health, as discussion became more often expressed in medical language than any other. The emergent theme here then is the political nature of madness. Only a political power shift could reframe the concept of madness in medical terms.

Medicalisation of mental illness

Mental health nursing is indirectly mentioned in early records. In the early 17th century Edward Jorden (1569–1632) despaired of medically curing the mentally ill and instead advocated that hysteria could be relieved by the 'ministrations of a kind person' (Nolan, 1990a: 21). Three very familiar elements were required: understanding, consent to treatment and community integration. This appears to be the first record describing nursing qualities without a related religious component.

John Strype (1642–1737) writes of three 'basket men' in his record of his own experience of hospitalisation. They were called basket men as their predecessors the monks used to gather alms and food in baskets. These basket men were probably the forerunners of mental health nurses, and Strype appears to credit his recovery to their care in Bethlem in the 1760s (Nolan, 1993: 27). Basket men were called 'keepers' around 1800, inferring a zoo-like relationship between keeper and beast. For example around this time the rationale for the legal assessment of insanity was called the wild beast test (Eigen, 1995). The importance of companionship was still stressed however. More literate patients wrote of the powerful effects of companionship in their recovery. Some of these keepers went on to deliver community care by supporting patients at home after they were discharged from hospital.

William Battie (1703–1776, and source of the slang term 'batty') trained in medicine as he could not afford to be a lawyer. He is widely credited with being the first to recognise the need to educate and train the 'servants' of the madhouses. He owned two madhouses thanks to a substantial inheritance. He observed that people recovered without medical treatment and concluded that a caring environment was more important than any medical treatment. Thomas Withers (1750–1809) held similar views and advocated occupational therapy delivered by trained nurses. Phillipe Pinel (1745–1826) credited his head attendant, Jean-Baptiste Pussin and his wife with instigating the reforms he became famous for; a strict nonviolent, nonmedical management of mental patients known as moral treatment (although psychological is probably a more accurate translation of the French 'moral'). George Jepson, the first head attendant at York Retreat was influential in the instigation of 'moral therapy' there. York Retreat was founded in 1793. The first institutional training for psychiatric nurses most likely occurred there.

Unfortunately, these initiatives were not representative of the majority. The early 19th century preceded a social decline, a function of huge population growth and the consequent poverty. A parliamentary inquiry in 1815 concluded that the law and practice of madhouses were in a 'state of unbelievable chaos' (Nolan, 1990a: 23). Although moral management was available it seemed more available to the rich than the poor (Parry-Jones, 1972). 'Pauper lunatics' overran workhouses and prisons. Against this backdrop the Lunacy Act of 1845 ordered the building of institutions where the insane could be treated separately from the criminal and the poor. The theme of segregation is an enduring factor in the story of mental health nursing.

The asylums

Johann Guggenbühl (1816–1863) has been credited with originating the idea of institutional care for the 'feebleminded'. He opened a training school for 'cretins' at Adenberg in Switzerland. He built it at 4000ft above sea level as he believed lower altitudes contributed to cretinism. He was initially widely praised for his efforts, but possibly as a result of his success and subsequent extensive travel the facility itself became understaffed, overcrowded and suspected of abuse. This is a lesson that would be relearned in the asylums, but his early efforts led others to open training schools for children with disabilities, mainly in the USA in the 1850s. It is certain he also had an influence on the asylum model adopted in the UK.

However, the main influence was money. Lunatic asylums were a social solution, sold by the now politically powerful medical profession to Victorian magnates as economically beneficial. The population of England had trebled within the previous century, resulting in a population of 14.8 million by 1840 and the concomitant widespread poverty, starvation and mental disease were not matched by resources. Public awareness was stirred by the media as the realities of economic disaster fuelled scapegoating of the insane. Some writers feel the actual numbers of lunatics were falsified to counter sensationalist articles such as this, found in *The Times* 5 April 1877:

> *If lunacy continues to increase as at present, the insane will be in the majority and freeing themselves, will put the sane in the asylums.*

Recipients of asylum care were expected to be grateful, as they were now held to be largely responsible for their own shortcomings (Nolan, 1990b). Responsibility was clearly the down side of the demise of externalisation of madness. The asylum system was supposed to get the insane back to work according to early conceptualisations. When this failed, keeping the insane away from society at large was promoted as economically sound to the financiers. Within the prevailing model of the therapeutic benefit of self-help, locating institutions by farmland made them simultaneously profitable and therapeutic. Asylums were judged primarily on their profits, not their standards of care. Economics is therefore another enduring theme.

Attendants

Attendants were central to the system, and were the buffer between medical staff and patients. Attendants were largely farm labourers, ex military men or prison warders and given no training. On the wards they were expected to behave like specialists in mental health care, but the work was of such low status and high stigma that workers were described as the 'dregs of society' (Scull, 1979). Superintendents valued attendants who could supervise farm labour and take orders without question. These men also administered treatments such as the 'bath of surprise', the swivel chair, the Turkish bath, poultices, enemas and suppositories. Superintendents defined what the work of the attendant should be and attendants obeyed (Nolan, 1990b). Wages were pitiful and retention of attendants was poor.

Rule keeping was of primary importance and transgression resulted in instant dismissal. Rule enforcing was likewise a primary role. Conformity was prized over initiative. Although higher level skills were agreed to be beneficial to patients, the pay and conditions did not encourage such skilled individuals. Some, like Tuke at the Retreat and John Thurman at the Wiltshire asylum saw attendants as spiritual guides, but most saw them as guards between rational society and the mentally ill (Abel-Smith, 1977).

Professionalisation

The first signs of professionalisation emerged around the time of the asylum, but not for the attendants. The term psychiatry was used for the first time in 1846 to describe that branch of medicine devoted specifically to this newly emergent discipline (Nolan, 1990b: 23). At this point there was no specialist training for doctors or attendants. John Conolly systematised medical training for junior doctors in the care of the mentally ill in 1842, but no certification existed. Dr Browne of Crichton Royal Mental Hospital gave attendants their first recorded series of lectures in 1854 including a

full, if popular, discussion of insanity in the different forms, intelligible by the shrewd and sensible if somewhat illiterate class of persons employed as attendants.

(Easterbrooke, 1940)

Nurse training is still delivered at the Crichton by the University of West of Scotland.

Psychological medicine was certified in 1885 by the Medico Psychological Association ('Royal' MPA from 1926). The RMPA subsequently created the post of registrar in 1892 to oversee the recording of a national training scheme for attendants. This training was founded on *The Handbook for the Instruction of Attendants on the Insane* which subsequently became known as the red handbook and sold thousands. The first attendants qualified in 1894, and the RMPA continued to register psychiatric nurses until 1951, alongside the General Nursing Council which established its own training scheme in 1923. The RMPA issued badges to qualified nurses, which were very popular. Eventually all hospitals had their own, promoting a sense of pride, identity and belonging (Harcourt Williams, 2001).

Running counter to this increased sense of pride and belonging were the apparently disparaging undertones directed at the attendants by the newly formed General Nursing Council (GNC). Mrs Ethel Bedford Fenwick appears as 'nurse number 1' in the first general nurse register of 1923 and famously said in 1896:

> *everyone will agree that no person can be considered trained who has only worked in hospitals and asylums for the insane.*

Mrs Fenwick is often portrayed as the nemesis of mental health nursing and the originator of some enduring conflict. However, her motivation was arguably to raise standards generally, not just to insult attendants. Her wider and primary agenda was in gaining equal rights for women.

This theme persisted into the 1950s where the continuing perception appears to be that mental health nursing was an activity carried out by working class males, and general nursing was carried out by middle class women. In making attempts to amalgamate training under general nurse control middle class females could be attracted into mental nursing, thus raising the standing of psychiatry (Nolan, 1993). The GNC ran a parallel course to the RMPA from 1923 until the RMPA ceased in 1951. From this point psychiatric nursing was partnered with general nursing for the purpose of registration, but maintained its own training.

The 1923 GNC course had a common foundation programme running for one year and the same final exam for all fields of nursing. Mental nurses and nurses certified in mental subnormality were eligible for admission to a supplementary register on completion of these standards. This option did not appeal to all mental health nurses of the time, hence the endurance of the RMPA qualification. While general nurses aspired to professional status mental nurses were more concerned with their working conditions (Nolan, 1990c). Mental nurses became psychiatric nurses by the 1950s, reflecting both their affiliation with psychiatry and the wider therapeutic shift to psychoanalytic theory. Nurse titles have always reflected contemporary understanding of the role according to Brooking (1985). If so then psychiatry has clearly been their biggest influence, directing the way mental health nurses define themselves. Given that psychiatry has itself had to fight its own corner in medicine and occasionally used mental health nursing in support the sense of the underdog has never really left mental health nursing. This is why as an emerging profession mental health nursing has historically found opportunities difficult to grasp. It is not used to being in control, and in fact appears to revel in not being so. The theme of underdog is therefore worth including.

One hundred years ago attendants were lowly paid, hard working and basically unable to secure any other employment. Their working day consisted of cleaning, polishing, bed making, dressing and supervising patients and serving meals. Somewhat surprisingly they also prescribed and administered drugs under their own authority (Nolan, 1993: 58), indicating the lack of significance this role held at that time. Tobacco was used as a tranquillizer as well as a reward for good behaviour. This practice made it into my early experience of long-stay psychiatry in the 1980s. Attendants also prescribed opium and hyoscine.

Work was the major therapy. It was hoped for the national economy that the mentally ill could be cured and thus return to work. Attendants, who supervised the work, themselves worked 90 hours a week with very little time off. Their official times of duty were 6 a.m. until 10 p.m. with one day off a month but in reality they could be called on 24 hours a day. Unions were discouraged and superintendents all powerful, with the right to dismiss at will. Attendants were trusted no more than the patients. This is exemplified by Broadgate Hospital superintendent Dr Mercer's encouragement of attendants to use their minimal spare time to help organise entertainment for the patients:

The attendants who organise [dances] have a wholesome pastime...which keeps them from indulging in less innocent pastimes.

(Curry, 1991: 22)

In the 1873 charter setting out general rules of the asylum (which became Broadgate Hospital in 1930) there were job descriptions for the superintendent, chaplain, clerk, matron/housekeeper and head male attendant. There is no job description for a nurse or attendant. Presumably these roles were beneath description or defined at the discretion of the people described above. However, there is evidence that the newly qualified nurses certified by RMPA did better than those not. In 1906 two nurses were given extra pay and responsibility, being the only two nurses in Broadgate Hospital with the qualification (Curry, 1991: 43).

By the 1920s life had become more tolerable due to the improvements in social conditions, although the work was still routine and unrewarding (Nolan, 1993: 17). When asked what they enjoyed about the work male nurses of the 1920s tended to concentrate on the job security and sporting facilities whereas female nurses focused on caring, companionship and interactions with patients (Nolan, 1993: 91). Nurses (females) received about two thirds of the attendant wage (Curry, 1991: 38), which is why it is easier to understand Mrs Fenwick in retrospect. Male and female staff were kept as separate as the male and female patients. Christian names were never used, and there are stories of rushed marriages which later failed no doubt due to inappropriate choices taken as a consequence of this enforced separation. There remained a tremendous stigma to the job, which could be highly detrimental to any burgeoning relationship with someone who was not also a nurse. Segregation of the sexes continued until the 1950s.

By the 1930s the atmosphere had comparatively relaxed however and a sense of camaraderie built around sports and social events. Unemployment was high and so those who applied for nursing/attendant posts were desperate for any job. Many were not particularly interested in the patients. Asylums formally became hospitals following the Mental Treatment Act 1930, which provided for the voluntary admission of patients to mental hospitals. The Local Government Act 1929 had already dismissed terms such as pauper and Poor Law. Thus pauper lunatics became 'rate-aided persons of unsound mind' by virtue of two acts of parliament. Patients remained of very lowly status however, while medical superintendents remained very much in charge. Custodial duties prevailed for the staff.

Mrs Welch worked at Broadgate between 1944 and 1947:

> *...it was a typical asylum was not it, in those days, because everything was under lock and key. Every door you went through was locked, and we had a bunch of keys round our waist...there was a lot of cleaning...I can remember having 80 [patients] on one ward but that was the biggest...I think 50 or 60 average.'*

(Curry, 1991: 68)

Bob Farrar seconds this picture

> *...they were all locked, all of 'em, and all the corridors was locked...it was secure, well it was like a prison...*

(Curry, 1991: 83)

During the Second World War beds were emptied for incoming wounded soldiers so other hospitals had to take the overflow resulting in massive overcrowding. This was a major factor in opening the locked doors of the institutions, but the discharge rates bore no relation to recovery rates. During this period nurses continued to carry out treatment regimes instigated by doctors and reported changes to them. Although clearly valued, independent thought was not encouraged. This was reinforced by the training philosophy of the time which was still run by doctors. Fisher's *Modern Methods of Treatment – A Guide for Nurses* had replaced the 'red handbook' by 1948 and taught the nurse to be of assistance to the doctor. However it also acknowledged that nurses had the power to influence well-being through role-modelling, orderly conduct and hope (Curry, 1991: 99).

Treatment

Although hope and care were advocated, administering it appeared difficult in the military type regime of the time. Patients were still 'aired' for five hours a day (four hours in inclement weather) and counted in and out of the 'airing courts' in many hospitals. Nurses and patients alike found this 'soul destroying' according to Nolan (1993: 109), and likewise found the endless cleaning and scrubbing futile. Many of these nurses had no idea what skills if any had got them the job in the first place. It seems a requirement of Broadgate staff was skills in music, sewing, sport, dancing, handicraft and singing according to Sister Edie Ashton (Curry, 1991: 73).

Bob Farrar started working at Broadgate in 1946 because he could not get a job in the police or the post office. However, there was some evidence of progress. Cec Wedge, a nurse at Broadgate in the 1950s recalled his interview where he was asked why he wanted to be a nurse. He said his father had been an attendant, and he was berated for using the terminology. 'A nurse', he said. 'That's better', said the chief male nurse. Cec recalls airing duties being just like a prison set up (Curry, 1991: 50), where people wandered aimlessly for hours, probably pondering escape. It was not just the patients either. He recalls instances where new staff would go for breakfast and never be seen again. I have seen that myself, in Guernsey in 1999. This job is not for everybody.

Efforts to define the role became systematic in the 1950s, but failed to find agreement due to the wide range of tasks and types of care provided. It is difficult to know if this lack of definition impacted on practice. It seems the majority of psychiatric nurses of the time were largely subservient to the medical profession and either quite happily so or unable to contemplate any other options. This was not the case with all nurses however, some of whom began to attempt change simply by building relationships with patients and trying to work with them. Some of this was structured, with the initiation of the forerunners of the primary nurse system. A lot was more spontaneous however, which supports both the long held belief in the power of the caring relationship and the nursing desire to seek it.

I was trained at Broadgate Hospital, Beverley and De La Pole Hospital in Willerby. De La Pole was known at the time for Dr Bickford's methods of occupational therapy developed in the 1950s. I remember being shown film of patients and staff engaged in all manner of sporting activity. Everybody appeared incredibly smartly dressed, and it all looked very stiff and formal. It was radical for its time though, and was clearly attempting to help people develop and integrate through purposeful activity. Dr Bickford always gave credit to the nursing staff for their commitment. The nurses took long-stay patients on holidays, and this appears to have been a trend of the time. In

Warrington for example a group of staff and patients went to Switzerland, complete with climbing gear (Bruton and Fox, 2007).

Cec Wedge, the nurse mentioned above was still working when I started my training at Broadgate. He once took a party of 26 patients and staff to Ostend, then on to Paris and Brussels. A Belgian man was so taken with the way the staff looked after the patients that he gave them all £10 for a drink, a huge amount of money at the time. Upon return one of the patients was asked where he had been and he said 'Oh, we've been to Hornsea!' (Curry, 1991). Hornsea is the closest seaside town to Beverley, about 10 miles from Broadgate. Nevertheless, these actions and activities showed that chronic patients previously thought intractably institutionalised could now potentially return to their community with the right kind of support. Undoubtedly one of the major factors in this was the relationships built between staff and patients.

Chlorpromazine

It was in this atmosphere of therapeutic activity and increasing discharge rate (Eisenberg, 2007) that chlorpromazine was launched. It was received very well by psychiatrists who now appeared to have in their armoury a potent weapon in the drive to cure chronic mental disease. Psychiatry was widely disparaged at the time. Consider Winston Churchill's (1951) view:

> *...it is very wrong to disturb large numbers of healthy, normal men and women by asking the kind of questions in which psychiatrists specialise. There are quite enough hangers on and camp followers already.*

Chlorpromazine therefore appealed greatly to psychiatry's mainstream medical aspirations. However it was soon noted that the atmosphere in which chlorpromazine was delivered remained a large factor in recovery. That is, drugs have a more powerful effect in a therapeutic setting. This was not lost on Smith, Kline and French who used Hildegard Peplau and other nurses to endorse the drug in a film shown to student nurses in the UK (Smoyak, 1991). By 1958 the 'open door' policy was more the norm, and the strictly custodial nature of the job diminished further.

According to Nolan (1993) this was an anxious time for nurses. They thought they would be made redundant by the new drug treatments, and if not by them by the upsurge of social workers and occupational therapists whose ranks were swelling at the time. Although it was clear psychiatric nurses were central to a lot of innovative activity they were not party to the wider debates in any formal way. They had no power. Training remained largely irrelevant and medicalised, despite the growing recognition of the value of nursing per se.

However, despite the increased discharge rate and reduction in length of stay, actual numbers of patients continued to rise. The Government responded with the 1959 Mental Health Act which challenged again the underpinning assumptions of institutional care. The notion of informal patients was introduced. The idea was that these patients would have the same rights as any other patient in the wider NHS. The population of the hospitals changed virtually overnight and the number of psychologists increased 10 fold in as many years (Bushfield, 1986) to treat this new informal population. The incoming psychologists and the social workers had no allegiance to the institutions. The move towards community care can therefore be attributed in part to this power shift triggered by the 1959 Mental Health Act. The dual themes of legislation and role anxiety emerge.

So what did mental health nurses do?

One of the main reasons for anxiety at this time was the fact that it remained unclear exactly what nurses did that was uniquely therapeutic, or indeed unique at all. Their role, previously largely taken for granted was now eroding according to historians. Certainly the custodial angle was substantially reduced after 1959 when padded rooms were dismantled, doors were opened and visiting became unrestricted. It must be clarified, however, that the custodial aspect did not disappear. My colleague Boyd Thomson was a psychiatric nurse in the 1970s, when patients were watched at Ravenscraig Hospital, Greenock in much the same way as mentioned by Cec Wedge at Broadgate in the 1950s. Nevertheless, therapeutic aspects of mental health nursing started to gain more attention. For instance psychiatric nurses appeared to be excellent in building, maintaining and positively exploiting caring relationships. Surely they must have a unique set of skills to be able to develop these 'professional' caring relationships?

Annie Altschul famously studied interpersonal relationships between nurses and patients in 1972, with the hypothesis that she would uncover theoretical or systematic underpinnings to these complex interactions. What she found was common sense. Henley and Brown (1974) went on to suggest that skills that professionals lay claim to are merely a smokescreen for them to make a living from the damaged psyches of desperate people. This is clearly an extreme view, but Henley and Brown did point to the difficulty in defining a professional caring relationship, which was about to become increasingly problematic for professionals apparently required to justify their existence.

1960–1989

The 1960s saw the rise of antipsychiatry, as discussed in *Chapter 1,* with the works of Goffman, Llaing and Szasz. This movement was timely for the Government. Just like the asylums 100 years previously the rationale for community care was primarily economic rather than philosophical. The Government could not afford to keep putting more and more money into the NHS. No pilot studies were ever undertaken of community care but it was initiated nonetheless. Unemployment was higher than it had been for decades by the early 1980s, and a transformation of the NHS was undertaken. Competitive tendering began and managerialism was introduced as a philosophy with nurses not being encouraged to apply for the senior posts.

This was very much the era of institutional investigations, and it has been argued that changes in mental health nurse training arose in direct response to one of these investigations criticising mental handicap services. The Jay Report of 1979 (DHSS, 1979) had concluded that mental handicap nurses were inadequately trained. Before this accusation could be levelled at mental health nursing the 1982 syllabus was hurriedly developed. The syllabus was based on a premise that institutionalisation was inherently negative. It consequently supported an uncritical view that community care was better. Hopton (1997) believed that mental health nursing at this point embraced uncritically the humanistic psychology inherent in the syllabus. This promoted a false image of mental health nursing as innovative and creative. This false image was based on the premise which suggested it had thoroughly embraced user-centred approaches to care, which Hopton believed was not the case. Instead he saw this blind adoption of naïve notions of humanistic psychology as instead masking the deeper structural problems inherent in mental health nursing. He suggested a more critical analysis should precede acceptance of any ideology, and recommended a deeper re-engagement with the original antipsychiatry movements in order to generate a more authentic identity.

However the vast majority of nurses of the 1960s and 1970s did not really appear to be searching for a coherent ideology. They were also less anxious than is inferred in the literature. Their reality remained pragmatic. It was one of delivering care, not contemplating the reason for their professional existence. The 1959 Mental Health Act had effectively lessened formality and encouraged therapeutic intervention but the job was still predominantly custodial and task-orientated, which maintained security inherent in routine, however boring this may have been. For example, cleaning duties were not removed from nursing (and patients) at Broadgate Hospital until 1972 (Curry, 1991: 101).Community nursing in Broadgate was initiated not as a therapeutic innovation or an expression of antipsychiatry but as a solution to the ambulance strike of 1973. Nurses went out in order to administer depot injections to patients unable to attend.

Theory and practice were very much seen as separate in this era which is why it is difficult to read Hopton's view as anything other than a historical analysis, however accurate that may be. Partnership between academia and practice has always been seen by nurses as secondary to the work they actually do. There is evidence this is changing as the concept of evidence-based practice is now more firmly embedded in the language of both, but this is a short history.

Ken Tracey was a nurse tutor when I started training in 1985 and he had established the first school of nursing at Broadgate in 1959. Initially he says that charge nurses had wanted nothing to do with the training of staff, not seeing it as their responsibility. Ken Tracey's story elaborates his part in convincing them otherwise. A series of more and more progressive syllabi moved nursing away from medicine and embraced more humanistic training, owned more by new students through an increasing sense of responsibility for their own training. This does not appear to have been entirely without criticism as Hopton suggests. One negative consequence of this evolution voiced by Tracey was the breakdown of the close association between the school and medical staff (Hopton, 1997: 116). He finishes his story somewhat ironically by suggesting that if psychiatry can provide evidence of success by working its way out of its function, then Broadgate can be considered a success. It closed on 21 May 1989 and is now the site of a housing estate. Training is therefore a major theme, as are the institutions that provide it.

The 1994 review of mental health nursing

The Broadgate class of 1985, along with the remaining patients and staff, moved into the community with trepidation. Tales of the *abandonati*, where ex patients aimlessly roamed the streets of Italy generated fears that we would make the same mistakes. Some argue that we have (Kendall, 2005). The Community Care Act 1990 provided the legal framework which defined responsibilities of local authorities and health services. This resulted in a more open system of accountability for the assessment and delivery of care packages to the mentally ill. Local authorities became responsible for inspection of all community services either purchased or provided by them. The Care Programme Approach simultaneously provided guidance for health authorities on how they should fulfil their duties under the Act. The practicalities of implementation remain an ongoing venture.

Hospital-based units were still seen to be required at this time for those whose needs could not be met anywhere else. Two wards were opened in Bridlington District General Hospital to accommodate these groups in 1990, which were not welcomed by everybody. Having an open door policy for the mentally ill in an old lunatic asylum appeared acceptable to the majority. Having an open door policy in the local general hospital raised many ancient fears, and one of the first duties of the new teams in the hospital was to assuage these. This was not easy when a lot of these fears were shared by the team. What made the practicalities justifiable was that people still needed care, and that is what mental health nurses do. However, this pragmatic attitude required refining and defining according to the instigators of the 1994 review of mental health nursing (Smith, 1994). Public expectation had risen on the wave of new drugs and therapies. Project 2000 had introduced higher education instead of hospital-based training, and the wider changes introduced by the 1990 Community Care Act meant the time was right for a review.

Working in Partnership: A Collaborative Approach to Care (Mental Health Nursing Review Team, 1994) explicitly attempted to identify the 'future role and function of mental health nurses and their potential contribution in a wide variety of settings' (1994: 6). The review team adopted a very wide remit and concluded that the relationship between nurse and service user was at the heart of nursing practice (Norman and Ryrie, 2004). They made 42 recommendations, among them the label change from 'psychiatric nursing' to 'mental health nursing'. The recommendation to continue mental health nursing as a pre-registration speciality was possibly the most valuable acknowledgment of the need for dedicated mental health nurses in this time of uncertainty. The report also questioned the value of psychiatric units attached to general hospitals and supported the value of clinical supervision. It urged increased partnership with patients, and suggested that nurses focus on patients with severe and enduring mental illness. Overall it contained little new however, and failed to specify what skills were needed to deliver specific therapies (Smith, 1994).

I spent five of the years since the review as a community psychiatric nurse (it seems the acronym CPN remained acceptable) in the older person mental health team in Greenock. In that period the 'team' grew from a group of geographically separate individuals managed in different cultures to a co-located joint managed team led by a jointly funded team leader, in this case a social worker. Infrastructure has slowly built around this model, supporting joint working principles (Scottish Executive, 2000). Single shared assessment (Scottish Executive, 2003) was adopted as the process by which care was managed. Care management became the core business. In practice this meant the team member with the most appropriate skills would become responsible for all aspects of a particular person's care. Whether care management should be part of a CPN role remains the subject of much debate regarding appropriate usage of skills. This naturally leads back to questions of what those skills are. As advanced roles developed across the profession, among them authority to prescribe, another review was felt to be timely.

Rights, relationships and recovery

Morris (2005) looked forward to the review in England

For nursing, the somewhat contentious prospect of medication prescribing and an expanded role in detaining patients are clearly part of the agenda although these are seemingly already well-worn debates, and perhaps the review should provide a definitive professional view.

It did not, which suggests either that the debate was not quite as well worn as had been presumed, or that the review was simply badly timed for inclusion of anything other than rhetoric. Evidence was certainly sparse in relation to mental health nurse prescribing.

As far as the Scottish review was concerned (Scottish Executive, 2006) it concluded from a similarly wide consultation that people want nurses who care about them, who listen, spend time, inspire hope and can equip them with skills and techniques they need to work towards recovery (ibid: 4). Although the language was more specific there are clear comparisons with the 1994 conclusions on what a nurse should do. Recovery constitutes a large part of the philosophy of both the English and Scottish reviews and the recovery approach (Barker, 2002) is suggested as the model for nursing care (Scottish Executive, 2006: 5).

The review goes on to say that people want more access to talking therapies (ibid: 5). The development of rights-based and person-centred care is stressed and is a requisite of the recovery approach. This is to be achieved through 'values and principles-based practice' set around a defined skill base (ibid: 5). The skills are defined by the 10 essential shared capabilities (ESCs) (Sainsbury Centre for Mental Health, 2004) (see *Figure 2.2*). The principles and values are those which underpin the Mental Health (Care and Treatment) (Scotland) Act 2003 shown are in *Figure 2.3*. The values, skills and the principles all have their roots in the Human Rights Act 1998 which itself can be traced back to the European Convention on Human Rights 1950 as discussed previously. The current mental health nurse value system amalgamates the skills in *Figure 2.2* and the principles in *Figure 2.3* onto a background of human rights shown in *Box 2.1*.

A primary attraction of the recovery approach is in its evolution from service user movements, which supports the theme of empowerment inherent in the 1950 convention, 1959 Mental Health Act, 1994 Review, 1998 Human Rights Act and the Mental Health Care and Treatment (Scotland) Act 2003. Recovery has been operationalised in the UK in part by Barker (2002) and his tidal model. Barker is unashamedly 'anti-psychiatry' although prefers the term 'pro-recovery' (Emerick, 2006), and like Hopton (1997) wishes mental

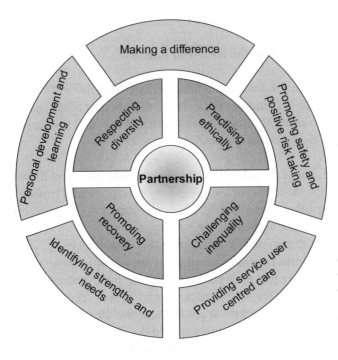

Figure 2.2. Ten essential shared capabilities (Sainsbury Centre for Mental Health, 2004).

health nurses would adopt a more critical appraisal of their core functions (Buchanan-Barker and Barker, 2005).

However, this is to presume that mental health nurses have core functions. Do they? These questions seem to occupy academics more than they do practising mental health nurses, who appear reasonably clear about the task in hand. For example, when attempting to assist an incontinent person with cognitive problems to the toilet the 'core function' is rarely a primary concern. However this is a cheap point. The value of having a clear philosophy is evident in the security and power afforded those professions that do. Hopton and Barker's criticism of the failure of nursing to have a cohesive philosophy does not necessarily detract from its ability to assist with recovery. Mental health nursing has been historically pragmatic, and therefore the 'mix and match' philosophies which appear to offend the academics may in practice be useful. What if there is no 'core' of nursing, or an all encompassing philosophy to underpin professionalism? What is left is what works, which is what has been done. This pragmatic approach does not appear as uncritical as Hopton suggests. With the acceptance of evidence-based practice and clinical supervision a more reflective application of contemporary thought has emerged. Consider the recovery approach. The recovery approach is based on the principle of empowerment, so in practice service users are given far more 'say' in their treatment than they have historically. The individual is seen as the person most likely to understand

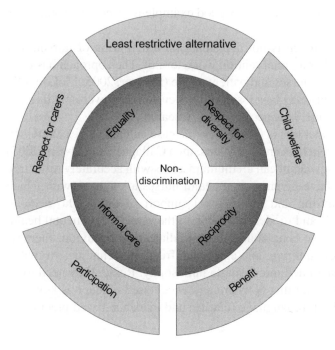

*Figure 2.3.
Principles of Mental
Health (Care
and Treatment)
(Scotland) Act
2003.*

Box 2.1. Human rights

- The right to life
- The right to freedom from slavery and indentured servitude
- The right to liberty, and freedom from arbitrary arrest or detention
- The right to freedom from torture, inhuman or degrading treatment or punishment
- The right to a fair and public hearing and to be presumed innocent until proven guilty
- The right to freedom of expression, including freedom of the press
- The right to respect for private and family life and the right to marry and found a family
- The right to freedom of thought, conscience and religion
- The right to freedom of assembly and associations, including the right to join a trade union
- The right to participate in fair and free elections
- The right to property
- The right to education

his or her own journey of recovery. A good example is respecting someone's wishes not to take medication.

The recovery approach is not dependant on a definition of nursing but on evidence of whether an intervention works or not. The approach has been well received so far by nurses and patients alike (Reisner, 2005; McLoughlin and Getter, 2006). This may be a result of its focus on empowerment through therapeutic relationship. This needs further research.

However, given that this is found to be the case and the values expressed in the reviews underpin these relationships, then Callaghan and Owen (2005) and the Scottish review team can credit themselves with accurately reflecting the zeitgeist. They have given mental health nurses a language with which to justify their enduring and professional support of those who need it. There are many tools and models available to the present day mental health nurse, such as cognitive behavioural therapy, dialectical behaviour therapy, neuro-linguistic programming, and emotional freedom technique. Arguably none needs to be integrated into a single philosophy. Rather they need to be rigorously evaluated, and this is where evidence-based practice is key. The final themes are therefore language (clarity) and evidence-based practice.

Conclusion

History shows that, although it has always been alluded to, mental health nursing had no 'official' place in the care of the mentally ill until the late 18th century. Prior to that care was custodial or delivered in the community. Ancient external views of the causes of mental illness were replaced with monotheistic views around the middle ages. Medicine in turn became the predominant language of mental illness as this view faded. Psychiatry became a sub-speciality of medicine around 1850, at which time nurses were called attendants and did what they were told by the medical superintendents of the asylums. The first signs of nursing becoming a profession emerged with certified training under the Royal Medico Psychological Association in 1894. However, although some notable exceptions existed, nurses had broadly similar status to patients. Nurses administered unusual treatments without question, their opinions were not sought, and their main function was to form a barrier between the general public (often including the medical superintendent) and the insane.

The profession grew as society became more liberal in the 20th century. Training became the remit of nurses instead of doctors; mental health legislation increasingly reflected human rights; treatments arguably became more effective; and everybody became more informed. Throughout this time mental health nurses held a course somewhere between custodian and therapist. They offered occupational therapy, refuge, routine, companionship, advice,

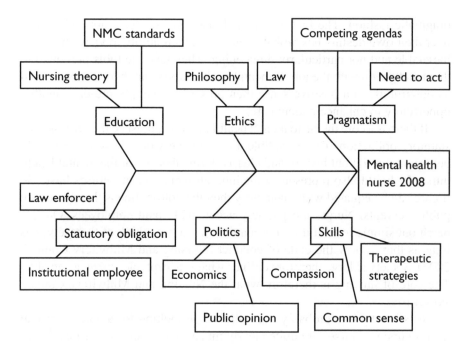

Figure 2.4. Themes of mental health nursing.

relationships, support, safety, structure, goals, physical care, compassion and concern at the same time as rule and law enforcement. Certainly mental health nurses have historically been more reactive than proactive, but does this necessarily reflect disempowerment in politics or just disinterest? They may be the same thing. Mental health nurses often appear to be on the edge of extinction due to their role ambiguity, whereas the reality seems to support their enduring flexibility in the face of constant change.

Is there a theme that underpins this endurance? Is there a core category of mental health nursing? The themes that have emerged during this chapter are illustrated in *Figure 2.4*.

For the purpose of identifying a core category, the majority of these themes appear to represent a series of impact factors as opposed to aspects of an emergent core. That is, these themes are mainly a summary of external demands and expectations. Mental health nurses have historically had little say in what their education and statutory duties should be, which themselves have been dictated by the prevailing politics and economics. The skills which have developed have largely been despite rather than because of these factors. Arguably there are elements of a trend towards autonomy but it is clear that historically mental health nurses have been told rather than asked what to do. This is not the whole picture however, as these factors in themselves have largely been absorbed by mental health nursing in a pragmatic fashion. The fact that mental health nurses have not had control over their own destiny has probably enhanced their ability to view change as inevitable and not particularly threatening. They take the tools presented to them and get on with the job. If mental health nurses can therefore be viewed as opportunist in a positive sense then prescribing simply presents another opportunity to enhance patient care.

If there is a core theme to mental health nursing it must be the profession's statutory obligation. To be credible a core theme would have to be largely persistent throughout history and clearly define the role of the mental health nurse. It should also represent something all mental health nurses have. So if core can be equated with mandatory then the bottom line is that nurses are public servants. Nurses are publicly accountable paid employees. On this harsh but simple level it does not matter what nurses think of themselves as long as they follow the code of conduct (Nursing and Midwifery Council, 2007). Society at large therefore defines what is acceptable and unacceptable. The core of nursing is therefore what the Nursing and Midwifery Council says it is.

This is why it is probably not useful to go looking for a core of mental health nursing. Nurses are quite clearly much more than a set of mandatory minimum standards. The Nursing and Midwifery Council recognises this. There are formal opportunities for nurses to expand their roles within this statutory framework (Nursing and Midwifery Council, 2007), and an opportunity has certainly been handed to mental health nursing with the new prescribing legislation. That is, the legislation was not primarily meant for mental health nurses. In fact, few people had thought about the impact on mental health practice, and were instead focused on the expansion of prescribing rights for those who had already demonstrated it to be safe and effective, namely district nurses and health visitors. However, now the legislation is here it would be foolish to let the chance go by. If mental health nurses do not take up the opportunity, the newly qualified pharmacy or even podiatry prescriber may feel competent enough to do so. The next chapter focuses on the history of prescribing in order to explore these issues.

Further reading

Foucault M (1965) *Madness and Civilisation: A History of Insanity in the Age of Reason*. New York: Random House

It is impossible to summarise Foucault, and it has been said that he is more often quoted than actually read. In this book he states, for example, 'Where there is a work of art there is no madness' (p. 274), and that madness is seen as the 'psychological effect of a moral fault' (p. 150). Throughout the book he combines in-depth historical and moral analysis of madness with unique insight into explanatory theories. Roy Porter suggested that the insights from this book have yet to be fully appreciated and absorbed.

Kutchins H, Kirk H (1997) *Making us Crazy. DSM: The Psychiatric Bible and the Creation of Mental Disorders.* New York: Simon and Shuster

This is a fascinating account of the politics underpinning the creation of categories of mental illness for the purpose of diagnostics. It combines in-depth analysis with classic examples to illustrate both the frailty and arguable necessity of this system.

Nolan P (1993) *A History of Mental Health Nursing.* London: Chapman Hall

This is the only comprehensive history of mental health nursing in the UK. Much of this chapter owes a debt to this book.

Porter R (2002) *Madness; a Brief History.* Oxford: Oxford University Press

This book is widely regarded as the best introduction to the history of madness.

Roberts A (2008) *Mental Health History Timeline.* Available from: www. mdx.ac.uk/www/study/mhhtim.htm

This remarkably detailed and deep resource is highly recommended.

References

Abel-Smith B (1977) *A History of the Nursing Profession.* London, Heinemann

Baldick C (1990) *The Oxford Concise Dictionary of Literary Terms.* Oxford, Oxford University Press

Barker P (2002) The Tidal Model: The healing potential of metaphor within the patient's narrative. *J Psychosoc Nursing* **40**(7): 42–50

Barker P (2006) Mental health nursing: The craft of the impossible? *J Psychiatric Ment Health Nursing* **13**(4): 385–7

Blackmore S (2005) *Conversations on Consciousness.* Oxford, Oxford University Press

Brooking JI (1985) Advanced psychiatric nursing in Britain. *J Adv Nursing* **10**: 455–68

Bruton R, Fox E (2007) The Standard 1972. Warrington, *Winwick Hospital Warrington Magazine*

Buchanan-Barker P, Barker P (2005) Observation: The original sin of mental health nursing? *J Psychiatric Ment Health Nursing* **12**(9): 541–9

Bushfield J (1986) *Managing Madness.* London, Unwin Hyman

Callaghan P, Owen S (2005) Psychiatric and mental health nursing: Past, present and future. *J Psychiatric Ment Health Nursing* **12**: 639–41

Churchill W (1951) *The Second World War.* Vol 4. London, Cassell

Clarke B (1975) *Mental Disorder in Early Britain.* Cardiff, University of Wales Press

Curry R (1991) *Across the Westwood. The Life and Times of Broadgate Hospital Beverley.*

Mental Health Unit. East Yorkshire Health Authority

Department of Health and Social Security (1979) *Report of the Committee of Enquiry into Mental Handicap Nursing*. London, HMSO

Easterbrooke CE (1940) *The Chronicle of Crichton Royal*. Dumfries, Courier Press

Eigen JP (1995) *Witnessing Insanity – Madness and Mad-Doctors in the English Court*. London, Yale University Press

Eisenberg L (2007) Furor Therapeuticus: Benjamin Rush and the Philadelphia Yellow Fever Epidemic of 1793. *Amer J Psychiatry* **164**(4): 552–6

Emerick R (2006) *"Antipsychiatry" and "Consumerism": Perspectives and Definitions Psychiatry*. Available from: http://ps.psychiatryonline.org/cgi/content/full/57/10/1514?etoc [Accessed 14 December 2006]

Foucault M (1965) *Madness and Civilisation: A History of Insanity in the Age of Reason*. New York, Random House

Goldstein JL, Godemont MML (2003) The legend and lessons of Geel, Belgium: A 1500-year-old legend, a 21st-century model. *Community Ment Health J* **39**(5): 441–58

Harcourt Williams M (2001) *An Outline of the History of the Examinations for Mental Nurses Organised by the (Royal) Medico-Psychological Association*. Available from: http://www.rcpsych.ac.uk/college/archives/history/nursinghistory.aspx [Accessed 22 June 2007]

Henley N, Brown P (1974) The myth of skill and the class nature of professionalism. In Radical Therapist/Rough Times Collective (eds) *The Radical Therapist*. Harmondsworth, Penguin

Hopton J (1997) Towards a critical theory of mental health nursing. *J Adv Nursing* **25**(3): 492–500

Hunter R, Macalpine I (1970) *Three Hundred Years of Psychiatry*. Oxford, Oxford University Press

Kendall T (2005) *Trieste: The Current Situation*. Available from: http://www.human-nature.com/hraj/trieste.html [Accessed 26 June 2007]

McLoughlin KA, Getter JL(2006) The Recovery Model and Seclusion and Restraint. *Psychiatric Services* **57**(7): 1045

Mental Health Nursing Review Team (1994) *Working in Partnership*. London, Department of Health

Morris M (2005) Review of mental health nursing is long overdue. *Brit J Nursing* **14**(5): 246

Nietzsche F (1895) *The Antichrist*. Transl HL Mencken in 1920 Available from: http://www.fns.org.uk/ac.htm [Accessed 12April 2008]

Nolan P (1990a) Psychiatric nursing – the first 100 years. *Senior Nurse* **10**(10): 20–3

Nolan P (1990b) Looking at the first 100 years. *Senior Nurse* **11**(1): 22–5

Nolan P (1990c) Psychiatric nursing: The first 100 years *Senior Nurse* **11**(2): 12–14

Nolan P (1993) *A History of Mental Health Nursing*. London, Chapman Hall

Nordenfelt L (1997) The stoic conception of mental disorder: The case of Cicero. *Philosophy, Psychiatry, and Psychology* **4**(4): 285–91

Norman I, Ryrie I (2004) Mental health nursing: Origins and orientation. In Norman I, Ryrie I (eds). *The Art and Science of Mental Health Nursing*. Buckingham, Open

University Press

Paley J (2002) Caring as a slave morality: Nietzschean themes in nursing ethics. *J Adv Nursing* **40**(1): 25–35

Ramsamy S (2001) *Caring for Madness. The Role of Personal Experience in the Training of Mental Health Nurses.* London, Whurr

Parry-Jones WL (1972) *The Trade in Lunacy.* London, Routledge and Kegan Paul

Plato (1901) *The Republic*, Translation by Benjamin Jowett. Stephanus page numbers used. Available from: http://www.mdx.ac.uk/www/study/xpla0.htm [Accessed 1 June 2007]

Porter R (2002) *Madness: A Brief History.* Oxford, Oxford University Press

Reisner AD (2005) The Common Factors, Empirically Validated Treatments, and Recovery Models of Therapeutic Change. *Psychological Record* **55**(3): 377–99

Roberts A (1981) *Mental Health History Timeline.* Available from: http://www.mdx.ac.uk/ www/study/mhhtim.htm Middlesex University. [Accessed 27 June 2007]

Sainsbury Centre for Mental Health (2004) *Ten Essential Shared Capabilities. A Framework for the Whole Mental Health Workforce.* London, Sainsbury Centre for Mental Health

Scottish Executive (2000) *Report of the Joint Future Group.* Available from: http://www. scotland.gov.uk/library3/social/rjfg-00.asp [Accessed 27 June 2007]

Scottish Executive (2003) *Framework to Assess Local Authority/NHS Partnerships' Performance on Joint Working.* Available from: http://www.scotland.gov.uk/ Publications/2003/03/16630/19312 [Accessed 27 June 2007]

Scottish Executive (2006) *Rights Relationships and Recovery.* Available from: http://www. scotland.gov.uk/Resource/Doc/112046/0027278.pdf [Accessed 14 December 2006]

Scull AT (1979) *Museums of Madness.* London, Penguin Books

Smith LN (1994) A review of the Report on Mental Health Nursing in England: Working in partnership. *J Psychiatric Ment Health Nursing* **1**: 179–84

Smoyak AS (1991) Psychosocial nursing in public versus private sectors. *J Psychosoc Nursing* **29**: 6–12

Wikipedia (2007) *Exorcism.* Available from: http://en.wikipedia.org/wiki/Exorcism [Accessed 18 May 2007]

CHAPTER 3

The history of prescribing

Chlorpromazine, imipramine and diazepam are all highly significant in the story of mental health treatment. So is the role of the mental health nurse. Of comparable significance is who controls the supply and demand of these resources. This chapter focuses on legislation and management of medication. Prior to 1906 there were no laws restricting the purchase of medicines. Medicines containing derivatives of morphine and cocaine were freely available as sedatives and tonics, respectively, and even if a prescription had been involved the pharmacist would have dispensed it without question. People could medicate themselves to excess with all manner of drugs including barbiturates and chloral hydrate without recourse to psychiatry or even medicine and, as with alcohol today, most people did not but some did. Opiates were clearly addictive hence socially problematic and thus came within the remit of law. It was as a direct consequence of the laws designed to restrict the use of opiates that prescription only medicines became the norm. This chapter tells the story of the regulation of medicines.

Following the tightening of drug laws it became more problematic for the average person to manage his or her own medication. The ensuing power shift away from the individual led many commentators to criticise the emergent medico-pharmaceutical complex as a unique and dishonest monopoly. That is, the consumer is considered by many to be captive to a degree unmatched by any other industry (Temin, 1980; Healy, 2004). This industry is worth vast sums of money which is certainly a factor in the huge array of literature criticising it. However, this state of affairs is not particularly new, and can be traced back to the 18th century when the main power sharing was between the apothecaries and the medical profession. Of major relevance from the mental health aspect is the recognition that psychiatry as opposed to general medicine rather fortuitously came to control the new psychotropic medicines. This is a consequence of how illnesses are conceptualised in the UK. In Japan for example drug laws are very similar, but psychosomatic medicine is in the hands of neurologists and physicians. Benzodiazepines do not produce comparable dependence in Japan, and in 2003 fluoxetine had not yet been marketed there as an antidepressant. This may not be simply a factor of differing genetics. Healy (2002: 67) believes market forces are a significant factor in determining culture. Non-medical prescribing has now resurfaced and with it comes a new dimension to the culture of medication management.

This chapter therefore builds on the themes raised in the last chapter in regard to who is responsible for mental health care and why, but here the focus will be specifically on the legal and practical aspects of prescribing. In order to understand the current situation this chapter starts with a broad history of medicine legislation. It then concentrates on developments within the 20th century which led to the return of non-medical prescribing. The chapter is immediately followed by a short summary integrating this chapter with the previous chapters to illustrate why mental health nurse prescribing is an end point of these combined histories.

Non-medical prescribing: Money

Although people have self-medicated throughout history a good place to start this chapter is with the story of patent medicines. A patent medicine is a medicine made and marketed under a patent and available without prescription. The name is still used in the US to refer to over-the-counter drugs. Patent medicines originated from the 1624 Statute of Monopolies in England, which granted 14 years of protected monopoly for the sale of a branded medicine. The main purpose of the statute was actually to restrict the King's right to create private monopolies in the domestic economy. The statute also aimed to encourage private business, and in granting a period of monopoly for a registered product it was thought this would give innovative ideas an advantage. Preparers of medicines had the right to use 'secret ingredients' until the Pharmacy and Medicines Act of 1941 required their disclosure for safety reasons. The business of patent medicines therefore had 300 years to grow.

The sale of these products expanded particularly rapidly in the 18th century. Brand names such as Mother Ashton and Mrs Gares were used to personalise the belief that each generation had a secret recipe that could cure all ills (marketing is an ancient skill). Analysis of one of the most popular ointments of the Victorian era, Dr. Roberts' original Poor Man's Friend ointment revealed that it consisted chiefly of paraffin. Brown's Herbal Ointment was essentially petroleum jelly. Manufacturers of these compounds were often coal merchants as their main trade hence their ease of access to carbon-based materials. The real power of these medicines lay broadly in their marketing, and I had very early personal experience of the power of this. As a five-year-old my grandmother gave me a large spoonful of Angiers emulsion (*Figure 3.1*) when I was sick. I cannot remember what it was supposed to do but it certainly did not stop me feeling sick. It was revolting and this was in 1966, some 25 years after the 1941 Act.

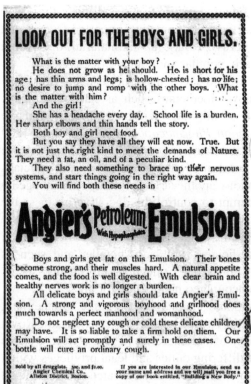

Figure 3.1. The benefits of Angiers emulsion.

There was (is) a lot of money to be made from illness, and those involved in the management of it would direct business each other's way (Porter and Porter, 1989). For example physicians would prescribe huge quantities of medicine to benefit the apothecary, who would in turn recommend those physicians as the best that he knew. This practice was widespread and commonplace, one of the reasons it came to the attention of the law. As a direct result of this unscrutinised back-scratching it became illegal for practitioners who certified insanity to accept recompense from the madhouse operators. This did not stop it happening however. John Conolly, the psychiatrist who formalised training for junior doctors and famous for his liberal approach to restraint has also become a subject of accusations in this regard (Schwieso, 1996).

Chemicals, patents, gullibility and power

Medicine became increasingly interested in drug treatments between 1600 and 1900 because there were more of them. Up until 1600 herb-based galenic formulations had prevailed for the previous 1300 years. This changed with the discovery and import of drugs from the Orient and the Americas. By the end of the 17th century several hundred exotic drugs had made their way to the public. For example, ipecacuanha (an emetic), imported from South America to France in 1672, and Peruvian Bark (an antimalarial) discovered by Europe in 1630 were particularly popular and highly effective.

Developments in chemistry around the same time also provided raw ingedients for the creation of novel medicines such as ferrous sulphate. Glauber's salt is the sodium salt of sulphuric acid and a highly effective laxative. Each edition of the *London Pharmacopoeia* from 1621 to 1809 showed an increase in chemically created cures, and demand drove supply. People actively sought these modern remedies, while physicians increasingly warned of unscrupulous apothecaries exploiting the allegedly ignorant masses. Partly in an attempt to control this lucrative business the hypochondria and drug dependence of that era were portrayed by those without vested business interests as the products of corruption of civilisation (Porter, 1983). Nevertheless, medicines were very popular and seen as a common right. Charities, as well as the College of Physicians, set up dispensaries for the poor which encouraged medication for all.

As far as the broader organisation of medicine went in the 19th century, medical professionals belonged to the Royal College of Physicians, the Royal College of Surgeons or the Society of Apothecaries. These reflected status groups in medicine as well as the differing duties and legal privileges within the medical community. Physicians were university educated and considered the most knowledgeable about medicine. Surgeons performed operations, and treated accident cases and skin disorders. They were apprenticed just as other traditional craftsmen. Apothecaries were responsible for the sale, compounding and supply of drugs. They were also able to provide medical advice and prescribe medication themselves thanks to the Apothecaries Act of 1815. They had actually been able to do this from 1704, as long as they only charged for treatment they sold and not the advice. Apothecaries, like surgeons, were apprenticed as skilled tradesmen. They became rich and moved to the very top of society, with many becoming members or Parliament and mayors. This publicly demonstrated that control of medication supply and demand could bring significant wealth and status.

In the late 19th century further advances were being made in medicine. The British Medical Association (BMA) began to take a leading role in influencing legislation on public health matters. This was mainly in response to the growing opiate addiction, which was framed as a medical issue in need of regulation. Also it turned out that a lot of the patent remedies were worse than ineffectual, they were dangerous. A BMA campaign in 1909 resulted in many patent medicine proprietors moderating the often exaggerated claims, while increased scrutiny ultimately caused the demise of many others.

These remedies did not just disappear. Still with us are Vick's vapour rub and milk of magnesia. I am not sure about Angiers emulsion. However, it is clear there is a residual power in customer loyalty. Consumers are still willing to pay significantly more for branded over-the-counter medicines (consider the price difference between generic ibuprofen and Nurofen). Although this may simply represent the power of branding (Gregory, 2003) and may appear to be the modern face of gullibility it also illustrates the importance of trust when it comes to medication management. From a positive perspective trust is an important aspect of a good therapeutic relationship, which is what mental health nurses excel at. The significance of this to concordance is clear. That is, medication concordance is improved as a consequence of partnership (Nolan and Badger, 2005; Benson and Britten, 2006). Recent conceptualisations of the mental health nurse role see it as one of partnership within a journey of recovery. Consequently mental health nurses are already very well placed to enhance concordance. Taking on the role of prescriber should further enhance concordance based on this established ability to engender trust. This argument will be returned to in *Chapter 7*.

Psychiatry: In the right place at the right time

Prior to the 1950s there were no antidepressants, and prevalence of clinical depression according to Porter (2002) was around 100 per million. Prevalence currently runs at 100000, a thousandfold increase. The reasons for this are complex, and include differing historical definitions of depression. For example the 'English malady' (Cheyne, 1773) has been hypothesised as 'depression before depression', and is the subject of a current PhD study at the University of Sunderland. The likelihood is that mood disorders have always been a problem for a substantial proportion of the population. Some of the best literature in history focuses on the darker side of people's feelings. How were these people treating themselves before 1950? This is difficult to know as modern concepts of depression clearly do not align with older ones. Also, in the pre-prescription chemotherapy era no records exist. One possibility is that people would have bought an occasional 'tonic' (cocaine) for milder forms. However, for more serious episodes warranting hospitalisation it is difficult to know as the discharge summary would not indicate medicinal treatment because the patients were expected to get this for themselves.

Early records from Broadgate Hospital in Beverley show the limits of physician prescribing in the early asylums around 1848 (Curry, 1992). Purgatives were used extensively, especially croton oil (mild laxative in small dose and an external irritant now used in cosmetic skin peels), calomel (highly toxic mercury-based laxative), colocynth (liver stimulant and diuretic) and senna. For mania sedatives were used with or without tonics or antimony (now used by vets as a skin conditioner in ruminants and a component of safety matches) and saline. For melancholia healthy digestion was encouraged, again using calomel as a purge. Epilepsy was treated according to severity and status. The healthy were given drastic purges with oleum terebinthinae (turpentine oil). Less well patients received tonics. Paralysis was treated with diuretics. In 'great apathy of the system' creosote (now known to be a carcinogenic laxative and cough suppressant, banned even as a wood preserver) and other stimulants with tonics and counter irritants were prescribed. As stated in the last chapter nurses could prescribe medication in hospital.

In the community it seems that hyoscine was popular for symptomatic treatment of depression (Norton, 1979). Hyoscine, which is extracted from henbane and mandragora, had been used for thousands of years for 'nerves'. It seems hyoscine is an effective and rapid treatment for depression as recently rediscovered by Furey and Drevets (2006). Hyoscine was used in combination with morphine, atropine and barbiturates in hospitals but was more often self-administered, due to the fact that any of these ingredients could be easily bought. More severe forms of depression prior to the 1950s were treated with various forms of convulsant therapy according to Norton (1979). Norton's paper is a very moving account of a psychiatrist doing his best with clearly inadequate tools. It is interesting to note that he did not treat anyone for depression during World War II.

Whether it was hyoscine, paraffin or creosote the prescription was generally self-administered. After 1906 control of substances considered likely to be abused became subject to increasing legislation. The notion of abuse itself has been the subject of much debate and criticism (Dally, 1995). However, opium and preparations containing more than 1% of the drug were restricted in the 1906 amendment to the Pharmacy Act 1869. The 1920 Dangerous Drugs Act further placed control on cannabis and preparations containing dihydrocodeine. Cocaine was also banned following stories of 'crazed soldiers' in World War I. Control of these substances for medicinal use was transferred to the medical profession, and by 1941 most medicines needed a prescription under the Pharmacy and Medicines Act 1941. Extension of this power to all new medicines in the 1950s effectively and fortuitously put psychiatry in charge of an area of mental health care previously largely ignored by it. The medicines discussed in *Chapter 1* fell into their hands. In other words, a system designed to protect society from addicts was rolled out to legislate and control all medication management, putting the medical profession firmly in charge. Psychiatry entered the modern era through a combination of wider legislation and fortuitous timing.

Thalidomide

This legislative system was quickly reviewed following the thalidomide disaster. In 1954 the German pharmaceutical company Chemie Grunenthal was hoping to find an inexpensive method of manufacturing antibiotics from peptides. The company's chief of chemical research heated a commercially available chemical and produced phthalimidoglutarimide, which the company labelled thalidomide. Although it showed no antibiotic properties or any other therapeutic indications in animals it appeared to be extremely safe. That is, it did not kill rabbits, dogs, mice or rats at huge doses. This encouraged the company to patent the drug and then look for a therapeutic niche. They began distributing the drug to physicians in 1955, with no rationale or follow up plan.

Physicians first tried the drug as an anticonvulsant, with no success, but patients reported having a deep and satisfying 'natural' sleep. In order to be licensed in Germany the company had to then go back and demonstrate this sedative effect in animals. They did this by creating a 'jiggle cage' which measured very slight movement of mice (Silverman, 2002). They claimed that mice remained awake after thalidomide but moved less, so therefore it was a demonstrably safe sedative. Because of its explicit safety claims thalidomide was sold over the counter in many countries following its worldwide release in 1957. What followed was an appalling lesson in the dangers of inadequate drug testing in humans. Even a single dose of the drug taken during pregnancy could cause birth defects if taken between the 34th and 50th day of pregnancy.

Lenz (1992) noted the following effects:

- Absence of ears and deafness: 35th–37th day.
- Absence of arms: 39th–41st day.
- Phocomelia with three fingers: 43rd–44th day.
- Thumbs with three joints: 46th–48th day.

About 40% of babies died before their first birthday. The drug was withdrawn in 1962. It is difficult to know the real extent of the damage as it was marketed differently in different countries and records are incomplete. An irony is that thalidomide has turned out to be therapeutic after all: it has revolutionised the care of leprosy (Silverman, 2002).

Medicines Act 1968

The thalidomide tragedy initiated a radical rethink about the safety of medicines which culminated in the UK with the Medicines Act 1968. The

Medicines Act governs the manufacture, administration and supply of medicine through a series of provisions and remains the primary legislation in the UK. For example Section 31 contains provisions pertaining to clinical trials. The Act also sets out criminal liability where the provisions are not followed. It introduced three categories of medicine: prescription only medicine (POM), which is available only from a pharmacist if prescribed by a doctor; pharmacy medicines (P), available only from a pharmacist but without a prescription; and general sales medicine (GSL) which may be bought from any shop without a prescription. It made possession of prescription drugs without a prescription an offence.

The Act sets out which groups of professionals can prescribe, and the manner in which prescription only medicines can be supplied and administered. Section 58 states that only doctors, dentists and veterinary surgeons have the legal authority to prescribe. It is this section which is amended by the Medicinal Products: Prescription by Nurses etc. Act 1992 to include registered nurses, midwives and health visitors 'who are of such a description and comply with such conditions as may be specified in the order'(Caulfield, 1999). These conditions are specified in statutory instruments. Viewed from this purely legal perspective doctors did not have sole control of prescriptive authority for long.

The return of non-medical prescribing

Nurse prescribing has crept into operation in stages. Jones (1999) provides an excellent narrative of the lobbying that went on behind the scenes that helped it into law. This tale involves private members bills getting fortuitous readings in the House of Commons, and a great deal of lobbying and media courting. It would have been even more interesting to hear from the politicians who voted it in as well. As in the 1970s when both antipsychiatry and the establishment (Government) wanted a shift of mental health care into the community, separate agendas appear to have converged on a mutually agreeable goal. It is likely that nurses were motivated in part by a desire to both improve patient care and become increasingly professional, and that the Government saw an opportunity to cut costs and disenfranchise the medical profession at the same time.

A significant moment was the Crown Review Group's (Department of Health, 1989) subsequently accepted recommendation that 'suitably qualified nurses working in the community should be able, in clearly defined circumstances, to prescribe from a limited list of items and to adjust the timing and dosage of medicines within a set protocol'.

Nurse prescribing was legalised for district nurses and health visitors with the introduction of the Medicinal Products, Prescription by Nurses Act

1992. They were called independent prescribers at the time but were only permitted to prescribe from a limited formulary of dressings and supplies. Since then there has been a rapid expansion of prescribing authority, starting with incremental changes in nurse prescribing formularies and culminating in virtually unrestricted prescribing. District nurse and health visitor prescribing is still formulary restricted and referred to as V100 community health practitioner prescribing. To qualify as extended independent prescribers and supplementary prescribers (V200/V300), nurses are now required to undertake a longer, more specific programme of preparation, which results in a recorded qualification on the Nursing Midwifery Council Register (Department of Health, 2006). The latest legislation allows nurses to prescribe independently within their sphere of competence (Scottish Executive, 2006c). The concept of the sphere of competence will be returned to at the end of this chapter.

By 2003 supplementary prescribing had been extended to pharmacists (Scottish Executive, 2001, 2002). Pharmacists are now able to become independent prescribers following completion of an accredited conversion programme for those who are currently supplementary prescribers (Royal Pharmaceutical Society, 2006). From September 2007 podiatrists, physiotherapists and radiotherapists have also had the authorisation to access the courses offered to nurses and pharmacists and will qualify as supplementary prescribers on completion of their studies. The expansion of prescribing rights is considerable.

The medical profession only had prescribing rights to itself for 50 years. Any challenge to this monopoly was bound to be poorly received by some. In response to Patricia Hewitt's announcement that the *British National Formulary* would be opened up to non-medical prescribers in 2005, the chairman of the British Medical Association said, 'I would not have me or my family subject to anything other than the highest level of care and prescribing, which is that provided by a fully trained doctor' (Day, 2005). Selections of equally emotive rapid responses followed Avery and Pringle's broadly positive article welcoming nurse prescribing in the *British Medical Journal* (Avery and Pringle, 2005). While often based on real concern for patient safety and hence deserving of genuine exploration these opinions are irrelevant as a point of law. So what has mental health nursing made of the opportunity to prescribe? This is best answered through analysis of policy responses to the initiative.

Rights, relationships and recovery

The overall message of *Delivering for Health* (Scottish Executive, 2005) was to shift the balance of care further into the community, and the focus is similar in England. Patients will be partners in care which will primarily be delivered at home. A key challenge is the action of establishing a new health and social care service in the community by 'developing practitioners with extended roles' (Key Actions: x). Nurse prescribing is not mentioned in the document as one of the extended roles. However prescribing is an extended role, and seems to fit with the trend of mental health nursing moving into these broader extended roles, such as care management, as discussed in *Chapter 2*.

Mental health nursing was reviewed in Scotland and England in 2005 following broad and inclusive consultation. The reports have been well received as recognising the profession's current direction and future needs. Unfortunately the reports came too soon to be informed by any primary evidence of the efficacy of nurse prescribing in mental health. As a result *Rights, Relationships and Recovery* (Scottish Executive, 2006a) provides a balanced view of the potential impact of nurse prescribing. It notes that mental health nurse prescribing is under-researched and could have positive or negative consequences. On the positive side it agrees with the wider view (Department of Health, 2006) that it could enhance medication access and choice. It may be cost-effective and seems to align well with the concept of developing extended roles. On the negative side it states that there is a perception that current training in nurse prescribing does not seem to be appropriate for mental health nurses. Service users have expressed concerns at nurses' level of competence to prescribe (Harrison, 2003). Knowledge of psychopharmacology is considered to be limited, which may have a detrimental effect on safety. The action point from the document is to develop mental health nursing's contribution to nurse prescribing. This translates into action 13 in the subsequent delivery action plan (Scottish Executive, 2006b). Action 13 states that mental health nursing's contribution to nurse prescribing should be developed by NHS board nursing directors (ibid: 11).

In other words, the role of nurse prescribing is unclear in mental health nursing. Medication management is not mentioned in the key messages at all. The first mention of pharmacological intervention in the review sees it as outmoded and restrictive, because its focus is on illness and deficits as opposed to 'person-centred recovery' (ibid: 11). It is difficult to see how medication management, which treats illness and disease, can align with recovery models that assist individual 'journeys' utilising interpersonal relationships based on the principles of partnership.

Medication management is first mentioned in a positive context on page 23, where 'supporting people receiving pharmacological interventions' is described as a core function of mental health nurses. This statement seems disconnected with the rest of the review. However, prescribing is included in this notion of support, and on page 35 a cautious but balanced welcome is extended to the initiative. The caution is explicitly due to the lack of primary evidence. The lack of evidence is due to the small number of mental health nurse prescribers in practice. It is within this 'Catch 22' that strategy for development of mental health nurse prescribing found itself in 2006.

From a wider perspective there is considerable evidence supporting the added value of different approaches to recovery. For example studies which compare efficacy of talking therapies with medication broadly support an equivalent efficacy in both (NICE, 2004). Although many authors claim the most effective strategies should therefore offer a combination of both talking therapies and medication (Ham et al, 2005; Feeney et al, 2006) this is not supported in all areas of mental health. For example some studies indicate a combination approach worsens outcome in panic disorder (Black, 2006). However, knowing what works best for whom and when supports the development of nurse prescribing within a recovery-based approach. A nurse with the requisite skills and knowledge to prescribe will be best placed to deliver the most comprehensive range of evidence-based therapeutic interventions based on individual strengths and needs.

That is, there is clear evidence of the potentially life changing benefit of taking medication, so prescribing works. In all 92% of people with mental health problems take prescribed medication (Healthcare Commission, 2007). Psychopharmacology and an underlying biology of mental illness are becoming better if not completely understood. There is also compelling evidence implying equivalent efficacy of various non-medical approaches to recovery (NICE, 2004) as supported by the reviews. *Rights, Relationships and Recovery* strongly supports the recovery approach to nursing intervention. Although it is philosophically difficult to align a treatment designed for addressing illness with an approach designed to distance itself from the concept of illness it is not difficult in practice (Kennedy, 2007). Nurse prescribing is likely to be an adjunct not an opposition to recovery. Admittedly this perspective is pragmatic, but as demonstrated in *Chapter 2* it seems that pragmatism suits mental health nurses better than philosophical purity.

Barker (2006) bemoans the fact that most consider the debate on mental health nurse prescribing over. Because prescribing is now legal for mental health nurses most argue that the focus should shift from justifying it to ways of operationalising it. This is premature however. Operationalising will be more effective with a clear direction, which itself depends on rational justification. As few mental health nurses are yet prescribing it seems there is still residual doubt, and this doubt is reasonable. Navigating this Catch 22 requires a first step outside the cycle. In other words, innovation is called for, which in turn becomes evidence and breaks the cycle. So where is the innovation? Are there any models of good practice to follow?

Research into mental health nurse prescribing

Nurse prescribing is widely accepted in the USA, but comparisons are not straightforward due to training, systemic and political differences. For example, in contrast to the UK where students may specialise in mental health nursing without a general nursing qualification, nursing professionals in the USA can only specialise at postgraduate level. Prescribing, diagnosing and treatment are the territory of masters degree trained advanced practitioners in the USA, whereas prescribing has been rolled out at undergraduate level in the UK. So although Nolan et al (2004) conclude that American mental health nurses feel prescribing has enhanced their practice and improved patient care, conclusions from this and other American studies may not be applicable in the NHS, given that all the nurses in Nolan's study were general trained and educated to Masters level by default. British mental health nurses in the main are not.

So is nurse prescribing the same in all the nursing disciplines in the UK then? Hall et al (2006) suggested that lack of confidence and an unsupportive infrastructure may be limiting prescribing practice when they found that many trained nurse prescribers were not actually prescribing routinely. Although not explicit in other studies, prescribing frequency may be lower than routinely inferred. Study samples are generally low, and the majority of respondents indicate low prescribing rates (While and Biggs, 2004). It would appear there are therefore similarities between the experience of mental health nurse prescribers and the wider nurse prescribing community in this regard.

However, Rungapadiachy et al (2004) noted student mental health nurses particularly feel that drug administration conflicts with patient advocacy. Although this is another study merely guessing at the possible impact of prescribing in mental health nursing it is one of many that hint at role conflict (Harrison, 2003; Jones, 2006) as already discussed in *Chapter 2*. That is, this role will somehow disturb a balance inherent within the (non-prescribing) therapeutic relationship between mental health nurses and their patients. This may be at the root of Barker's (2006) anxiety, and there is empirical evidence to support this. Snowden (2007) found that mental health nurse prescribers are qualitatively different to their non-mental health colleagues, mainly in their concern over this therapeutic relationship. He also demonstrates that mental health nurse prescribers differ from their non-mental health colleagues in that they are younger, more likely to be male, less likely to work in primary care, less likely to prescribe once qualified but more likely to utilise supplementary prescribing when they do. They have more senior roles, yet are not as academic or experienced in terms of years spent nursing. They are more likely to look up drug interactions and drug reactions, probably as a result of their comparative inexperience. Mental health nurse prescribers are also less sure about nurse prescribing having a positive impact on quality of care.

If mental health nurses are less experienced prescribers perhaps they can only guess as to the impact nurse prescribing may have, which may explain their caution. District nurses and health visitors have been prescribing for four years and more believe they know what impact it has had. This could explain why mental health nurses worry about policy and guidelines whereas district nurses worry about workload. Although these findings could be a result of differing operational experience they could also be signs that mental health nurse prescribing may be fundamentally different. For example, there may be a different approach required to prescribing antidepressants to that needed to prescribe laxatives or contraceptives. Do registered mental nurses feel confident to prescribe psychotropic medication? Do patients feel confident with them doing so? From anecdotal evidence this would appear unclear (Jones, 2006).

Jones et al (2005) conducted a qualitative study on the impact of mental health prescribing, and reported that service users benefited from the initiative. This appears to be the first evidence from service users in the UK, and some key themes emerged. Service users reported that nurse prescribers provided a greater focus on collaboration and treatment options, apparently supporting the notion that choice is improved (Brimblecombe, 2005) and concordance enhanced. Service users thought that the nurse listened to their concerns, acknowledged difficulties associated with using psychiatric drugs, and provided information on how to minimise the risks of use. Most of the psychiatrists reported that nurse prescribing made their life easier and improved the knowledge base of the team. Both they and the nurses worked in a way that was more evidence based, which also improved practice as a result. It would seem therefore that mental health nurse prescribing is both qualitatively and quantitatively different to other forms of prescribing and also potentially very positive.

The practicalities of prescribing. A personal perspective

I completed the nurse prescribing course in 2005, and it took me a year to write my first prescription. The reason it took me a year was because the infrastructure was not there to support mental health nurse prescribing when I first qualified. This was a common issue around this time (Pollock and Dudgeon, 2006). I consequently spent much of this year attending meetings with GPs, practice managers, administrators and colleagues attempting to put my qualification into practice. Eventually the team had template letters and a policy to support supplementary prescribing. So, my first prescription was not really a prescription. It was a template letter to the GP prescribing a reduction in a medication as part of a clinical management plan we had all (consultant, GP, patient, and myself) agreed upon.

As it turned out this letter actually delayed the reduction in the medication, as the pharmacist would not take my word as a prescriber. Had I telephoned the pharmacist and said 'the doctor has reduced this medication' I am reasonably sure the medication would have been instantly reduced. So not only did it take me a year to prescribe but when I did it made things worse for the patient. This evidence is purely anecdotal, and undoubtedly one of the many teething problems bound to emerge from a new venture. However, on reflection a more fundamental reason why it did not work smoothly was because the older person mental health team I worked for had been running effectively without nurse prescribing for years. There was no need for it. Adding a tier of administration did not help the patient. However, this was when supplementary prescribing was the only option available to mental health nurse prescribers. Independent prescribing may not have added that tier.

It is quite easy to identify where nurse prescribing should work if aspects of this example are accepted. It will work where there is a need for it. The need should be generated by service users. Where those needs are already being met effectively, adding more to the system may actually make things less effective. The benefits of operationalising nurse prescribing across mental health services are therefore not clear, albeit there are likely to be areas where it will prove highly beneficial. This may be stating the obvious, but as with any new initiative a period of experimentation and review will help clarify relevant issues. Innovation is necessary at this stage, but it will have to be rational. If there is minimal planning and forethought in how prescribing will enhance local practice there is a very good chance the employer will not support it.

The sphere of competence

Before summarising this section it is important briefly to discuss the application of the concept of 'sphere of competence', as this underpins safe prescribing practice as specified by the Nursing and Midwifery Council (2006) in regard to nurse prescribing. Although this sphere of competence is a consistent theme in the consultation on nurse prescribing which preceded the opening up of the *British National Formulary* to nurses (Medicines and Healthcare Regulations Agency, 2006) at no point is it made explicit what this means. Despite this it appears that the legal and professional implication of the wide extension of prescribing rights for nurses is that it is now the sole responsibility of the individual practitioner to operate in a safe manner 'within their sphere of competence'. There is no external legislation limiting prescribing behaviour. It is therefore crucial to understand what the term competence means and how it can be assured, as practising outside the sphere of competence would likely be construed as not simply unprofessional but illegal.

There are many definitions of competence but Mollerup and Mortensen (2004) provide a useful distinction between two forms: formal competence and real competence. Formal competence describes competence assumed due to qualifications, and the specific duties which may be performed as a consequence of those qualifications. Thus qualifying as a prescriber meets the criterion for formal competence. The Nursing and Midwifery Council (2006: 35) describes competence at this level as 'relat[ing] to the need for the student to demonstrate their "capability" in certain skill areas to a required standard at a point in time'.

Real competence is defined by Mollerup and Mortensen as the ability to apply knowledge to clinical situations, to practise and use skills safely, and to demonstrate attitudes appropriate to the specific situation. This is very much a précis of Benner's (1984) work on describing the process of growing from novice to expert, and summarises nicely the issues needing to be addressed in claiming competence in (expert) prescribing practice. However, this is not as easy to define as formal competence, because it assumes aspects of autonomy, and nurses are not yet autonomous (Collin Jacques and Smith, 2005). So again nurses find themselves in a less than clear situation. GPs are autonomous and insured against error. Nurse prescribers are 'semi-autonomous' and are covered for vicarious liability by their employer, but only within the remit of their job description, which may or may not cover drug errors depending on the situation. They are therefore advised to join a union to cover this eventuality. From a practical perspective then in order to practise 'within the sphere of competence' clinical governance needs to be solid.

This means clear and systematic engagement with clinical audit, patient involvement, risk management, evidence of clinical effectiveness, continuing professional development, use of IT and staff management (Goldstein and Reilly, 2007). This is not new for nurses. There is evidence to suggest that nurses are very good at following protocols (Manias et al, 2005). This quality has been subject to thinly veiled criticism inferring that nurses are somehow inflexible. I would argue that following protocols is ideally suited to prescribing and that any other method is thinly veiled unsafe practice rationalised as 'clinical judgement'. The point is, if clinical governance procedures are followed then prescribing practice may not be innovative or radical but it will be safe and demonstrably so. This is crucial because the legislation is almost incomprehensible at times (West, 2007).

Organisational responsibilities are summarised by Pollock and Dudgeon (2006):

- NHS Boards should develop non-medical prescribing strategies to support the development of independent prescribing by nurses and ensure clinical governance systems are put in place to support nurse prescribing.
- Nurse directors should work with local managers and financial colleagues to make sure that budgets are set up for all nurse prescribers and collaborate with pharmacy colleagues to ensure that nurse prescribing practices are monitored and reviewed.
- Nurse directors should work with local educationalists of nurse prescribing programmes to select appropriate prescribing students, and ensure mentoring and continuing professional development systems are in place to support nurse prescribing.
- The blockages to developing electronic prescribing need to be explored locally and nationally and steps taken to put this in place in all areas. These recommendations to the Scottish Government move towards defining an operational clarity missing from the review on mental health nursing. Uptake of these recommendations will result in mental health nurse prescribers operating safely in a supported manner.

Conclusion

This chapter has shown that 100 years ago responsibility for medication management lay with the individual. Opinions that this should be the case now appear extreme until viewed in this context. That is, prior to legislation primarily aimed at prevention of addiction people were able to medicate themselves with whatever was available to them. Patent medicines were the norm for 300 years. Following a campaign by the British Medical Association opium and preparations containing more than 1% opium were restricted in the 1906 amendment to the Pharmacy Act 1869. Further incremental restrictions led to the 1941 Pharmacy Act whereby control of addictive substances was effectively transferred to the medical profession, and by 1941 most other medicines needed a prescription. Extension of this power to all new medicines in the 1950s put psychiatry in charge of psychotropic medicines just at the time the most effective ones appeared.

The thalidomide tragedy initiated a radical rethink of the safety of medicines which culminated in the UK with the Medicines Act 1968. This Act remains the primary legislation in the UK and came to include nurses from 1992 following extensive lobbying. Section 52 of the Medicines Act was amended by the Medicinal Products: Prescription by Nurses etc.

Act 1992 to include registered nurses, midwives and health visitors. This allowed nurses to prescribe from a restricted formulary. In 2006 legislation was passed to allow nurses to prescribe independently within their sphere of competence (Scottish Executive, 2006c).

Mental health nurses were not at the forefront of any of these discussions and were not prepared for the opportunity. Recent reviews of mental health nursing have been vague in their response to prescribing responsibilities. Evidence for its efficacy is sparse and largely anecdotal. Not all of the evidence is positive or transferable. However, this evidence is very useful and highly relevant to this stage of development. 'Dead ends' are as useful as positive outcomes in establishing a broader view of what works and where.

Although the medical monopoly of prescribing has now been effectively ended it is unlikely that self-prescribing will return in the near future. The trend appears to be towards greater legislation rather than less. Therefore for the purpose of increasing treatment options for people it is sensible for nurses to engage with this opportunity rather than reject it without a deeper critical analysis. This engagement needs to be safe and therefore clearly supported by the employing organisation. This chapter has outlined the personal and organisational issues of safety which need to be addressed. Mental health nurse prescribing practice can then emerge which genuinely informs debates on care provision for people with mental health problems.

Further reading

Jones M (1999) *Nurse Prescribing. Politics to Practice*. London: Bailliere Tindall. RCN
This is an excellent account of the lobbying and behind the scenes activism which drove nurse prescribing onto the political agenda and legislature. It would be even better if a Government account were included for a future edition, as the Government also clearly had a lot to gain with the introduction of non-medical prescribing.

Porter R, Teich M (1995) *Drugs and Narcotics in History*. Cambridge: Cambridge University Press
As this chapter reveals, a great deal of legislative action happened as a result of societal concern about drugs of addiction. This book is a collection of essays which explore this angle in greater depth. It looks at the 'war on drugs' from a contemporary perspective, details the history of opium use and abuse and discusses regulation in Britain before the 18th century.

Nurse Prescribing. MA Healthcare
Because of the speed at which developments occur it is useful to have an

up to date account of events. This monthly journal is dedicated to the topic of nurse prescribing and has dedicated sections on law and clinical research which reflect current practice and thinking.

References

Avery AJ, Pringle M (2005) Extending prescribing by UK nurses and pharmacists. *Brit Med J* **331**: 1154–5

Barker P (2006) Mental Health Nursing: The craft of the impossible? *J Psych Ment Health Nursing* **13**(4): 385–7

Benner P (1984) *From Novice to Expert: Promoting Excelence and Power in Clinical Nursing Practice.* Wenlo Park: Addison-Wesley

Benson J, Britten N (2006) What effects do patients feel from their antihypertensive tablets and how do they react to them? Qualitative analysis of interviews with patients. *Fam Pract* 23: 80–7

Black DW (2006) Efficacy of Combined Pharmacotherapy and Psychotherapy Versus Monotherapy in the Treatment of Anxiety Disorders. *CNS Spectrums* **11**(Suppl 12): 29–33

Brimblecombe N (2005) Medication and mental health nurses: Developing new ways of working. *Ment Health Pract* **8**(5): 12–14

Caulfield H (1999) Nurse prescribing. A legal minefield? In Jones M (ed) *Nurse Prescribing. Politics to Practice.* London: Bailliere Tindall

Cheyne G (1773) *The English Malady.* Delmar, NY: Scholars' Facsimiles & Reprints, 1976

Collin-Jacques C, Smith C (2005) Nursing on the line: Experiences from England and Quebec (Canada). *Human Relations* **58**(5): 5–33

Curry R (1991) *Across the Westwood. The Life and Times of Broadgate Hospital Beverley. Mental Health Unit.* Beverley: East Yorkshire Health Authority.

Dally A (1995) Anomalies and mysteries in the 'War on Drugs'. In Porter R, Teich M (eds) *Drugs and Narcotics in History.* Cambridge: Cambridge University Press

Day M (2005) UK doctors protest extension to nurses' prescribing powers. *Brit Med J* **331**: 1159

Department of Health (1989) *Report of the Advisory Group on Nurse Prescribing.* London: Department of Health

Department of Health (2006) *Improving patients' access to medicines: A guide to implementing nurse and pharmacist independent prescribing within the NHS in England.* Available from: http://www.dh.gov.uk/assetRoot/04/13/37/47/04133747.pdf [Accessed 24 April 2006]

Feeney GFX, Conner JP, Young RMcD, Tucker J, McPherson A (2006) Combined acamprosate and naltrexone, with cognitive behavioural therapy is superior to either medication alone for alcohol abstinence: A single centre's experience with pharmacotherapy. *Alcohol and Alcoholism* **41**(3): 321–7

Furey ML, Drevets WC (2006) Antidepressant efficacy of the antimuscarinic drug scopolamine: A randomized, placebo-controlled clinical trial. *Arch Gen Psychiatry* **63**(10): 1121–9

Goldstein R, Reilly R (2007) A practical guide to clinical governance for non-medical prescribing. In McKinnon J (ed) *Towards Prescribing Practice*. Chichester: John Wiley and Sons

Gregory JR (2003) *The Best of Branding: Best Practices in Corporate Branding*. London: McGraw-Hill

Hall J, Cantrill J, Noyce P (2006) Why don't trained community nurse prescribers prescribe? *J Clin Nursing* **15**(4): 403–12

Ham P, Waters BD, Norman OB (2005) Treatment of panic disorder. *American Family Physician* **71**(4): 733–9

Harrison A (2003) Mental health service users' views of nurse prescribing. *Nurse Prescribing* **1**: 2

Healthcare Commission (2007) *Talking about Medicines: The Management of Medicines in Trusts Providing Mental Health Services*. London: Commission for Healthcare Audit and Inspection

Healy D (2002) *The Creation of Psychopharmacology*. Cambridge, Massachusetts: Harvard University Press

Healy D (2004) *Let Them Eat Prozac*. New York and London: New York University Press

Jones M (1999) *Nurse Prescribing. Politics to Practice*. London: Bailliere Tindall

Jones A (2006) Supplementary prescribing: Potential ways to reform hospital psychiatric care. *J Psychiatr Ment Health Nursing* **13**: 132–8

Jones M, Miller D, Lucas B, Bennett J, Gray R (2005) Extended prescribing by UK nurses and pharmacists: Supplementary prescribing by mental health nurses seems promising *Brit Med J* **331**: 1337

Kennedy S (2007) The mental health perspective. In McKinnon J (ed) *Towards Prescribing Practice*. Chichester: John Wiley and Sons

Lenz W (1992) *The history of Thalidomide*. Available from: http://www.thalidomide.ca/en/information/history_of_thalidomide.html [Accessed 13 June 2007]

Manias E, Aitken R, Dunning T (2005) How graduate nurses use protocols to manage patients' medications. *J Clin Nursing* **14**: 935–44

Medicines and Healthcare Regulation Agency (2006) *Summary of Replies to Consultation MLX 320*. Available from: http://www.mhra.gov.uk/home/dcplg?IdcService=GET_FIL E&dID=17984&noSaveAs=1&Rendition=WEB [Accessed 4 July 2007]

Mollerup A, Mortensen PS (2004) Nurses' perception of their own level of competence. Connect: *The World of Critical Care Nursing* **3**(3): 70–3

NICE (2004) *Depression: Management of depression in primary and secondary care. NICE Guideline 23*. Available from: http://www.nice.org.uk/pdf/CG023quickrefguide.pdf [Accessed 6 June 2007]

Nolan P, Badger F (2005) Aspects of the relationship between doctors and depressed patients that enhance satisfaction with primary care. *J Psych Ment Health Nursing* **12**(2): 146–53

Nolan P, Bradley E, Carr N (2004) Nurse prescribing and the enhancement of mental health services. *Nurse Prescriber* **1**(11): 1–9

Norton A (1979) Depression. *Brit Med J* **2**(6187): 429–30

Nursing and Midwifery Council (2006) *Standards of Proficiency for Nurse Prescribers Without a Specialist Practice Qualification to Prescribe from the Community Practitioner Formulary*. Available from: http://www.nmc-uk.org/aDisplayDocument.

aspx?DocumentID=2477 [Accessed 27 August 2007]

Pollock L, Dudgeon N (2006) *The Scottish Nurse Prescribing Audit*. Available from: http://www.scotland.gov.uk/Resource/Doc/924/0038125.doc [Accessed 4 July 2007]

Porter R (1983) The rage of party: A glorious revolution in English psychiatry? *Medical History* **29**: 35–50

Porter R (2002) *Madness; A Brief History*. Oxford: Oxford University Press

Porter R, Porter D (1989) The Rise of the English Drugs Industry: The Role of Thomas Corbyn. *Medical History* **33**: 277–95

Royal Pharmaceutical Society of Great Britain (2006) *Curriculum for the Education and Training of Pharmacist Supplementary Prescribers to Become Independent Prescribers*. London: Royal Pharmaceutical Society of Great Britain

Rungapadiachy DM, Madill A, Gough B (2004) Mental health student nurses' perception of the role of the mental health nurse. J *Psych Ment Health Nursing* **11**(6): 714–24

Schwieso JJ (1996) 'Religious fanaticism' and wrongful confinement in Victorian England: The affair of Louisa Nottidge. *Social History of Medicine* **9**(2): 159–74

Scottish Executive Health Department (2001) *Caring for Scotland, The Strategy for Nursing and Midwifery*. Edinburgh: Scottish Executive Health Department

Scottish Executive Health Department (2002) T*he Right Medicine. A Strategy for Pharmaceutical Care in Scotland*. Edinburgh: Scottish Executive Health Department

Scottish Executive (2005) *A Report on the Future of the NHS in Scotland*. Available from: http://www.scotland.gov.uk/Publications/2005/05/23141307/13104 [Accessed 18 December 2007]

Scottish Executive (2006a) *Rights Relationships and Recovery*. Available from: http://www.scotland.gov.uk/Resource/Doc/112046/0027278.pdf [Accessed 14 December 2006]

Scottish Executive (2006b) *Rights Relationships and Recovery: Action Plan*. Available from: http://www.scotland.gov.uk/Resource/Doc/112046/0027279.pdf [Accessed 14 December 2006]

Scottish Executive Health Department (2006c) *Non Medical Prescribing in Scotland Guidance for Nurse Independent Prescribers and for Community Practitioner Nurse Prescribers in Scotland: A Guide for Implementation*. Available from: http://www.scotland.gov.uk/Publications/2006/08/23133351/29 [Accessed 11 September 2007]

Silverman WA (2002) The schizophrenic career of a monster drug. *Paediatrics* **110**(2): 404–6

Snowden A (2007) Is mental health nurse prescribing qualitatively different? *Nurse Prescribing* **5**(5): 66–73

Temin P (1980) T*aking your medicine. Drug regulation in the United States*. Cambridge, MS: Harvard University Press

West J (2007) Legislation, regulation and accountability in prescribing. In McKinnon J (ed) *Towards Prescribing Practice*. Chichester: John Wiley and Sons

While AE, Biggs KSM (2004) Benefits and challenges of nurse prescribing. *J Adv Nursing* **45**(6): 559–67

Summary of Section 1

In order to bring this section to a close it is useful to look at some of the themes which permeate the histories as described above. This way all three chapters can be discussed together where common themes emerge (*Figure 1*).

The most enduring themes have been power (authority) and regulation, determined in general by the prevailing rationality. For example in the 17th century money was made from the mentally ill through private madhouses which were justified on the basis of containment of a social evil (Foucault, 1965). The asylums were introduced as an economic measure in 1850. Human rights dominate current thought, but many argue that these mask rather than address current inequalities, as real power remains with psychiatry and not the individual. There is the further issue that human rights are themselves socially constructed and subsequently also subject to the prevailing rationality.

With specific regard to medicine management the general population exercised the power of choice by freely purchasing over-the-counter remedies prior to the 20th century. England in particular was an easy target for profits generated from a gullible population:

The English are easier than any other nation infatuated with the prospect of universal medicines, nor is there any other country in the world where the doctors raise such immense fortunes
(Mrs Montague, 18th century writer and critic, quoted in Campbell, 1971: 116)

Money and power are closely linked so it is of no real surprise that the battle for control of the lucrative medication market is ongoing, involving suppliers, entrepreneurs, administrators and legislators. Arguments for control are regularly framed in moral terms which the public suspects mask less virtuous profit-focused agendas. Consider debates on embryonic stem cell research, or the rationing of expensive drugs like herceptin.

These themes filter through the history of the care of the mentally unwell. Mental health nursing did not appear as a factor in the care of madness until later on in these stories, but money was certainly a major factor when they did. Attendants were paid as little as possible and did what they were told. Mental health nurses are currently regulated to protect the public, and a large part of the role remains custodial.

Although the psychotropics discovered in the 1950s and 1960s initially promised cures for chronic mental illness, they subsequently came under attack by the antipsychiatrists of the 1970s as the scope of mainstream psychiatry grew while the psychotropics turned out to 'cure' nobody. Although antipsychiatrists were considered 'fringe' players (Kennedy, 2007) their themes persist today in the debates over normality and the pathologising of everyday behaviour. This is also about power, but less overtly financial, although some argue that pathologising everyday behaviour suits drug companies and some prescribers very well financially (Healy, 2002, 2004; Kutchins and Kirk, 1997).

An enduring theme is the place of luck. Antipsychotic medication was discovered while looking for a pre-anaesthetic agent. Antidepressants arose while looking for more antipsychotics, and the first monoamine oxidase inhibitor was discovered while looking for a cure for tuberculosis. Psychiatry

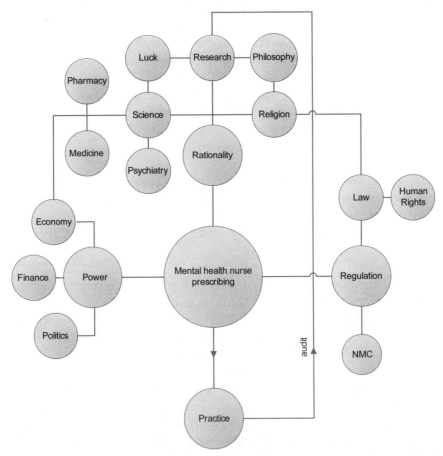

Figure 1. Themes of mental health nurse prescribing.

came to control the supply of these drugs due to legislation primarily aimed at restricting addictive drugs and just happened to be in the right place at the right time. The first therapeutic effects of chlorpromazine were noticed by a surgeon not a psychiatrist.

Mental health nurses have been conspicuous by their absence in these events. Again this can be explained in terms of power, as mental health nurses historically have not had any. In order to address this academics from the 1950s onwards have sought a coherent mental health nursing philosophy. However, in practice mental health nurses simply got on with the job. Pragmatism is therefore a major theme when the history of mental health nursing is considered in any depth. Once considered the very dregs of society mental health nurses now arguably stand on the verge of autonomy, and this is a remarkable rise. Pragmatism must therefore count as one of its more effective traits. That is, despite or possibly because of a history of being done to, a breed of professional has emerged that naturally builds relationships with people (Altschul, 1972) by valuing them while simultaneously managing the moral balancing act of being therapist and custodian.

It is because of the ubiquitous presence of competing agendas such as these that mental health nurses have become quite comfortable in the 'swampy lowlands of practice' (Schon, 1983). As such, philosophical incompatibilities such as prescribing and recovery become just another grey area of practice which the mental health nurse will manage and make sense of. Mental health nurses now have the option of prescribing, and this was not planned by them. However, now it is here mental health nurses will most likely apply it where it is useful to their patients. The next section deals specifically with how to do that.

References

Altschul A (1972) *Patient Nurse Interaction: A Study of Interactive Patterns in Acute Psychiatric Wards.* Edinburgh: Churchill Livingstone

Campbell WA (1971) *The Chemical Industry.* London: Longmans

Foucault M (1965) *Madness and Civilisation: A History of Insanity in the Age of Reason.* New York: Random House

Healy D (2002) *The Creation of Psychopharmacology.* Cambridge, MA: Harvard University Press

Healy D (2004) *Let Them Eat Prozac.* New York and London: New York University Press

Kennedy S (2007) The mental health perspective. In McKinnon J (ed) *Towards Prescribing Practice.* Chichester: John Wiley and Sons

Kutchins H, Kirk H (1997) *Making Us Crazy. DSM: The Psychiatric Bible and the Creation of Mental Disorders.* New York: Simon and Shuster

Schön D (1983) *The Reflective Practitioner.* London: Basic Books

Section 2

Prescribing for mental illness

Introduction

Section 2 focuses on the practicalities of prescribing in mental health. It specifically focuses on clinical decision making in respect to pharmacological treatment for psychosis, depression and anxiety. Within each of these areas the only treatment options discussed in detail are the most commonly prescribed drugs. The rationale is that in covering these options in some depth more advanced decisions can be given a solid grounding. For example, if you want to prescribe venlafaxine as an antidepressant then your rationale will be supported by a comprehensive defence of why you would not prescribe fluoxetine, citalopram or lofepramine. It is suggested that most prescribing decisions can be made by applying the framework provided in this section.

Underpinning appropriate treatment is accurate diagnosis, and therefore systematic methods of consultation will be explored first. Although this may at first appear daunting, in fact most of the principles of good consultation are inherent to mental health nursing. For example, systematic and reflexive enquiry, coupled with a genuine desire to understand the problem as the patient sees it, is not only good prescribing practice, it correlates exactly with the principles of communication in mental health nursing. However, it remains the case that this process needs to be rigorous and explicit to counter the evidence which suggests that nurses in general are not as good at communicating as they think they are (Brereton, 1995). There is no place for uncorroborated assumptions in prescribing.

In practice, patients seek help because of their belief in the presence of a problem. They also believe the problem can benefit from professional intervention. The professional then seeks to resolve the issue to the patient's satisfaction. As 80% of diagnoses can be made from health history and interviewing alone (Epstein et al, 2000), this aspect is focused on here. References are given throughout the chapters where laboratory or physical tests supplement this process.

Consultation theory

Most consultation theory is medical in origin (Allen, 2007) and contributions from other disciplines are sparse. However, this is beginning to change. For example for nursing there is the Consultation Assessment Improvement Instrument for Nurses (CAIIN) (Redsell, 2002, Hastings and Redsell, 2006). However, all consultation theory basically encompasses the process of discovering why the person has presented in order to then take appropriate action. Therefore communication is at the heart of this process whichever theory is adopted. Specifically for the purpose of consultation communication needs to be directive. That is, without direction it is possible to interview someone at length without obtaining pertinent aspects of their health history. Lloyd and Craig (2007) provide an excellent guide to taking a person's history. However, Allen (2007) argues that even an accurate health history can miss relevant supplementary information. Both are therefore crucial aspects of consultation which elicit different information. Allen refers to this supplementary information as 'need to know, nice to know and nuts to know' (ibid: 154). In order to minimise the latter category she suggests structuring the interview.

Mnemonics are very useful for the novice in this regard. In common use is SWIPE: When did it Start? What makes it Worse? What causes Improvement? Is there a Pattern? What is the Evaluation (what is being currently being done to make it better)? Along the same lines but more detailed is TROCARSSS: Time, Rapidity, Occurrence, Characteristics, Associations, Relief, Site, Spread, Severity. Naturally these are not exclusive, but they provide examples of a focus to the interview which generates a good chance of asking all the pertinent questions and validating answers within a structured framework.

Arguably, consultation in mental health is more detailed still (Harrison, 2004), with more focus on subtle communication such as nuance, tone and cognition. History is often much more detailed, possibly an artefact of its psychodynamic roots, but the approach remains systematic. For example the following issues are suggested as having direct correlation with concordance in mental health treatment (Nolan et al, 2004). They should be established on first contact:

- How the person presents – their general demeanor.
- How they talk about their problems.
- What the condition means to them.
- Why they think their illness has occurred at this time.
- Whether they have felt this way before.
- What they think the appropriate treatments should be.
- What they think about other treatments.
- What their family and friends think about (e.g. depression) and its treatment.
- Whether they intend to comply with whatever treatments are prescribed.
- What important things they are currently not able to do.
- What important things they would most like to do.
- How long they think it will take before they are well again.

Giving patients time and space to describe their problems is the key. Studies suggest that patients do not reveal problems in any particular order

(Allen, 2007: 154), and this has certainly been the case in my experience. However the fact that communication issues are the biggest source of complaints in the NHS (Department of Health, 2005) suggests patients' problems are not being heard by those they seek help from. As Brereton (1995) suggested even those professionals who believe they are good at communicating may not necessarily be so. For example in a recent study of nurse prescribing Latter et al (2007) found that nurses were not practising the principles of concordance despite believing they were. However, in these nurses' defence the attempt seems to have been appreciated in that all of the patients were satisfied with their care. Snowden (2008) suggests that Latter et al's findings may have more to do with the problematic nature of the concept of concordance than anything else.

Assuming that the information elicited in the consultation is pertinent and comprehensive then a prescribing decision follows based on a synthesis of this information. A hypothesis emerges as a result of clinical and diagnostic reasoning. This hypothesis may then be tested through further reasoning and other diagnostic tests which may confirm or deny the validity of the original. A substantial part of this process is therefore the knowledge underpinning this diagnostic reasoning, and this is what is provided in the following chapters. The other major aspect is the ability to elicit and integrate information into this reasoning process. Paul and Heaslip (1995) suggest that all reasoning has nine common elements, and they argue that if these are understood then reasoning in clinical practice can be explained. They are (the brackets are my own):

- The purpose, goal or end product (e.g. concordance/compliance/ adherence).
- The question or issue to be resolved (e.g. patient distress).
- The professional perspective (e.g. diagnosis).
- The empirical dimension (e.g. how the patient presents).
- The conceptual dimension (e.g. understanding of health/illness).
- Assumptions (e.g. 'I can/can't help').
- Inferences (e.g. if x worked last time it should work this time).
- Implications (e.g. side effects).
- Implicit and explicit elements (e.g. attitudes and resources).

Paul and Heaslip are so definitive about this list because of their findings that uncritical 'intuition' is often used by expert practitioners to the detriment of practice. In other words, where this process is not followed, reasoning in clinical practice cannot be explained. They realise there is nothing wrong with subjective knowledge as long as it is interpreted as such. It may then be integrated into a systematic and explicit assessment encompassing physiological, psychological and social factors. It follows that this will create a rational prescribing decision with an explicit justification grounded in the primary evidence.

There are two major categories of prescribing decision which follow: autocratic and collaborative. A main advantage of the former is that it is quick. It is also useful in emergency situations or where clear expertise differences occur. However, in these cases the recipient feels as if they have made no contribution, and ownership of the prescription is with the 'expert'. A well-acknowledged consequence of this is low compliance (Jones, 2003). Collaborative decisions by contrast have been shown to enhance concordance (Nolan and Badger, 2005), which has nothing to do with compliance.

In practice however, an ideal collaboration where each partner is of equal status is unlikely. This is a complex area of social interaction which has been the subject of much philosophical debate (Foucault, 1965; Paley, 2002). In practical terms the professional is likely to know more about medication in general and the recipient will naturally know more about how they really view that particular medication. However, partnerships are rarely between people of identical attributes or there would arguably be no need for them. Attempting to explore and understand each other's opinion can at least express a desire to approach the goal of concordant partnership. As seen in Latter et al's (2007) study this may well be significant in itself. These factors enhance the therapeutic relationship which is in turn likely to encourage further fruitful communication. In this way a deeper understanding of why there may be a place for medication, whether the person would like to take it, what it is likely to do and whether the effects will be tolerable will lead to a more informed person-centred choice and hence approach the ideal of concordance (Benson and Britten, 2006; Prinjha et al, 2005).

The following chapters take this systematic enquiry into action by exploring the manifestation and pharmacological treatment of schizophrenia and psychosis, depression, and anxiety and insomnia. They should ideally be read in order, as the latter chapters assume some knowledge detailed in the preceding ones. For example pharmacokinetics is discussed in depth in *Chapter 4*, and this knowledge is assumed in the following chapters. However, the chapters still stand alone and can be used as a quick reference, for example in relation to the side effects of fluoxetine. The final chapter looks at some issues unique to mental health nurse prescribing and suggests possible future directions.

Further reading

Cohen R (2003) *Objective Structured Clinical Examination for Psychiatric Trainees* (Vols 1 and 2). London: Quay Books

This is a practical revision book aimed at psychiatric trainees sitting Objective Structured Clinical Examinations (OSCEs) in the MRCPsych and similar examinations. It is also highly relevant to the above discussion. The text is divided into four sections: history-taking skills; examination skills; procedure skills and communication skills.

Lloyd H, Craig S (2007) A guide to taking a patient's history. *Nursing Standard* **22**(13): 42–8
    This is an excellent and concise article on the art of taking a history, focusing on the nurse's role. It emphasises the need for structure and gives examples of sequence, cardinal symptoms and the rationale for adherence to NMC guidance.

References

Allen C (2007) Consultation and Decision Making.In McKinnon J (ed) Towards Prescribing Practice. Chichester: John Wiley and Sons

Benson J, Britten N (2006). What effects do patients feel from their antihypertensive tablets and how do they react to them? Qualitative analysis of interviews with patients. Fam Pract 23: 80–7

Brereton ML (1995) Communication in nursing: The theory-practice relationship. J Adv Nursing 21(2): 314–24

Epstein O, Perkins GD, Cookson J, de Bono DP (2000) Clinical Examination. London: Moseby

Department of Health (2005) Report of the Independent Complaints Advisory Service. London: Stationery Office

Foucault M (1965) Madness and Civilisation: A History of Insanity in the Age of Reason. New York: Random House

Harrison TC (2004) Consultation for Contemporary Helping Professionals. New Zealand: Pearson Education

Hasting A, Redsell S (2006) The Good Consultation Guide for Nurses. Oxford: Radcliffe Publishing

Jones G (2003) Prescribing and taking medicines. Brit Med J 327(7419): 819

Latter S, Maben J, Myall M,Young A (2007) Perceptions and practice of concordance in nurses' prescribing consultations: Findings from a national questionnaire survey and case studies of practice in England. Int J Nursing Studies 44(1): 9–18

Lloyd H, Craig S (2007) A guide to taking a patient's history. Nursing Standard 22(13): 42–8

Nolan P, Badger F (2005) Aspects of the relationship between doctors and depressed patients that enhance satisfaction with primary care. J Psych Ment Health Nursing 12(2): 146–53

Nolan P, Bradley E, Carr N (2004) Nurse prescribing and the enhancement of mental health services. Nurse Prescriber 1(11): 1–9

Paley J (2002) Caring as a slave morality: Nietzschean themes in nursing ethics. J Adv

Nursing 40(1): 25

Paul RW, Heaslip P (1995) Critical thinking and intuitive nursing practice. J Adv Nursing 22(1): 40–2

Prinjha S, Chapple A, Herxheimer A, McPherson A (2005). Many people with epilepsy want to know more: A qualitative study. Fam Pract 22: 435–41

Redsell SA (2002) Consultation Assessment and Improvement Instrument for Nurses (CAIIN). Leicester: Department of General Practice and Primary Health Care, University of Leicester

Snowden A (2008) Medication management in older adults: A critique of concordance. Brit J Nursing 17(2): 114–21

CHAPTER 4

Schizophrenia and psychotic symptoms

Section 1 provided a background on the origins of mental health treatments from the biochemical, neurological and the social construction perspective. While it is acknowledged that some people believe mental illness may be a construct of the pharmaceutical industry, a cultural anomaly, an indication of psychic pain or a pathologising of normal behaviour, these perspectives are not the focus of the following chapters. These perspectives are written about in great detail elsewhere (Porter, 2002; Healy, 2002; Shean, 2004). This chapter focuses on the evidence for and against drug treatment of schizophrenia and psychotic symptoms.

For the purpose of a generalised introduction psychotic symptoms are best understood within the history of schizophrenia. That is, schizophrenia may be viewed as a composite of psychotic symptoms although psychotic symptoms can occur in isolation. All of these symptoms have been treated successfully to varying degrees with anti-psychotic medication. In order to discuss the treatment options in detail an understanding of the issues surrounding the history, aetiology and diagnosis of schizophrenia provides a solid foundation.

What is schizophrenia? Early history of diagnosis

There is no consensus on the definition of schizophrenia. For example Japan has no such definition. My personal experience of caring for people labelled with it is that it can be highly distressing for the individual concerned and very difficult to understand as a carer. It is uniquely alienating. However, this chapter does not intend to add to the debate on what it may or may not be, but rather to describe the framework within which medication can be safely and therapeutically prescribed based upon the clinical evidence.

Diagnosis of schizophrenia has swung in the last century from descriptions of absolute objective criteria based on a disease model to a relative and dimensional diagnosis based on psychosocial factors. Most clinicians accept that it is a devastating disorder or group of disorders affecting about 1% of people worldwide. Beyond that people hold different viewpoints, from the biological to the philosophical (Shean, 2004).

The history of schizophrenia starts with its description by Bleuler and Kraepelin. It probably existed before this but not as the set of symptoms currently understood. By contrast, the term psychosis was first used by Ernst von Feuchtersleben in 1845 (Beer, 1995) as an alternative to the much longer established labels of mania and insanity. Kraepelin was the first to clarify objective descriptions and diagnostic criteria for the precursor to schizophrenia. He named the disorder dementia praecox in 1893, a term first used by Benedict Morel earlier in the century (*démence precoce*) to describe a mental disorder which initially struck males when they were in their teens or were young adults.

Kraepelin was attempting to systematise various diagnostic criteria of the time by looking for patterns of symptoms as opposed to similarities of major symptoms. That is, he recognised that major symptoms could be present in various different syndromes and were therefore not diagnostic in themselves. He was the first to separate mood disorders from other forms of psychosis. Kraepelin believed dementia praecox to be a disease of the brain, identified by a common unique pattern of early onset (praecox) and inexorable decline (dementia).

Under this umbrella he placed disorders like catatonia, hebephrenia and paranoia, which were previously (and consequently) thought to be separate. He thought that two broad types of symptoms were common to all types of dementia praecox presentation: the presence of bizarre, disorganised thoughts that do not remit, and a marked weakening of volition or motivation. He grouped these previously disconnected disorders because he believed the underlying cause was the same. Therefore, there would be a linear cause, onset, course and outcome, just like any other physical disease. Along with his colleague Alois Alzheimer, Kraepelin also discovered Alzheimer's disease (Maurer and Maurer, 2003). He thought there would be a pathological basis to all major mental illness.

Eugene Bleuler was a Swiss Psychiatrist and director of Zürich's Burghölzi Asylum from 1898. He was a colleague of Freud and employed Karl Jung as a junior doctor. It is therefore unsurprising to find he accepted psychosocial explanations of behaviour as well as medical. Consequently he disagreed with Kraepelin's purely organic formulation and introduced the term schizophrenia in 1911. He felt this was more appropriate as a description of what he saw happening. Schizophrenia means split (schiz-) mind (phren-) in Greek. Bleuler chose this as he saw the primary problem as one of disconnection between emotion, thoughts and behaviours.

From a purely diagnostic point of view Bleuler also found the disease did not always end in a state of dementia as Kraepelin's model had suggested. He introduced a different set of diagnostic criteria, memorable as 'the four As', which emphasised symptoms over course and outcome (Bleuler, 1924).

The four As were his fundamental symptoms:

- flattened Affect,
- Ambivalence,
- Autism (social relatedness deficit), and
- impaired Association of ideas.

Bleuler is credited with introducing the terms ambivalence and autism. He believed fundamental symptoms were present in all cases of the disorder, but impaired 'associations of ideas' were the most important symptoms. Accessory symptoms could not be diagnostic as they may be present in other disorders. His belief that people were curable was unique at the time.

However, being in agreement Freud did not necessariliy enhance credibility within the mainstream psychiatric establishment of the time in Europe. Despite the fact that his criteria were widely accepted they were still criticised for being vague and descriptive. Like Freud they became more accepted in the USA than in Europe. Bleuler's attempt at clarification actually resulted in the opposite effect (Shean, 2004: 5). By elaborating how he understood schizophrenia it became clear his definition had fuzzy boundaries. For example, he believed the fundamental symptoms may not necessarily be florid, but quite difficult to detect. This meant they could potentially include behaviours and thought patterns difficult to differentiate from the norm. Current thinking continues to attempt to quantify these apparently subtle issues he was referring to. Nevertheless, his generalised descriptions formed the basis of the DSM-I and DSM-II criteria for schizophrenia and remained until DSM-III was published in 1980.

One of the reasons DSM-III took a radically different approach to diagnosis was because of the lack of uniformity. Vague descriptions led to vague diagnoses. For example lack of clarity was largely blamed for finding diagnostic rates in the US double those in the UK in 1971 (Wing, 1971). Europe was by this time using diagnosis based on first rank (Schneider, 1959) observable symptoms which narrowed diagnosis while practitioners in the US were using wide Bleulerian terms. Psychiatrists were unable to conduct meaningful worldwide research and had to face accusations of being unscientific by their peers. This was unacceptable to psychiatrists who had fought hard to establish credibility within medicine. Confusion regarding schizophrenia was therefore a major factor not only in the revision of the diagnosis of schizophrenia but also in the revision of DSM as a whole.

DSM-III set out to abandon the general descriptive terminology of DSM-1 and DSM-II and replace it with specific inclusion and exclusion criteria. This method has been described as 'neo-Kraepelinian' (Double, 1990). In an attempt to be specific, Bleuler's fundamental symptoms were replaced by

Schneider's first rank symptoms and Feighner's six month duration. This cut the diagnostic frequency in half within five years of its inception (Loranger, 1990) by separating out disorders such as brief reactive psychosis, various personality disorders, and schizophreniform disorder.

The six month duration idea came from the Feighner criteria, which were the basis of new research and diagnostic criteria specifically developed for their objectivity (Feighner et al, 1972). Kurt Schneider's first rank symptoms were initially used as diagnostic criteria in Europe in 1937 (Loftus et al, 2000), and were also developed in part to reject the vague description associated with Bleuler. They attempted to differentiate between symptoms indicative of schizophrenia and other psychotic disorders. They are (Schneider, 1959):

- Hallucinated voices speaking the patient's thoughts aloud.
- Hallucinated voices talking or arguing among themselves about the patient.
- Hallucinated voices describing the patient's activity as it takes place.
- Delusional percepts: a two-stage phenomenon consisting of a normal perception followed by a delusional interpretation of it as having a special and highly personalised significance.
- Somatic passivity: Patients believe they are the passive recipient of bodily sensations imposed from the outside.
- Thought insertion: Patients believe thoughts are put into their mind by an external force.
- Thought withdrawal: Patients believe their thoughts are being removed from their mind by an outside force.
- Thought broadcast: Patients believe their thoughts are somehow transmitted to others.
- Patients believe their affect is controlled by an outside force.
- Patients believe their impulses and/or motor activities are controlled by an outside force.

These symptoms are more often summarised as: third person hallucinations, running commentary, thought echo, thought broadcasting, thought withdrawal, thought insertion and delusions of control (Loftus et al, 2000). Like many commentators Bertelsen (2002) believes these criteria are also unreliable. He suggests a worldwide classification system, such as the ICD-10 system currently relies more on these first rank symptoms than does DSM-IV. The real issue is more likely to be a genuine absence of objective symptoms, which partly underpins the Japanese decision to abandon the term schizophrenia altogether (Sato, 2004), preferring instead ¨

' (Togo-shitcho-sho) which would probably have sat well with Bleuler. Nevertheless, the first rank symptoms are understood and often used descriptively by clinicians all over the world, suggesting at least some sort of common language is being understood.

The current classification systems continue attempts to clarify schizophrenia as a psychotic disorder as distinct from all other psychotic and affective disorders. Whether this remains meaningful in the long term is open to question. The appendix of DSM-IV contains an experimental approach for future classification based on three relative dimensions: psychoticism, negative symptoms and disorganisation. This approach abandons the all or nothing concept inherent in neo-Kraepelinian classifications and moves back towards a more Bleuler inferred description by degrees. This will be evaluated for DSM-V due 2011.

To summarise, the tendency to support a particular classification system largely depends on theoretical position. That is, if schizophrenia is seen as mainly biological in origin a categorical diagnostic model logically follows. If psychosocial factors predominate then a dimensional model will make more sense. As schizophrenia is widely thought to be a combination of both with knowledge evolving of each then the need for ongoing revision of classification systems becomes understandable. However, although ICD-10 places more explicit faith in the first rank symptoms the two sets of criteria are currently very similar in principle. The current criteria as defined by DSM-IV are shown in *Box 4.1*.

The ICD-10 recognises a further two subtypes:

- Post-schizophrenic depression: A depressive episode arising in the aftermath of a schizophrenic illness where some low-level schizophrenic symptoms may still be present (ICD code F20.4).
- Simple schizophrenia: Insidious but progressive development of prominent negative symptoms with no history of psychotic episodes (ICD code F20.6).

Vital for a diagnosis is the presence of distress or dysfunction. There may be many people for whom some if not most of these criteria may pose no problem. Two in three people hear voices without seeking or needing psychiatric help (Adams, 2007). I personally have nursed people for whom hallucinations and delusions pose them or others no risk at all. However, there has often been a clear organic component to these cases and this will be discussed next.

Psychotic symptoms

As mentioned in the introduction schizophrenia is composed of psychotic symptoms, but psychotic symptoms are not exclusive to schizophrenia. They

Box 4.1. DSM-IV criteria for schizophrenia

A *Characteristic symptoms*
Either one or more of the following:
1. Bizarre delusions. Clearly implausible and non-understandable delusions, including delusions of control over mind and body
2. Hallucinations in the form of voices commenting or conversing

Or two or more of the following
1. Other delusions
2. Other hallucinations occurring in a clear sensorium (sum of perception)
3. Disorganised speech
4. Grossly disorganised or catatonic behaviour
5. Negative symptoms. That is, flat affect, alogia (poverty of speech), avolition

The characteristic symptoms must be present for a significant proportion of time throughout a one-month period, or less if successfully treated. This is the active phase. There may also be prodromal (early symptoms) or residual phases during which time either negative symptoms alone or at least two attenuated (weakened) characteristic symptoms are present.

B *Social/occupational dysfunction*
For a significant period of time since the onset of the disturbance one or more major areas of functioning such as work, interpersonal relationships or self-care is markedly below that before onset.

C *Six month duration*
Continuous signs of disturbance for at least six months including an active phase of at least one month (or less if treated). Exclusion criteria include mood disorder and pervasive developmental disorders such as Asperger's syndrome and autism. Organic disorders also preclude diagnosis, which can be confusing as many consider the disorder to be organic.

The DSM contains five sub-classifications of schizophrenia
- *Paranoid type:* Delusions and hallucinations are present but thought disorder, disorganised behaviour, and affective flattening are absent (DSM code 295.3/ ICD code F20.0)
- *Disorganised type:* 'hebephrenic schizophrenia' in the ICD. Thought disorder and flat affect are present together (DSM code 295.1/ICD code F20.1)
- *Catatonic type:* Prominent psychomotor disturbances are evident. Symptoms can include catatonic stupor and waxy flexibility (DSM code 295.2/ICD code F20.2)
- *Undifferentiated type:* Psychotic symptoms are present but the criteria for paranoid, disorganised, or catatonic types have not been met (DSM code 295.9/ICD code F20.3)

can be part of a mood disorder (e.g. manic depression), delirium or drug withdrawal, or they can occur in individuals without any concurrent mental illness (e.g. adverse drug reactions, extreme stress).

Symptoms are generally described as functional or organic, differentiated by whether there is a pathophysiological basis (organic) or not (functional). As well as schizophrenia functional causes of psychosis include:

- bipolar disorder/manic depression
- severe clinical depression
- severe psychological stress
- sleep deprivation.

Organic causes include:

- Alzheimer's disease (Lesser and Hughes, 2006)
- Lewy body dementia (McKeith, 2002)
- Parkinson's disease (Wedekind, 2005)
- Lyme disease (Fallon and Nields, 1994)
- syphilis (Kararizou et al, 2006)
- multiple sclerosis (Rodriquez Gomez, 2006)
- sarcoidosis (Bona et al, 1998)
- brain tumour (Lisanby et al, 1998).

Electrolyte disturbances can cause psychotic symptoms, for example:

- hypocalcaemia (Rossman and Vock, 1954)
- hypercalcaemia (Rosenthal et al, 1997)
- hyponatraemia (Haensch et al, 1996)
- hypernatraemia (Jana and Romano Jana, 1973)
- hypophosphataemia (Nanji, 1984)
- hyperkalaemia (Hafez et al, 1984).

Hypoglycaemia can also mimic many neurological signs and should always be considered in any change of mental state according to Padder et al (2005). The same may be true of all the electrolyte disturbances, which can be ruled out by basic urea and electrolyte blood tests.

Psychosis has also been caused by AIDS, lupus and malaria and has even been found as consequential to flu (Maurizi, 1985), the latter perhaps not altogether surprising as influenza is a symptom of Lyme disease, which has also been causative. Psychoactive drugs such as alcohol and barbiturates (particularly in withdrawal), amphetamines, cocaine and LSD can also cause psychotic symptoms, as can prescription drugs such as benzodiazepines, antidepressants and anticonvulsants. Even antihistamines, the founding molecules of antipsychotic medication have been shown to cause psychosis at therapeutic doses (Sexton and Pronchik, 1997).

This list is not exhaustive, but what it means is that psychosis in these cases is secondary to these diseases/imbalances/intoxications. Therefore antipsychotic medication would not be a first line treatment. A careful history and differential diagnosis is vital, which is achieved through following the advice given at the beginning of this section. Once a diagnosis is made a prescription for an antipsychotic may be considered.

NICE guidelines

NICE clinical guidelines support the role of healthcare professionals in providing care in partnership with patients, taking account of their individual needs and preferences, and ensuring that patients (and their carers and families, where appropriate) can make informed decisions about their care and treatment.

(NICE, 2007: 1)

The NICE guidelines are based on a hierarchy of evidence as illustrated in *Table 4.1*. The concept is developed from Eccles and Mason's (2001) 'how to develop cost-conscious guidelines', which in turn replicates a general consensus on research quality. They grade evidence based on source quality and whether the evidence is primary or not. So, for example, grade A evidence is directly based on data from meta-analyses (category 1) whereas grade B evidence may be extrapolated from the recommendations of that meta-analysis. Grade D may simply be expert opinion.

With specific regard to schizophrenia the 2002 guidance is currently being updated and is due to be complete in January 2009. This is because new evidence of the efficacy of psychological interventions and antipsychotic drugs needs to be incorporated. Data on medication is regularly reviewed and updated in technology appraisals, but these will be incorporated into the new guidance (NICE, 2007: 3, 4.3 a–d, h). In the spirit of this process the following section therefore examines the latest evidence for the efficacy of pharmacological intervention in psychosis and schizophrenia.

What do antipsychotics do?

The first antipsychotics were discovered in the 1950s as described in *Chapter 2*, and were successful despite any understanding of how they worked. To a large extent this remains the case. Dopamine is known to

Table 4.1 NICE hierarchical grading of clinical evidence (Eccles and Mason, 2001)

Recommendation grade	Evidence
A	Directly based on category I evidence
B	Directly based on: • category II evidence, or • extrapolated recommendation from category I evidence
C	Directly based on: • category III evidence, or • extrapolated recommendation from category I or II evidence
D	Directly based on: • category IV evidence, or • extrapolated recommendation from category I, II, or III evidence

Evidence category	Source
I	Evidence from: • meta-analysis of randomised controlled trials, or • at least one randomised controlled trial
II	Evidence from: • at least one controlled study without randomisation, or • at least one other type of quasi-experimental study
III	Evidence from non-experimental descriptive studies, such as comparative studies, correlation studies and case-control studies
IV	Evidence from expert committee reports or opinions and/or clinical experience of respected authorities

be involved but not as straightforwardly as initially hoped. Serotonin appears implicated via the 5HT2 receptor, and the therapeutic lag suggests structural changes in the cell via an intracellular cascade of activity. Just about every neurotransmitter discovered since acetylcholine appears to be implicated in some way, with glutamate arguably currently of greatest interest (Moghaddam, 2005). However, the drugs appear to exert their effect mainly by initially targeting specific neurotransmitter systems. The subsequent cascade and feedback reactions which follow are much less well understood. Therefore, from a prescribing point of view the most important information to focus on is both pragmatic and clinical. That is, what do they actually do in practice? How do they measurably affect people clinically? Do they work, and if so, at what cost?

As illustrated in *Table 4.1* the highest level of evidence regarding clinical trials remains meta-analyses of randomised double blind controlled trials. Put simply, this is a statistical overview of a number of high quality trials. Conclusions can then be drawn from all the data. It must be noted that this process is often largely dependent on published clinical trials. Trials which do not find significant results do not tend to get published. As a result, even a systematic review or meta-analysis may not have all the relevant information to begin with. However, authors of systematic reviews published by the Cochrane Collaboration do their best to find unpublished data as well as published, and are widely agreed to meet the highest standards possible. 'It is the best single source of reliable evidence about the effects of health care' (Cochrane Collaboration, 2007). Its originator Archie Cochrane marched through London in 1938 bearing a placard reading 'All effective treatments should be free'. He called for a central international register of clinical trials while working as an epidemiologist in 1972 (Cochrane, 1972). His vision of a 100% accurate medical database is now a reality according to Grimshaw (2004).

The following evidence is summarised from the Cochrane library, and would be categorised as grade A by NICE.

Risperidone and schizophrenia

Risperidone was entered as a search term into the Cochrane database title, abstract or keyword, combined with the same search strategy for 'schizophrenia'. This generated 4941 results. The search was then limited to Cochrane reviews only. The following information is summarised from those 15 reviews.

Hunter et al (2003) undertook a systematic review of trials comparing efficacy of risperidone with haloperidol in schizophrenia. They concluded that risperidone was less likely to cause movement disorders (extrapyramidal syndrome) and that more people continued treatment with risperidone in some trials, suggesting patients found it preferable to haloperidol generally. Significantly fewer people had to use concomitant antiparkinsonian drugs. Risperidone was more likely to improve both positive and negative symptoms in the short and long term, and more likely to reduce relapse at one year than haloperidol. Four studies showed it was more likely to cause weight gain than the typical antipsychotics and some results indicated it was more likely to cause rhinitis.

However, Hunter et al noted that the data on relapse were generated by researchers affiliated with the drug company and would therefore need to be repeated in studies less liable to accusations of bias. They concluded that any marginal benefit demonstrated by risperidone had to be contrasted with the higher probability of weight gain and the higher cost. However the cost will reduce because from December 2007 Janssen's patent expires.

Gilbody et al (2000) looked at risperidone versus other atypical drugs, as the majority of studies tended to compare atypicals with typicals, as above. Their objective was to determine the efficacy of risperidone compared with other atypicals for schizophrenia. In an analysis of nine studies they found little difference between risperidone, olanzapine and amisulpride. They did not find enough evidence to suggest risperidone was as effective as clozapine in treatment-resistant schizophrenia, a conclusion supported by Tuunainen et al's (2000) review focusing on the efficacy of clozapine. These reviews need to be updated.

More recent reports have shown that risperidone and olanzapine account for nearly half of all the antipsychotics prescribed and more than 90% of the atypical antipsychotics prescribed in the UK (Jayaram et al, 2006). Jayaram et al conducted a comparison of risperidone versus olanzapine to determine the relative clinical effects, safety and cost-effectiveness of both in treating schizophrenia. They concluded there was little to separate the two except on the basis of differing adverse events. Attrition rates were high in all 16 studies examined. They concluded that both drugs were effective in terms of improvement of symptoms but risperidone was associated with movement disorders and sexual dysfunction whereas olanzapine is associated more with weight gain.

At least 0.1% of the world's elderly population have a diagnosis of late onset schizophrenia, but Arunpongpaisal et al (2003) found no trial-based criteria on which to base guidelines for treatment. They concluded that clinicians must therefore be prescribing based on clinical judgement and habit alone. The danger of this has already been discussed.

In summary, in the treatment of schizophrenia risperidone appears less likely to cause extrapyramidal side effects than haloperidol while being of similar efficacy. It may not be as effective as clozapine in treatment refractory schizophrenia, but it is as effective as olanzapine and causes less weight gain. It causes more movement disorders than olanzapine. The attrition rates from all the reviews may be relevant from a relapse perspective, and could well be addressed in a nursing relationship. That is, if people are not taking their medication perhaps their nurse may be in the right place to find out why and seek more acceptable supportive alternatives.

Risperidone and psychotic symptoms

Risperidone has also been used to treat a variety of psychotic symptoms and a summary of the relevant Cochrane reviews follows.

Rendell et al (2006) reviewed risperidone as a treatment for mania, either as a stand alone treatment or as an adjunct to lithium or valproate. They concluded that it was effective as both monotherapy and adjunct, and that its efficacy was comparable to haloperidol. Significant side effects in this review were weight gain, extrapyramidal symptoms and sedation. Overall risperidone caused less extrapyramidal disorder, more weight gain and comparable sedation to haloperidol. There are currently no trials on the long-term use of risperidone in mood disorders (Rendell and Geddes 2006); although there is emerging evidence that 'combination treatment' of antidepressants and antipsychotics is a better treatment option than either alone for psychotic depression (Wijkstra et al, 2005). More worrying, considering the history of the randomised control trial in humans, is the lack of evidence supporting the use of any antipsychotic in pregnancy. Webb et al (2004) believe this may be a paradoxical result of ethical constraints concerning experimental treatment in pregnant women.

Ballard et al (2006) reviewed the efficacy of atypicals in regard to psychosis and aggression in people with Alzheimer's disease. They found nine high quality trials and concluded risperidone was effective in reducing psychotic symptoms and aggression. However, it also caused a significantly higher incidence of cerebrovascular events including stroke and death, extrapyramidal symptoms, upper respiratory infections and oedema. Again, there was a significant incidence of attrition. They concluded that risperidone should not be used unless there was a serious risk of physical harm to those living or working with the patient. Schneider et al (2005) checked mortality rates for all the atypicals and found no drug to be significantly worse than any other. They did find a significant overall risk of death (3.5%) when any atypical was compared to placebo (2.3%). Caution should therefore be exercised in prescribing any atypical for this group. Although not reviewed by Cochrane, Schneider's data included Cochrane trials and a number of unpublished trials. It was peer reviewed by the *Journal of the American Medical Association.*

Lonergan et al (2007) studied the atypicals in respect to their efficacy in delirium. This is relevant here as the authors again contrasted haloperidol with risperidone, quetiapine and olanzapine, and measured efficacy and adverse events, thereby giving a broader view of the adverse event spectrum. Like Hunter et al's (2003) review Lonergan et al (2007) found similar efficacy in treatment outcomes across the drugs, but unlike Hunter et al found that average dose levels generated no difference in adverse events. It was only when doses were increased that haloperidol showed more extrapyramidal symptoms.

In summary, risperidone would appear to be of similar efficacy to haloperidol in addressing psychotic symptoms, while causing fewer extrapyramidal symptoms but more weight gain. It appears to carry a significant risk of cerebrovascular accident and death in dementia as well as upper respiratory infections, oedema and extrapyramidal symptoms. Comparisons of its efficacy in relation to other atypicals appear similar.

Olanzapine and schizophrenia

The manufacturers of olanzapine claim it causes fewer extrapyramidal symptoms than typical and other atypical antipsychotics. Duggan et al (2005) tested this through systematic review, but found most of the available studies were run or sponsored by the companies marketing the drugs they were testing. They concluded that olanzapine seemed to be an effective antipsychotic that produces less adverse events for movement. It appears more likely to cause weight gain. They did not find any difference in its claimed ability to target negative symptoms. It was as effective as other atypicals. Rummel et al (2003) concluded similarly in their review on atypicals as first-line treatment for first episode schizophrenia.

In the reviews discussed already, Gilbody et al (2000) found 'little to choose' between risperidone and olanzapine, whereas Tuunainen et al (2000) found olanzapine to have fewer extrapyramidal symptoms than the newer atypicals. Jayaram et al (2006) found olanzapine to cause more weight gain than risperidone while also recognising extrapyramidal symptoms were less frequent. With regard to older people with schizophrenia Marriott et al (2006) felt unable to come to any conclusions based on the small amount of data available.

Olanzapine and psychotic symptoms

Lonergan et al (2007) found no difference between the atypicals in the treatment of delirium, or the adverse events reported. Ballard et al (2006) found a comparable risk to risperidone with regard to cerebrovascular risk in people with Alzheimer's disease. In assessing olanzapine for the treatment of mania Rendell et al (2003) concluded olanzapine was more effective than the anticonvulsant divalproex (sodium valproate and valproic acid), a finding supported by MacRitchie et al (2003) in their review of the efficacy of divalproex. Both reviews found olanzapine more effective but less well tolerated by patients, with more likelihood of weight gain and sedation. There is no evidence of difference in efficacy between haloperidol and risperidone, olanzapine, and valproate according to Cipriani et al (2006). Cipriani et al (2003) are currently reviewing olanzapine as a long-term treatment in bipolar disorder.

Olanzapine is available as an intramuscular preparation and oral dispersible tablet for rapid tranquillisation of acutely disturbed people due to serious mental illness. Belgamwar and Fenton (2005) assessed its effectiveness. However, they also found all the studies to be sponsored by the company and therefore concluded that more studies are required. They felt able to say that intramuscular olanzapine probably has a place where more traditional treatments cannot be given. It causes fewer movement disorders than haloperidol and more than lorazepam. They felt unable to comment on the dispersible tablet.

In summary, olanzapine would appear to be of similar efficacy to both haloperidol and risperidone in addressing psychotic symptoms, while causing fewer extrapyramidal symptoms but more weight gain than both. As with risperidone it appears to carry a significant risk of cerebrovascular accident and death in dementia.

Quetiapine and schizophrenia

Quetiapine should theoretically cause fewer movement disorders. This was reviewed along with its efficacy by Srisurapanont et al (2004). They wanted to determine the effects of quetiapine for schizophrenia in relation to placebo and other antipsychotics. They found quetiapine to be an effective treatment for schizophrenia, but no more so than the older typical antipsychotics or risperidone. They did find it to have a lower risk of movement disorder, but a greater incidence of dizziness, dry mouth and sleepiness. As such they felt unable to conclude anything other than 'more clearly reported pragmatic randomised controlled trials should be carried out to determine its position in everyday clinical practice'.

Quetiapine and psychotic symptoms

There are no current Cochrane reviews focusing on the efficacy of quetiapine in psychosis. The following evidence is from clinical trials and other reviews within the Cochrane library.

A meta-analysis from 1999 concluded that quetiapine was as effective as haloperidol, with less frequent need of antiparkinsonian medication (Leucht et al, 1999). This was the only other review. There were 193 clinical trials in the database. What follows is a very brief summary of six of the more recent trials directly related to quetiapine in the treatment of psychosis.

Quetiapine and risperidone have broadly comparable clinical efficacy according to Zhong et al (2006). Both improve cognitive and social functioning and in this study neither had a clinically significant effect on weight or glucose. Somnolence was more common with quetiapine. Extrapyramidal symptoms and elevated prolactin rates were significantly higher with risperidone (Zhong et al, 2006). Thase et al (2006) found that quetiapine, like risperidone (Rendell et al, 2006) and olanzapine (Cipriani et al, 2006) is an effective monotherapy for mania. Its use in longer term bipolar disorder also seems effective. It has been shown to be effective as an anxiolytic in bipolar I depression, but less so in bipolar II (Hirschfeld et al, 2006). This may be because bipolar I depression is defined by its more severe psychotic symptoms, and that may be where quetiapine exerts its therapeutic effect.

Kinon et al (2006) conducted a six month randomised double blind comparison of 346 patients receiving either quetiapine or olanzapine in the treatment of schizophrenia with predominantly negative symptoms. They concluded both were equally effective, although olanzapine showed greater improvement in positive symptoms.

In a small open label study quetiapine was shown to be more effective than haloperidol in treating behavioural disturbances associated with Alzheimer's disease (Savaskan et al, 2006). This does not add to the debate on safety however. The atypicals' efficacy is not in question overall. Tariot et al (2006) found efficacy to be comparable between haloperidol and quetiapine in a much larger better controlled study.

In summary, there is not as much high quality evidence for quetiapine as there is for olanzapine and risperidone. It is difficult to know why, especially as evidence supports equivalent efficacy among the atypicals. Quetiapine has slightly more affinity for the H1 histamine receptor and this is what is thought to cause the increase in drowsiness in comparison with its peers.

So what do atypical antipsychotics do?

The atypical antipsychotics reduce symptoms for the sufferer better than placebo:

- They reduce distressing hallucinations and delusions.
- They reduce aggression and agitation where there is a serious underlying mental illness.
- They reduce the likelihood of mania in bipolar disorder and help with psychotic depression.
- They appear to help with some of the negative symptoms of schizophrenia.
- They are generally better tolerated than the older typicals.

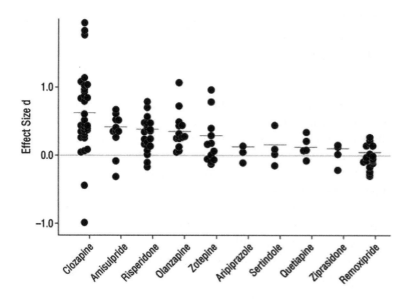

Figure 4.1. The efficacy of antipsychotics (Reproduced with permission from Davies et al, 2007).

However, in the main they have a similar profile of action to the typical antipsychotics, but they achieve their effects with less adverse events. Tardive dyskinesia appears to have been all but eradicated, although it may be too early to say. Risperidone appears to generate the most extrapyramidal symptoms of the three, olanzapine the most weight gain and quetiapine the most drowsiness. However, they are not without adverse events. Risperidone and olanzapine are certainly implicated in cerebrovascular events in people with dementia, and the same may be true of quetiapine.

It is not straightforward to translate clinical trial data directly to practice as even the most valid conclusions are based on probabilities. That is, the aim of a clinical trial is to demonstrate statistical support of the hypothesis, which naturally amalgamates disparate (individual) results. Results would be crystal clear if every person presented the same, was treated the same and had the same metabolism and social circumstance. Then researchers could be sure that the differences observed would be a factor of the differences in treatment and nothing else. These are the criteria clinical trials attempt to control, and they succeed to varying degrees. Bias is all but eradicated with a double blind placebo controlled randomised trial. The vast majority of the literature just discussed met this standard. The knowledge this generates is as objective as possible and of the highest relevance. However, no two people are alike and therefore safe prescribing practice depends to a large extent on a working knowledge of worst case scenarios. These may not necessarily be highlighted in these trials, as their incidence is not necessarily the focus of study. Arguably then, the most important question to consider first is:

What is the worst that can happen?

The aim of a prescription is safe and effective clinical treatment. However, this is not always the case. In the case of atypical treatment in schizophrenia it is only the case 50% of the time. Side effects often necessitate stopping treatment. In very rare instances severe adverse reactions occur. This section looks at these reactions and suggests ways of preventing them or managing them should they happen. Extrapyramidal symptoms will be explained in detail as these are the most common. Tardive dyskinesia will be discussed as it is not clear that this has been totally eradicated. Hyperprolactinaemia will be covered, as will torsade de pointes. First, neuroleptic malignant syndrome.

Neuroleptic malignant syndrome (NMS)

Neuroleptic malignant syndrome is increasingly rare (0.07–0.2%, Benzer, 2005), probably as a consequence of the shift to atypicals and a better recognition of the condition, but it is potentially fatal. Key symptoms according to Kohen, 2004) are

- alteration of conciousness – mild confusion to coma,
- autonomic disturbance – fluctuating blood pressure, tachycardia, hypersalivation, incontinence, excessive sweating (diaphoresis),
- elevated temperature, and
- severe muscle rigidity.

An easy way to remember this is with the mnemonic FEVER:

- Fever,
- Encephalopathy (alteration of conciousness),
- Vital sign fluctuation,
- Enzyme elevation (creatine phosphokinase, discussed below)
- Rigidity.

Mild confusion can often be mistakenly attributed to the sedating properties of the drug. Hypertension should raise suspicions, especially as most antipsychotics lower blood pressure. Fever is almost always present.

Muscle rigidity can be localised to the tongue and face, manifesting as limitations in speaking, eating and swallowing. These symptoms often indicate the initial stages prior to the full blown syndrome where severe rigidity is associated with high mortality. It is thought to be caused by dopamine receptor blockade and central dopamine hypoactivity.

NMS usually happens 4 to 11 days after start or increase of treatment. Of those patients who develop NMS, 90% will do so within 10 days (Benzer, 2005) although some cases have been reported after long-term use. The full blown syndrome is easy to recognise but the development of the syndrome may be more difficult due to its fluctuating course and similarity to other effects and side effects of the drug. This is compounded by the fact that there are no tests specific to NMS. However, creatine phosphokinase (CPK) is often elevated, and although not diagnostic (e.g. CPK is raised following strenuous exercise or muscle injury) it is a useful marker for measuring clinical improvement.

Several conditions can present as similar to NMS such as heat exhaustion, serotonin syndrome (discussed in *Chapter 5*), thyrotoxicosis and tetanus. Anticholinergic delirium can also resemble it (Stevens, 2007). However, the exclusive feature of NMS is muscle rigidity and diaphoresis. For example heat exhaustion presents with muscles flaccid and skin hot and dry. The muscles may be rigid in anticholinergic delirium but the skin will be dry.

Management

All neuroleptic medication should be stopped. Two hourly observations of vital signs should be started and CPK levels taken. The patient should be cooled and rehydrated. Medical colleagues should be consulted for advice on any concurrent medical condition. The patient may need to be transferred to intensive care. Benzodiazepines do not prevent the development of NMS but can help with relaxing the muscles. Dantrolene appears the most effective agent in reducing mortality (Shalev et al, 1989).

All antipsychotics have been associated with NMS, but haloperidol appears to carry the greatest risk. NMS can also occur with a sudden stoppage of antiparkinsonian drugs. The best way to avoid it is to minimise high doses of psychotropic medication and increase doses gradually. NMS can recur. See Bristow and Kohen (2002) for a detailed review on restarting psychotropic medication following an episode of NMS.

Extrapyramidal syndromes (EPS)

The extrapyramidal system is extremely old in evolutionary terms and remains the primary motor system in reptiles, birds and lower mammals. It

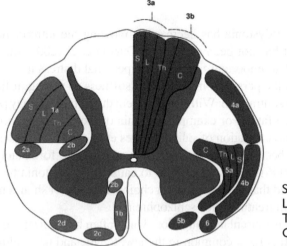

S: Sacral
L: Lumbar
Th: Thoracic
C: Cervical

Motor and descending (efferent) pathways (left)
1. Pyramidal tracts
1a. Lateral corticospinal tract
1b. Anterior corticospinal tract
2. Extrapyramidal tracts
2a. Rubrospinal tract
2b. Reticulospinal tract
2c. Vestibulospinal tract
2d. Olivospinal tract

Sensory and ascending (afferent) pathways (right)
3. Corsal column medial lemniscus system
3a. Gracile fasciculus
3b. Cuneate fasciculus
4. Spinocerebellar tracts
4a. Posterior spinocerebellar tract
4b. Anterior spinocerebellar tract
5. Anterolateral system
5a. Lateral spinothalamic tract
5b. Anterior spinothalamic tract
6. Spino-olivary fibres

Figure 4.2. Pyramidal and extrapyramidal tracts. From: http://en.wikipedia.org

maintains rhythmic and phasic movement such as walking in humans but does not initiate movement, the latter is thought to be under the control of the pyramidal system. However, it is difficult to separate both structurally and functionally. The main difference is that the pyramidal system is continuous from cortex to spinal cord without synapse, whereas the extrapyramidal system represents all other motor components (*Figure 4.2*).

The extrapyramidal side effects of neuroleptics are the most well-known adverse events, recognised very soon after the drugs entered clinical practice in the 1950s. Four key syndromes are recognised (Dursun et al, 2004):

• acute dystonia
• akathisia
• parkinsonism
• tardive dyskinesia.

Acute dystonia

The incidence of acute dystonia has decreased following the introduction of atypicals. However, it has not been eradicated. Dursun et al (2004) quote an incidence of 32% and an important feature is the personal distress it causes. It has a rapid onset with the person complaining of stiffness or aching, followed quickly by full muscle contraction. Without treatment the symptoms may persist for days and have been fatal. For example dystonia of the pharangeal muscle can lead to choking and inhalation of saliva (Stones et al, 1990). However, the fact that this has not been reported since 1990 suggests it is fortunately not common. Joy et al (2006) found haloperidol to cause more dystonia than the atypicals and concluded that where there is a choice haloperidol should not be used as a first option in treatment for schizophrenia.

The key symptom is muscular contraction which often has a bizarre quality (Dursun et al, 2004). It is most common in the jaw, tongue and neck, although it can involve any site. It is rarer with atypicals but not absent. The recent literature consists mainly of case studies of these incidences, suggesting it is not widespread (Desarker and Sinha, 2006). Chakos et al (1995) found acute dystonia was associated with a short period in remission, indicating greater risk when treatment may not be under control. In a small study of 39 schizophrenic patients Kondo et al (1999) found young males to be at highest risk.

Management is by administration of anticholinergic drugs, either orally in mild conditions, intramuscularly in moderate or intravenously in severe conditions, the latter resolving any crisis in minutes.

Akathisia

Akathisia is a feeling of 'inner restlessness' manifesting in actual restlessness, often located in the lower limbs. It can be highly distressing and often mistaken for anxiety. It means 'not sitting' in Greek and can manifest as impatience, irritability, and impaired attention and concentration. Incidence is generally stated to be around 5–15%, but Nassir Ghaemi et al (2006) found a much higher incidence in clinical practice. They found akathisia to be less common with olanzapine and quetiapine as opposed to risperidone. This research needs to be repeated with a larger sample as it challenges some common assumptions about the safety of atypicals.

The pharmacological mechanism of akathisia is unclear, but may reflect an overactive noradrenergic system combined with a depressed dopaminergic system. The person will be unable to sit still and may shuffle the feet, walk on the spot, rock from foot to foot or sit and stand repeatedly. It usually appears soon after starting or increasing the dose of an antipsychotic, worsens on further increase and lessens on reduction.

Management is by reduction of dose and then by switching to another antipsychotic. Anticholinergics, benzodiazepines and propanolol have all been effective as treatment.

Parkinsonism

Parkinsonian symptoms are present to a degree in virtually all patients taking conventional antipsychotic drugs. The highest incidence is with haloperidol (Dursun et al, 2004), although the problem appears to be dose related with all the antipsychotics. Parkinsonism occasionally occurs with selective serotonin reuptake inhibitors (SSRIs) as well.

These symptoms are classed as parkinsonian because of their presentation. However, Parkinson's disease is primarily a disease of the nigrostriatal pathway and not the extrapyramidal system. Loss of dopaminergic neurons in the substantia nigra leads to faulty regulation of the extrapyramidal system. Since this system regulates posture and skeletal muscle tone, a result is the characteristic dyskinesia of Parkinson's disease. Parkinsonism as a syndrome presents as a triad of bradykinesia, tremor and rigidity caused by psychotropic medication. The pharmacological mechanism is D2 blockade in the striatum.

Key symptoms are the characteristic gait with small, shuffling steps, resting tremor of the hands, mask-like expression, lack of arm swing, absence of blink, sialorrhoea (excessive saliva secretion) and seborrhoea (excessive sebum secretion leading to oily coating, crust or scales on the skin).

It usually appears within three months of starting or increasing an antipsychotic. Diagnosis is through observation of the above symptoms and by testing for leadpipe or cogwheel rigidity and reduced glabellar tap. Leadpipe rigidity is the term used to describe the hypertonicity felt in a parkinsonian limb throughout the range of movements of a joint and indicates increased tone in all the surrounding muscles. With cogwheel rigidity the examiner may be able to feel passive flexion or extension of a limb resulting in a series of catches in rapid succession. The glabellar tap is a primitive response where the reflex is to blink when a point between the eyebrows is tapped. This is normally habituated in about five taps. In parkinsonism this reflex is never overcome.

Parkinsonism is managed by reducing or changing the antipsychotic or prescribing an anticholinergic.

Tardive dyskinesia

The most distressing adverse syndrome associated with EPS is tardive dyskinesia. Tardive refers to the late onset of the disorder and it manifests itself in various involuntary movements which can be deeply embarrassing to the sufferer as these movements have become synonymous with schizophrenia. Tardive dyskinesia was widely thought to be an incurable relic of the older typical regime, but both these assumptions have recently been questioned.

The movement disorders present as tics, myoclonic jerks (sudden contraction of large body muscles), chorea (brief, irregular contractions that are not repetitive or rhythmic, but appear to flow from one muscle to the next), dystonia, but not tremor. It most commonly affects the bucco linguo masticatory muscles resulting in lip smacking, tongue protrusion, grimacing and pursing of the lips. Choreiform movements of the trunk and limbs are also seen. People with tardive dyskinesia have difficulty not moving. It is thought to be caused by supersensitivity of the striatal post-synaptic D2 receptors (Dursun et al, 2004), secondary to their continued blockade by antipsychotics. It usually takes at least six months of antipsychotic treatment for symptoms to appear and may not manifest for years.

Nassir Ghaemi et al (2006) found that 7.8% (4/51) of trials led to mild 'de novo' tardive dyskinesia. Even though their study was small this finding appears to be supported by Margolese et al (2005) who studied the incidence of tardive dyskinesia over 40 years between 1965 and 2004. They concluded that cases of de novo tardive dyskinesia have been reported but reporting is not always reliable so the actual incidence may be higher. However, they also found the newer atypicals ameliorated pre-existing tardive dyskinesia and that the overall incidence is significantly lower with atypicals than typicals.

Hyperprolactinaemia

Hyperprolactinaemia can cause the range of symptoms illustrated in *Table 4.2*. As with all adverse events there is great individual variability in the presence of these symptoms. They can present within a short period of time following initiating an antipsychotic or develop after a long time on an apparently stable dose (Wieck and Haddad, 2004).

Clinical manifestations of hyperprolactinaemia

Higher doses of antipsychotics are more likely to cause hyperprolactinaemia but it can occur with relatively low doses, e.g. 200mg chlorpromazine (Meltzer and Fang, 1976). It is more likely with typical antipsychotics but risperidone and olanzapine can cause it, particularly at high doses. It has also been known with SSRIs, tricyclic antidepressants and monoamine oxidase inhibitors (MOAIs).

The pharmacological mechanism is thought to relate to the blockade of D2 receptors on pituitary lactotroph cells, or by enhanced serotonergic

Table 4.2 Clinical manifestations of hyperprolactinaemia (Wieck and Haddad, 2004: 72)

- Galactorrhoea
- Gynaecomastia
- Infertility
- Menstrual irregularities
    Oligomenorrhoea
    Amenorrhoea
- Sexual dysfunction
    Decreased libido
    Impaired arousal
    Impaired orgasm
- Decreased bone mineral density (increased risk of osteoporosis)
- Increased risk breast cancer in women
- Acne and hirsutism in women

transmission via the antidepressants. It is confirmed by blood test and exclusion of other causes, e.g. pregnancy, primary hypothyroidism, severe liver disease, Cushing's disease.

Management options include switching to a prolactin sparing antipsychotic and reducing the dose of the causal agent (Smith et al, 2002). Smith et al support the correlation of dosage to severity and found in females that the level of hyperprolactinaemia was also correlated with the degree of suppression of the hypothalamic-pituitary-gonadal axis. Quetiapine is not associated with long-term raised prolactin, and should therefore be considered as first line treatment of young women requiring antipsychotic medication if hyperprolactinaemia with hypogonadism is found to be present.

Torsade de pointes and sudden death

Torsade de pointes (TDP) is a polymorphic (multiple possible states) ventricular tachycardia. It can be asymptomatic or cause dizziness and syncope (faint). In rare cases it may progress to fibrillation which presents as cardiac arrest and potentially sudden death. Sudden death has been defined as

Death within the hour of symptoms (excluding suicide, homicide and accident) which is both unexpected in relation to the degree of disability before death and unexplained because clinical investigation and autopsy failed to identify any plausible cause.

(Jusic and Lader, 1994)

Table 4.3. Classification of antipsychotic medication in terms of risk of cardiac arrhythmia (Abdelmawla and Mitchell, 2006: 101)

Drug	Chemical structure	Risk of cardiac arrhythmia
Typical antipsychotics		
Chlorpromazine	Aliphatic phenothiazine	Higher
Pimozide	Diphenylbutylpiperidine	Higher
Thioridazine	Piperidine	Higher
Trifluoperazine	Piperazine	Lower
Haloperidol	Butyrophenone	Lower
Sulpiride[1]	Substituted benzamide	Lower
Atypical antipsychotics		
Clozapine	Dibenzodiazepine	Higher
Quetiapine	Dibenzothiazepine	Lower
Risperidone	Benzisoxazole	Lower
Amisulpride	Substituted benzamide	Lower
Olanzapine	Thienobenzodiazepine	Lower
Zotepine	Dibenzothiepine	Lower

[1]Some regard sulpiride as an atypical antipsychotic

Both typical and atypical antipsychotics have cardiac complications. This is further compounded as they also increase the likelihood of diabetes and weight gain, contributory factors to cardiac complications in themselves (Abdelmawla and Mitchell, 2006). Abdelmawla and Mitchell suggest thinking of antipsychotics in terms of high and low risk (*Table 4.3*).

They also suggest clinicians prescribing these medications should be able to interpret an ECG, particularly the relevance of QTc prolongation in this regard. QTc is a corrected value for the QT interval incorporating heart rate. Bazett's formula is most commonly employed (*Figure 4.3*), although the Friedericia formula corrects more accurately at higher rates (Ferrier 2004). If excessive QTc prolongation is identified then the responsible drug should be stopped. Management of arrythmias is the remit of physicians. However, prevention is the remit of the prescriber. Monitoring supports prevention, so a clear idea of the potential risks and diagnostic investigation is the key.

Although the risk of sudden death is small with antipsychotic drugs, it is clearly a crucial adverse event to minimise. Sertindole was voluntarily withdrawn from the UK market in 1998 following evidence associating it

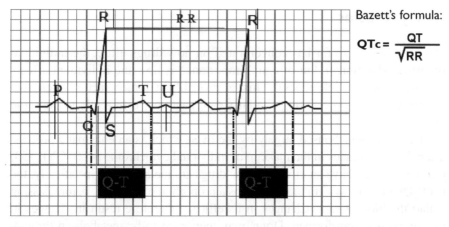

Bazett's formula:

$$QTc = \frac{QT}{\sqrt{RR}}$$

Figure 4.3. QT interval adjusted for heart rate = QTc

with malignant arrhythmia. Thioridazine was withdrawn in 2005 in response to similar concerns. The known risk factors in TDP are shown in *Table 4.4* and should be considered in the prescribing decision.

Periodic monitoring of the ECG is therefore advocated in high risk individuals (Taylor et al, 2003), although the cost-benefit analysis of such an approach has yet to be studied.

Table 4.4. Risk factors for torsade de pointes (Ferrier, 2004: 60)

Clinical risk factors	Pre-existing repolarisation abnormality
	Previous episode of TDP
	Left ventricular hypertrophy
	Cardiac failure
	Electrolyte imbalance
	Female gender
	Liver disease
	Restraint?
	Psychological distress?
	Drug and alcohol misuse?
Pharmacological risk factors	Overdose
	Prescribed high dose of antipsychotic
	Slow metaboliser status
	Pharmacokinetic interactions
	Pharmacodynamic interactions
	Diuretics

Idiosyncrasies

Most discussion so far has concentrated on how drugs affect the individual (pharmacodynamics), but of equal importance is how the individual affects the drug (pharmacokinetics). This is probably a major factor when two people apparently presenting similarly can react very differently to the same drug and dose.

Drugs are metabolised largely by the liver, which is an enzymatic process. Therefore differences in the makeup of individual cytochrome p450 (CYP 450) enzyme systems have an effect on how drugs are metabolised. Specifically, the CYP 450 enzyme system biotransforms a proportion of the drug, before passing it into the bloodstream. Changes in its efficacy therefore result in changes in that proportion transformed. Drugs may then need to be metabolised through less efficient means, which in the worst case could lead to toxic blood levels at apparently therapeutic drug dosages. In general, it may be useful to consider people either normal metabolisers, or poor or ultra-rapid metabolisers (Nagata and Yamazoe, 2002). For example, CYP 450 enzyme 2C9 is missing in 1–3% of caucasians; CYP 2C19 has reduced activity in about 20% of Japanese and Chinese people; and 5–10% of Caucasians are poor metabolisers via the enzyme CYP 2D6, whereas less than 1% of Japanese are.

A more common issue is the potential for drug interactions, as the metabolism of one drug may alter the level of available enzyme for the metabolism of another. For example nicotine is metabolised by the same enzyme as caffeine (CYP 1A2). Therefore one result of stopping smoking is an increase in plasma caffeine levels. Another would be an increase in olanzapine levels, as this is also metabolised by 1A2. In other words, cigarette smoking can lower olanzapine levels (Stahl, 1999). Grapefruit juice also inhibits CYP 1A2, as does fluvoxamine. Fluoxetine inhibits CYP 2C19, which, as seen above, is already compromised in 20% of Japanese people, which may also be a factor in its absence from their market. However, fluoxetine also inhibits CYP 2D6, which is missing in 5–10% of Caucasians. As risperidone and olanzapine are metabolised via 2D6, concomitant use of fluoxetine or any other 2D6 inhibitor will raise plasma levels. Any drug metabolised by 2D6 will always carry some risk as patients are not routinely screened for genetic polymorphism of the 2D6 enzyme (Medicines and Healthcare Regulation Agency, 2006).

According to Stahl (1999) the clinical significance of these interactions is unclear. That is, risperidone's net efficacy appears unchanged when given with 2D6 inhibitors. Olanzapine levels do not generally need to be adjusted in smokers or people taking SSRIs. However this is a relatively new field of study. Recent research supports the idea that greater understanding of specific CYP 450 genotyping could result in fewer adverse events and hence greater adherence to medication regimens (Bondy and Spellman, 2007). Bray et al (in press) go further and suggest that there are now genotyping tests available which provide information on the individual's ability to metabolise psychotropic medication. A single case study is then presented to suggest that this could be a major factor.

Certainly caution is necessary in combining phenytoin with quetiapine. Phenytoin can lower quetiapine levels to the extent that dosage increase may be necessary. However few combinations must be absolutely avoided. What is perhaps more relevant is that different atypicals have clinically distinctive effects in different patients, and pharmacokinetics may well underpin some of these differences. In the absence of solid evidence of the clinical significance of these findings caution and an open mind is required. It may be these factors that support success when trying another atypical if the first or second fails.

Uncorroborated evidence

Whether or not it is these factors, it is clear that in some cases a second atypical will have a therapeutic effect where the first choice did not. This may well be a combination of individual phamacodynamics, genomics and unique properties of individual drugs. However this is difficult to demonstrate and so this is where clinical judgement takes precedence. Stahl (1999) refers to this level of knowledge as 'clinical pearls'. At best this evidence is grade D (Eccles and Mason, 2001) and most of it would not be considered at even this criterion. These observations are often anecdotal or minimally researched. However, it is worth mentioning some in regard to the antipsychotics discussed here.

Stahl (1999: 61) suggests the atypicals may be useful in treating aggression and depressive symptoms in schizophrenia and as discussed may be more effective in treating negative symptoms than the typicals. There is better compliance, fewer hospitalisations and hence reduced overall treatment costs. There is a less disruptive downhill course. With regard to specific drugs he suggests that risperidone is a well-accepted treatment for schizophrenia, and many anecdotal reports support its efficacy in positive psychotic symptoms not associated with schizophrenia. There is less weight gain than with the other atypicals, but risperidone is the only atypical to elevate prolactin levels. In these cases less may be more. By reducing the dose side effects are often eliminated without loss of efficacy (Stahl, 1999: 77). Risperidone may have the fewest clinically relevant drug interactions of all the atypicals. The plasma half-life suggests twice daily administration but clinical experience suggests once daily is sufficient for efficacy, especially if total dose is less than 4mg (ibid: 109).

Olanzapine is also well accepted for schizophrenia, particularly in difficult cases (ibid: 79). Again there is anecdotal evidence for its efficacy in treatment refractory cases and psychotic symptoms not associated with schizophrenia. Cognitive symptoms of schizophrenia have improved in some clinical trials despite the fact that olanzapine's muscarinic antagonist properties would suggest the opposite. It causes more weight gain than other atypicals. Doses in clinical practice are often higher than those quoted in clinical trials, as dosage appears tolerable at higher doses without increase in adverse events. Women may have higher plasma levels and thus require lower doses (ibid: 109). Cigarette smoking can decrease olanzapine levels, whereas inhibitors of 2D6 (e.g. fluoxetine, paroxetine) may raise olanzapine levels. The clinical significance of this is unclear however. Administration once daily is fine.

Some patients respond to quetiapine when other atypicals have failed (ibid: 82). It may be the preferred antipsychotic for psychosis in Parkinson's disease. Again there is anecdotal evidence for its efficacy in treatment refractory cases and psychotic symptoms not associated with schizophrenia. Studies support its use in hostility/aggression, cognition and affective symptoms in schizophrenia. There is essentially no EPS or prolactin elevation at any dose. Clinical experience suggests twice daily dosing is optimal (ibid: 110). Phenytoin can lower quetiapine levels necessitating dosage increase for quetiapine.

In summary, different atypicals often have clinically distinct effects in different patients, and atypicals in general do not always work as fast as typicals. They are thus often less effective at treating agitation and acute psychoses than the typicals. There is a mismatch between optimal doses used in clinical trials and optimal dosages used in practice. However, atypicals undoubtedly have a better side effect profile. They reduce negative symptoms more effectively, possibly as a result of this. They also reduce cognitive and affective symptoms, again possibly secondary to their increased tolerability. The magnitude of these differences underpins the rationale for making atypical antipsychotics the first line treatment for psychosis (NICE, 2002).

Summary

Psychotic symptoms are only problematic if they cause distress. If help is required then accurate, replicable, structured and systematic diagnosis is the key to pharmacological intervention. Concordance is best achieved through mutual understanding and this takes skilled communication based upon the current principles of partnership and recovery in mental health nursing (Scottish Executive, 2006). Prescribing decisions will

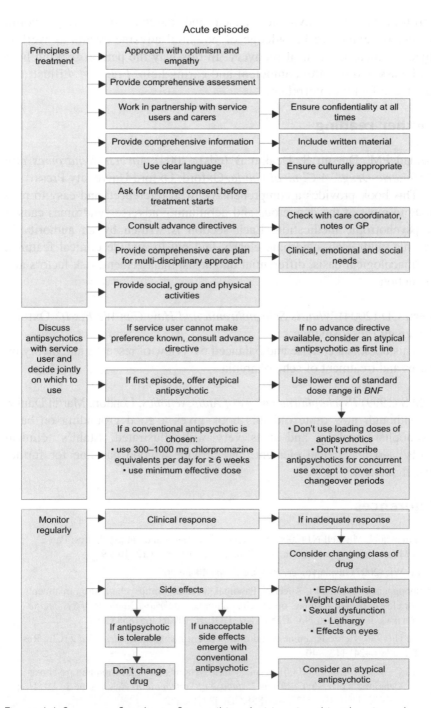

Figure 4.4. Summary flowchart of prescribing decisions in schizophrenia and psychosis (NICE, 2002).

therefore be clear, evidence based and agreed. Monitoring should encompass extensive knowledge of potential adverse events as well as objective measurement of recovery. In this way the person seeking help can be assured of safe, competent and caring help. *Figure 4.4* illustrates how these factors interrelate.

Further reading

Haddad PM, Dursun S, Deakin B (eds) (2004) *Adverse Syndromes and Psychiatric Drugs. A Clinical Guide.* Oxford: Oxford University Press

This book provides a comprehensive, well-referenced and easy to read guide to most of the dangerous and debilitating adverse syndromes caused by psychotropic medication. Each section is written by an authority in the area, with each syndrome clearly laid out to include clinical features, pharmacological basis, differential diagnosis, management, risk factors and prevention.

Shean GD (2004) *What is Schizophrenia and How Can We Fix It?* Oxford: University Press America

This book is a concise and balanced overview of research and theory on causes and treatment of schizophrenia

Stahl S (1999) *Psychopharmacology of Antipsychotics.* London, Martin Dunitz

Although now quite old this book gives a good grounding on basic psychopharmacology and it is very well illustrated. Stahl's 'clinical pearls' add a practical element, and provide a good baseline for further investigation.

References

Abdelmawla N, Mitchell NJ (2006) Sudden cardiac deaths and antipsychotics: Part 2 – Monitoring and prevention. *Adv Psychiatric Treatment* **12**: 100–9

Adams WL (2007) Inside voices. *Psychol Today* **40**(1): 26

Arunpongpaisal S, Ahmed I, Aqeel N, Paholpak S (2003) Antipsychotic drug treatment for elderly people with late-onset schizophrenia. *Cochrane Database of Systematic Reviews*, Issue 2. Art. No.: CD004162. DOI: 10.1002/14651858.CD00

Ashton H (1984) Benzodiazepine withdrawal: An unfinished story. *Brit Med J* (Clin Res Ed) **288**(6424) 1135–40

Ballard C, Waite J, Birks J (2006) Atypical antipsychotics for aggression and psychosis in Alzheimer's disease. *Cochrane Database of Systematic Reviews*, Issue 1. Art. No.: CD003476. DOI: 10.1002/14651858.CD003476.pub2

Beer MD (1995) Psychosis: From mental disorder to disease concept. *Hist Psychiatry* **6**(22(II)): 177–200

Belgamwar RB, Fenton M (2005) Olanzapine IM or velotab for acutely disturbed/agitated people with suspected serious mental illnesses. *Cochrane Database of Systematic Reviews*, Issue 2. Art. No.: CD003729. DOI: 10.1002/14651858.CD003729.pub2

Benzer E (2005) *Neuroleptic Malignant Syndrome*. Emedicine http://www.emedicine.com/ EMERG/topic339.htm [Accessed 15 June 2007]

Bertelsen A. (2002) Schizophrenia and related disorders: Experience with current diagnostic systems. *Psychopathology* **35**(2–3): 89–93

Bleuler E (1924) *Textbook of Psychiatry* (trans AA Brill from Lehrbuch der Psychiatrie 4th ed) New York: Macmillan

Bona JR, ,Fackler SF, Fendley MJ, Nemeroff CB (1998). Neurosarcoidosis as a cause of refractory psychosis: A complicated case report. *Am J Psychiatry* **155**(8): 1106–8

Bondy B, Spellmann I (2007) Pharmacogenetics of antipsychotics: Useful for the clinician? *Curr Opin Psychiatry* **20**: 126–30

Bray J, Clarke C, Brennen G, Muncey T (in press) Should we be 'pushing meds'? The implications of pharmacogenomics. *J Psych Ment Health Nursing*

Bristow M, Kohen D (2002) Predicting the effects of rechallenge with antipsychotics following NMS: A review of cases from neuroleptic malignant syndrome database. *Brain Pharmacology* **1**: 181–7

Chakos M, Alvir J, Koreen A, Sheitman B, Geisler S, Lieberman J (1995) Incidence and correlates of acute extrapyramidal symptoms in first episode schizophrenia. *Biol Psychiatry* **37**(9): 660–1

Cipriani A, Rendell J, Geddes J (2003) Olanzapine in long-term treatment for bipolar disorder. (Protocol) *Cochrane Database of Systematic Reviews*, Issue 2. Art. No.: CD004367. DOI: 10.1002/14651858.CD004367

Cipriani A, Rendell JM, Geddes JR (2006) Haloperidol alone or in combination for acute mania. *Cochrane Database of Systematic Reviews*, Issue 3. Art. No.: CD004362. DOI: 10.1002/14651858.CD004362.pub2

Cochrane A (1972) *Effectiveness and Efficiency*. London: Nuffield Provincial Hospitals Trust

Cochrane Collaboration (2007) *Cochrane Reviews and the Cochrane Library: An Introduction* http://www.cochrane.org/reviews/clibintro.htm [Accessed 22 August 2007]

Davies SJC, Lennard MS, Ghahramani P, Pratt P, Robertson A, Potokar J (2007) PRN prescribing in psychiatric inpatients – potential for pharmacokinetic drug interactions. *J Psychopharmacol* **21**(2) 153–60

Desarker P, Sinha VK (2006) Quetiapine-induced acute dystonia and akathisia. *Aust NZ J Psychiatry* **40**(6–7): 607–8

Double DB (1990) What would Adolf Meyer have thought of the neo-Kraepelinian approach? *Psychiatric Bull* **14**: 472–4

Duggan L, Fenton M, Rathbone J, Dardennes R, El-Dosoky A, Indran S (2005) Olanzapine for schizophrenia. *Cochrane Database of Systematic Reviews*, Issue 2. Art. No.: CD001359. DOI: 10.1002/14651858.CD001359.pub2

Dursun S, Haddad PM, Barnes TRE (2004) Extrapyramidal syndromes. In Haddad P, Dursun S, Deakin B (eds) *Adverse Syndromes and Psychiatric Drugs. A Clinical Guide*. Oxford: Oxford University Press

Eccles M, Mason J (2001) How to develop cost-conscious guidelines. *Health Technology Assessment* **5**: 16

Fallon BA, Nields JA. (1994) Lyme disease: A neuropsychiatric illness *Am J Psychiatry* **151**(11):1571–83

Feighner JP, Robins E, Guze SB, Woodruff RA, Winokur G, Munoz R (1972) Diagnostic criteria for use in psychiatric research. *Arch Gen Psychiatry* **26**: 57–63

Ferrier N (2004) Torsade de Pointes and sudden death. In Haddad PM, Dursun S, Deakin B (eds) *Adverse Syndromes and Psychiatric Drugs. A Clinical Guide.* Oxford: Oxford University Press

Gilbody SM, Bagnall AM, Duggan L, Tuunainen A (2000) Risperidone versus other atypical antipsychotic medication for schizophrenia. *Cochrane Database of Systematic Reviews* Issue 3. Art. No.: CD002306. DOI: 10.1002/14651858.CD002306

Grimshaw J (2004) So what has the Cochrane Collaboration ever done for us? A report card on the first 10 years. *Can Med Assoc J* **171**(7): 747–9

Haensch CA, Hennen G, Jorg J(1996) Reversible exogenous psychosis in thiazide-induced hyponatremia of 97 mmol/l. *Der Nervenarzt* **67**(4): 319–22

Hafez H, Strauss JS, Aronson MD, Holt C (1984) Hypokalemia-induced psychosis in a chronic schizophrenic patient. *J Clin Psychiatry* **45**(6): 277–9

Healy D (2002) *The Creation of Psychopharmacology.* Cambridge, MA: Harvard University Press

Hirschfeld RM, Weisler RH, Raines SR, Macfadden W, for the BOLDER Study Group (2006) Quetiapine in the treatment of anxiety in patients with bipolar I or II depression: A secondary analysis from a randomized, double-blind, placebo-controlled study. *J Clin Psychiatry* **67**(3): 355–62

Hunter RH, Joy CB, Kennedy E, Gilbody SM, Song F (2003) Risperidone versus typical antipsychotic medication for schizophrenia. *Cochrane Database of Systematic Reviews* Issue 2. Art. No.: CD000440. DOI: 10.1002/14651858.CD000440

Jana DK, Romano-Jana L (1973) Hypernatremic psychosis in the elderly: Case reports. *J Am Geriatrics Soc* **21**(10): 473–7

Jayaram MB, Hosalli P, Stroup S (2006) Risperidone versus olanzapine for schizophrenia. *Cochrane Database of Systematic Reviews*, Issue 2. Art. No.: CD005237. DOI: 10.1002/14651858.CD005237.pub2

Joy CB, Adams CE, Lawrie SM (2006) Haloperidol versus placebo for schizophrenia. *Cochrane Database of Systematic Reviews*, Issue 4. Art. No.: CD003082. DOI: 10.1002/14651858.CD003082.pub2

Jusic N, Lader M (1994) Post modern antipsychotic drug concentrations and unexplained deaths. *Brit J Psychiatry* **165**(12): 787–91

Kararizou E, Mitsonis C, Dimopoulos N, Gkiatas K, Markou I, Kalfakis N (2006) Psychosis or simply a new manifestation of neurosyphilis? *J Int Med Res* **34**(3): 335–7

Kohen D (2004) Neuroleptic malignant syndrome. In Haddad P, Dursun S, Deakin B (eds) *Adverse Syndromes and Psychiatric Drugs. A Clinical Guide.* Oxford: Oxford University Press

Kondo T, Otani K, Tokinaga N, Ishida M, Yasui N, Kaneko S (1999) Characteristics and risk factors of acute dystonia in schizophrenic patients treated with nemonapride, a selective dopamine antagonist. *J Clin Psychopharmacol* **19**(1): 45–50

Lesser JM, Hughes S (2006) Psychosis-related disturbances. Psychosis, agitation, and disinhibition in Alzheimer's disease: Definitions and treatment options. *Geriatrics* **61**(12): 14–20

Leucht S, Pitschel-Walz G, Abraham D, Kissling W (1999) Efficacy and extrapyramidal side-effects of the new antipsychotics olanzapine, quetiapine, risperidone, and sertindole compared to conventional antipsychotics and placebo: A meta-analysis of randomized controlled trials. *Schizophrenia Res* **35**(1): 51–68

Lisanby SH, Kohler C, Swanson CL, Gur RE (1998) Psychosis secondary to brain tumor. *Seminars in Clinical Neuropsychiatry* **3**(1): 12–22

Loftus J, DeLisi LE, Crow TJ (2000) Factor structure and familiality of first-rank symptoms in sibling pairs with schizophrenia and schizoaffective disorder. *Brit J Psychiatry* **177**: 15–19

Lonergan E, Britton AM, Luxenberg J (2007) Antipsychotics for delirium. *Cochrane Database of Systematic Reviews*, Issue 2. Art. No.: CD005594. DOI: 10.1002/14651858.CD005594.pub2

Loranger AW (1990) The impact of DSM III on diagnostic practice in a university hospital: A comparison of DSM II and DSM III in 10,914 patients. *Arch Gen Psychiatry* **47**: 329–44

Macritchie K, Geddes JR, Scott J, Haslam D, de Lima M, Goodwin G. (2003) Valproate for acute mood episodes in bipolar disorder. *Cochrane Database of Systematic Reviews* Issue 1. Art. No.: CD004052. DOI: 10.1002/14651858.CD004052

Margolese HC, Chouinard G, KolivakisTT, Beauclair L, Miller D, Annable L (2005) Tardive dyskinesia in the era of typical and atypical antipsychotics. Part 2: Incidence and management strategies in patients with schizophrenia. *Can J Psychiatry* **50**(11): 703–14

Marriott RG, Neil W, Waddingham S (2006) Antipsychotic medication for elderly people with schizophrenia. *Cochrane Database of Systematic Reviews*, Issue 1. Art. No.: CD005580. DOI: 10.1002/14651858.CD005580

Maurer K, Maurer U (2003) *Alzheimer: The Life of a Physician and Career of a Disease.* New York: Columbia University Press

Maurizi CP (1985) Influenza and mania: A possible connection with the locus ceruleus. *Southern Med J* **78**(2): 207–9

McKeith IG (2002). Dementia with Lewy bodies. *Brit J Psychiatry* **180**: 144–7

Medicines and Healthcare Regulation Agency (2006) *Pharmacovigilance Working Party Public Assessment Report on Neuroleptics and Cardiac safety, in particular QTprolongation, cardiac arrhythmias, ventricular tachycardia and torsades de pointes* MHRA portal: http://www.mhra.gov.uk/home/idcplg?IdcService=SS_GET_PAGE&nodeId=936 [Accessed 20 December 2007]

Meltzer HY, Fang VS (1976) The effect of neuroleptics on serum prolactin in schizophrenic patients. *Arch Gen Psychiatry* **33**: 279–86

Moghaddam B (2005) *Current Hypotheses*. Available from: http://www. schizophreniaforum.org/for/curr/Moghaddam/default.asp [Accessed 1 August 2007]

Nagata K, Yamashoe Y (2002) Genetic polymorphism of human cytochrome P450 involved in drug metabolism. *Drug Metabolism and Pharmacokinetics* **17**(3): 167–89

Nanji AA (1984) The psychiatric aspect of hypophosphatemia. *Can J Psychiatry* **29**(7): 599–600

Nassir Ghaemi S, Hsu DJ, Rosenquist KJ, Pardo TB, Goodwin FK (2006) Extrapyramidal side effects with atypical neuroleptics in bipolar disorder. *Progress in Neuro-Psychopharmacology and Biological Psychiatry* **30**(2): 209–13

NICE (2002) *Management of the acute episode of schizophrenia and management in the early-post-acute phase.* Available from: http://www.nice.org.uk/nicemedia/pdf/CG1individualalgorithms.pdf [Accessed 30 January 2008]

NICE (2007) *Schizophrenia (update): Draft scope for consultation.* Available from: http://www.nice.org.uk/nicemedia/pdf/SchizophreniaUpdateDraftScope.pdf [Accessed 29 January 2008]

Padder T, Udyawar A, Azhar N, Jaghab K (2005) Acute Hypoglycemia Presenting as Acute Psychosis. *Psychiatry Online*

Porter R (2002) *Madness: A Brief History.* Oxford: Oxford University Press

Rendell JM, Geddes JR (2006) Risperidone in long-term treatment for bipolar disorder. *Cochrane Database of Systematic Reviews*, Issue 4. Art. No.: CD004999. DOI: 10.1002/14651858.CD004999.pub2.

Rendell JM, Gijsman HJ, Bauer MS, Goodwin GM, Geddes JR (2006) Risperidone alone or in combination for acute mania. *Cochrane Database of Systematic Reviews*, Issue 1. Art. No.: CD004043. DOI: 10.1002/14651858.CD004043.pub2

Rodriguez Gomez D, Elvira Gonzalez V, Óscar Perez C (2005) Acute psychosis as the presenting symptom of multiple sclerosis. *Revista de Neurología* **41**(4): 255–6

Rosenthal M, Gil I, Habot B (1997) Primary hyperparathyroidism: Neuropsychiatric manifestations and case report. *Israel J Psychiatry and Related Sci* **34**(2): 122–5

Rossman PL, Vock RM (1956) Postpartum tetany and psychosis due to hypocalcemia. *California Medicine* **85**(3): 190–3

Rummel C, Hamann J, Kissling W, Leucht S (2003) New generation antipsychotics for first episode schizophrenia. *Cochrane Database of Systematic Reviews*, Issue 4. Art. No.: CD004410. DOI: 10.1002/14651858.CD004410

Sato M (2004) Renaming schizophrenia: A Japanese perspective. *World Psychiatry* **5**(1): 53–5

Savaskan E, Schnitzler C, Schröder C, Cajochen C, Müller-Spahn F, Wirz-Justice A (2006) Treatment of behavioural, cognitive and circadian rest-activity cycle disturbances in Alzheimer's disease: Haloperidol vs. quetiapine. *Int J Neuropsychopharmacol* [Official scientific journal of the Collegium Internationale Neuropsychopharmacologicum (CINP)] **9**(5): 507–16

Schneider K (1959) *Clinical Psychopathology.* New York: Grune and Stratton

Schneider L, Dagerman KS, Insel P (2005) Risk of death with atypical antipsychotic drug treatment. *J Am Med Assoc* **294**(15): 1934–43

Scottish Executive (2006) *Rights, Relationships and Recovery.* Available from: http://www.scotland.gov.uk/Resource/Doc/112046/0027278.pdf [Accessed 14 December 2006]

Sexton JD, Pronchik DJ (1997) Diphenhydramine-induced psychosis with therapeutic doses *Am J Emerg Med* **15**(5): 548–9

Shalev A, Hermesh H, Munitz H (1989) Mortality from neuroleptic malignant syndrome. *J Clin Psychiatry* **50**: 18–25

Shean GD (2004) *What is Schizophrenia and How Can We Fix It?* Oxford: University Press America

Smith S, Wheeler MJ, Murray R, O'Keane V (2002) The effects of antipsychotic induced hyperprolactinaemia on the hypothalamic-pituitarygonadal axis. *J Clin Psychopharmacol* 22(2): 109–14

Stahl S (1999) *Psychopharmacology of Antipsychotics*. London: Martin Dunitz

Stevens HE (2007) Oral candidiasis secondary to adverse anticholinergic events of psychotropic medication. *J Child and Adolescent Psychopharmacol* 17(1): 145–6

Stones M, Kennedy DC, Fulton JD (1990) Dystonic dysphagia associated with fluspirilene. *Brit Med J* **301**: 668–9

Srisurapanont M, Maneeton B, Maneeton N (2004) Quetiapine for Schizophrenia. *Cochrane Database of Systematic Reviews*, Issue 2. Art. No.: CD000967. DOI: 10.1002/14651858.CD000967.pub2.

Tariot PN, Schneider L, Katz IR, Mintzer JE, Street J, Copenhaver M, Williams-Hughes C (2006) Quetiapine treatment of psychosis associated with dementia: A double-blind, randomized, placebo-controlled clinical trial. *Am J Geriatric Psychiatry* **14**(9): 767–76

Taylor D, Paton C, Kerwin R (2003) T*he Maudsley 2003 Prescribing Guidelines*. London: Martin Dunitz

Thase ME, Macfadden W, Weisler RH, Chang W, Paulsson B, Khan A, Calabrese JR, and BOLDER II Study Group (2006) Efficacy of quetiapine monotherapy in bipolar I and II depression: A double-blind, placebo-controlled study (the BOLDER II study). *J Clin Psychopharmacol* **26**(6): 600–9

Tuunainen A, Wahlbeck K, Gilbody SM (2000) Newer atypical antipsychotic medication versus clozapine for schizophrenia. *Cochrane Database of Systematic Reviews*, Issue 2. Art. No.: CD000966. DOI: 10.1002/14651858.CD000966

Webb RT, Howard L, Abel KM (2004) Antipsychotic drugs for non-affective psychosis during pregnancy and postpartum. *Cochrane Database of Systematic Reviews*, Issue 2. Art. No.: CD004411. DOI: 10.1002/14651858.CD004411.pub2.

Wedekind S (2005) Depressive syndrome, psychoses, dementia: Frequent manifestations in Parkinson disease. *MMW Fortschr Med* **147**(22): 11

Wieck A, Haddad PM (2004) *H*yperprolactinaemia. In Haddad PM, Dursun S, Deakin B (eds) *Adverse Syndromes and Psychiatric Drugs. A Clinical Guide*. Oxford: Oxford University Press

Wijkstra J, Lijmer J, Balk F, Geddes J, Nolen WA (2005) Pharmacological treatment for psychotic depression. *Cochrane Database of Systematic Reviews*, Issue 4. Art. No.: CD004044. DOI: 10.1002/14651858.CD004044.pub2 Wikipedia (2006a) Chlorpromazine http://en.wikipedia.org/wiki/Chlorpromazine [Accessed 15 December 2006]

Wing JK (1971) International comparisons in the study of the functional psychoses. *Brit Med Bull* **27**(1): 77–81

Zhong KX, Sweitzer DE, Hamer RM, Lieberman JA (2006) Comparison of quetiapine and risperidone in the treatment of schizophrenia: A randomized, double-blind, flexible-dose, 8-week study. *J Clin Psychiatry* **67**(7): 1093–103

CHAPTER 5

Depression

Introduction

Depression is arguably even more emotive a subject than schizophrenia. There is a wealth of literature describing psychological, social, economic, cultural and philosophical implications of the label, and remedial suggestions abound. This chapter is grounded in the view that clinical depression exists within the population. It focuses on the practical and empirical aspects of prescribing medication for clinical depression, and like the last chapter frames discussion in terms of diagnosis, pharmacological treatment effects and side effects. It focuses on disorders that may present as depression but are not, and gives advice on when and when not to prescribe, based on the best current evidence incorporating NICE guidelines. The chapter acknowledges but does not focus on the other potentially equally effective approaches. However, first it is worth discussing some background epidemiology, with particular focus on fluoxetine. This is one of the reasons why depression is so emotive.

Fluoxetine

Fluoxetine raises more eyebrows than just about any other prescription drug at present. Type Prozac into a search engine and 13.5 million entries appear, slightly more than heroin (13.4 million). Only valium generates more hits at 17.4 million. By comparison citalopram only generates 1.4 million and lofepramine only 96 000. Before concentrating on the clinical evidence which largely supports equivalent efficacy between these three antidepressants it is worth very briefly examining why fluoxetine has generated so much furore.

As was discussed in the first section it is only through the failure of zelmid that fluoxetine happened to become a blockbuster (zelmid only generates 570 hits now). It is difficult to estimate the worldwide consumption of fluoxetine as many different companies now market and manufacture it since Eli Lilly's patent expired in August 2001 (at which time their sales had reached $2.5 billion). However, adult use of antidepressants in the USA almost tripled between the periods 1988–1994 and 1999–2000, with Prozac taking a significant and major share. This increase has been mirrored elsewhere, leading many commentators to question the rationale behind it.

Depression was the third leading cause of burden among all diseases in the year 2002, and it is expected that this rising trend will continue during the coming 20 years (Imperidore et al, 2007). A whole body of literature has interpreted the success of Prozac as indicative of the medicalisation of unhappiness (Barondes, 2003) or as a demonstration of the power and immorality of the drug companies (Healy, 2002, 2004). In other words Prozac has often borne the brunt of critiques of this more general trend. However, alternative views point to the historical underdiagnosis of depression. For example Isacsson (2000) found that a fivefold increase in the use of antidepressants was followed by a 25% decrease in the Swedish suicide rate.

This increase in antidepressant consumption has slowed down in Scotland. That is, although still increasing, the annual rate of increase in the prescribing of antidepressant drugs continues to fall, down from a peak of 15.0% in 1997/98 to 1.4% in 2006 (Information and Statistics Division, 2007). However, a total of 3.53 million items were prescribed in Scotland during 2005/06, an increase of 49000 from the previous financial year. A total of 8.7% of the Scottish population between the ages of 15 and 90 make daily use of antidepressants. Actual costs dropped as patents expired, and amitriptyline remains the most prescribed item, despite advice to the contrary (NICE, 2007). Direct comparison with rest of the UK is difficult. In England the Prescribing Pricing Division (PPD) (2006) states that overall prescribing of antidepressants in England has increased by 36% over the last 5 years with selective serotonin reuptake inhibitors (SSRIs) accounting for half of the items and the cost. Tricyclic prescribing has remained stable at 35%. Antidepressant prescribing trends in Scotland are shown in *Figure 5.1*.

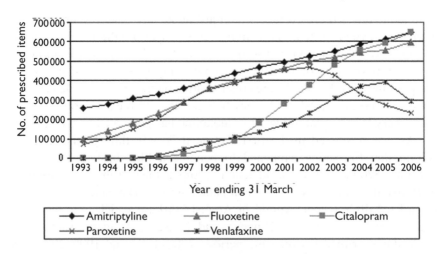

Figure 5.1. Antidepressant prescribing trends in Scotland (Reproduced with permission from Information and Statistics Division, 2007).

Diagnosis

Clinical depression is currently categorised by ICD-10 as a mood or affective disorder, and constitutes categories F30–F39 (WHO, 2007) of the mental and behavioural disorders. F30–F39 includes mania and bipolar disorder. The fundamental source of distress in this group of disorders is the change in mood which manifests itself in a change in normal activity. Most symptoms are best understood therefore as being consequential to this. Onset can often be stress related, and recurrence is common.

F30 and F31 describe mania and bipolar disorder respectively, which are outside the remit of this book. F33–F39 are defined in terms of how often they do or do not fit with the major categories F30, F31 and F32. The focus here is therefore on F32: 'depressive episode'. Recurrent depression F33 follows a similar treatment regime. The WHO (2007) definition of F32 follows.

ICD-10 criteria for depressive episode

In typical mild, moderate, or severe depressive episodes, the patient suffers from lowering of mood, reduction of energy, and decrease in activity. Capacity for enjoyment, interest, and concentration is reduced, and marked tiredness after even minimum effort is common. Sleep is usually disturbed and appetite diminished. Self-esteem and self-confidence are almost always reduced and, even in the mild form, some ideas of guilt or worthlessness are often present. The lowered mood varies little from day to day, is unresponsive to circumstances and may be accompanied by so-called 'somatic' symptoms, such as loss of interest and pleasurable feelings, waking in the morning several hours before the usual time, depression worst in the morning, marked psychomotor retardation, agitation, loss of appetite, weight loss, and loss of libido.

It includes single episodes of: depressive reaction, psychogenic depression and reactive depression, and excludes adjustment disorder (F43.2), recurrent depressive disorder (F33.-) and when it is associated with conduct disorders in F91.- (F92.0).

Depending upon the number and severity of the symptoms, a depressive episode may be specified as mild, moderate or severe:

F32.0: Mild depressive episode
Two or three of the above symptoms are usually present. The patient is usually distressed by these but will probably be able to continue with most activities.

F32.1: Moderate depressive episode
Four or more of the above symptoms are usually present and the patient is likely to have great difficulty in continuing with ordinary activities.

F32.2: Severe depressive episode without psychotic symptoms

An episode of depression in which several of the above symptoms are marked and distressing, typically loss of self-esteem and ideas of worthlessness or guilt. Suicidal thoughts and acts are common and a number of 'somatic' symptoms are usually present.

This latter category is further subdivided with the presence of psychotic features:

F32.3: Severe depressive episode with psychotic symptoms

An episode of depression as described in F32.2, but with the presence of hallucinations, delusions, psychomotor retardation, or stupor so severe that ordinary social activities are impossible; there may be danger to life from suicide, dehydration, or starvation. The hallucinations and delusions may or may not be mood-congruent.

Single episodes of:
- major depression with psychotic symptoms
- psychogenic depressive psychosis
- psychotic depression
- reactive depressive psychosis.

F32.8: Other depressive episodes

Atypical depression

Single episodes of 'masked' depression with no other symptoms.

F32.9: Depressive episode, unspecified

Depression with no other symptoms.
Depressive disorder with no other symptoms.

DSM-IV-TR criteria

DSM-IV-TR criteria are similar in that they grade severity based upon the number of symptoms present. However, either anhedonia or depressed mood must have been present for at least two weeks. A useful mnemonic for remembering all the symptoms is DEAD SWAMP (de Beer, 2002)

- Depressed mood
- Energy (lack of)
- Anhedonia
- Death (thoughts of)
- Sleep
- Worthlessness/guilt
- Appetite

- Mentation (lack of/rumination)
- Psychomotor (retardation).

These criteria lend themselves to a stepped care approach, as depression is seen as a continuum of possible severity. This is the rationale underpinning the NICE (2004: 3) guidelines for doing just that (*Table 5.1*). It is also clear there is a place for nursing care at every level.

In clinical practice it is usually obvious if someone is at the extremes of these criteria. I remember asking an 84-year-old patient if he was basically satisfied with his life, the first (and most important) question of the Geriatric Depression Scale (Sheikh and Yesavage, 1986) and he could not answer because he was so depressed. I am not sure if he forgot the question, thought it preposterous, could not concentrate, or something else. No further assessment was necessary in this case however as (a) I knew him and his personal history very well and (b) he was physically healthy and not normally cognitively impaired. He was accompanied to hospital as he was clearly severely depressed. I had other cases at the opposite end of the spectrum where, due to the length of the waiting list and the lack of immediate risk indicated by the referral, by the time I visited the person he or she had apparently spontaneously recovered and was in good health. I learned from them also. Sometimes doing nothing is the right thing and should always be considered as a serious option. NICE calls this 'watchful waiting'.

NICE also specifies pharmacological treatment options, and it is these which will now be discussed in further detail. *Figure 5.2* shows a flowchart of potential nursing activity from GP referral through to discharge of someone who presents with moderate symptoms of depression. In this model the nurse prescriber supports the patient through the episode of care utilising a variety of therapeutic strategies. These include prescribing and amending prescriptions as required, in line with NICE guidelines and local protocols. Fluoxetine and citalopram have been chosen as first line treatments because they are cheap, relatively safe and effective and therefore more likely to be approved by local formulary managers. Lofepramine has been chosen as a second line antidepressant as it is the safest tricyclic, thereby also likely to be approved by local formulary managers. It was very popular just before the emergence of the even safer SSRIs, due to its lack of toxicity in overdose in comparison with the older tricyclics.

What do antidepressants do?

The first modern antidepressants were discovered in the 1950s as described in *Chapter 2*. Like the antipsychotics they were successful despite any knowledge of how they exerted their effect. It is now clear the drugs exert their effect by initially

Table 5.1. The stepped care model (NICE, 2004a: 3)

The recommendations in this guideline are presented within a stepped care framework that aims to match the needs of people with depression to the most appropriate services, depending on the characteristics of their illness and their personal and social circumstances. Each step represents increased complexity of intervention, with higher steps assuming interventions in previous steps.

Step 1: Recognition in primary care and general hospital settings
Step 2: Treatment of mild depression in primary care
Step 3: Treatment of moderate to severe depression in primary care
Step 4: Treatment of depression by mental health specialists
Step 5: Inpatient treatment for depression

	Who is responsible for care	*What is the focus?*	*What do they do?*
Step 5:	Inpatient care, crisis teams	Risk of life, Severe self-neglect	Medication, combined treatments, ECT
Step 4	Mental health specialists, including crisis teams	Treatment-resistant, recurrent, atypical and psychotic depression, and those at significant risk	Medication, complex psychological interventions, combined treatments
Step 3	Primary care team, primary care mental health worker	Moderate or severe depression	Medication, psychological interventions, social support
Step 2	Primary care team, primary care mental health worker	Mild depression	Watchful waiting, guided self-help, computerised CBT, exercise, brief psychological interventions
Step 1	GP, practice nurse	Recognition	Assessment

targeting specific neurotransmitter systems. The subsequent cascade reactions which follow are much less well understood. Therefore, from a prescribing point of view the most important information to focus on is pragmatic and clinical. That is, what do they actually do in practice? How do they measurably affect people clinically? Do they work, and if so, at what cost?

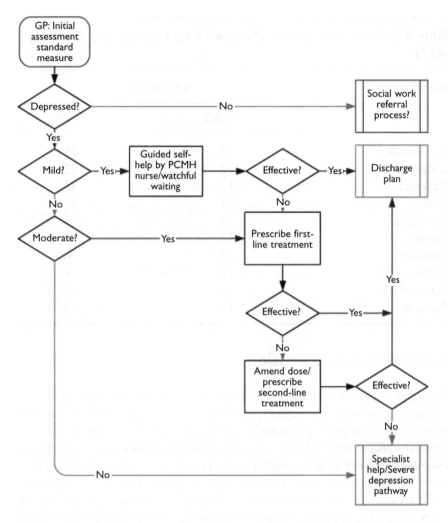

Figure 5.2. Prescribing actions in moderate depression in primary care. PHMH: primary health mental health.

SSRIs are currently the drugs of choice due largely to their improved side effect profile (*Table 5.2*) hence NICE (2004) suggests them as first line treatment. However, as can be seen this is relative. The antimuscarinic effects are improved, but unpleasant excitatory effects remain, and in some instances increase. Some clinicians believe it is these excitatory side effects which may be responsible for the SSRI potential to apparently increase suicidal ideation (Osterwell, 2007). The following section examines the evidence with regard to fluoxetine, citalopram and lofepramine.

Table 5.2. Side effect profile SSRIs v TCAs (Ausejo and Glennie, 1997)

Side effect	%Reported	
	SSRIs	TCAs
Dry mouth	21	55
Constipation	10	22
Dizziness	13	23
Nausea	22	12
Diarrhoea	13	5
Anxiety	13	7
Agitation	14	8
Insomnia	12	7
Nervousness	15	11
Headache	17	14

Fluoxetine and depression

Fluoxetine works by initially blocking the serotonin reuptake pump. It desensitises serotonin receptors, particularly 5-HT1A, and presumably increases serotonergic neurotransmission as a result (Stahl, 2006). It also has antagonist properties at 5-HT2C receptors which could increase dopamine and norepinephrine neurotransmission. The Cochrane Library was searched for high quality randomised controlled clinical trials. Cipriani et al (2005) undertook a comprehensive systematic review, collating data from 132 randomised controlled trials comparing fluoxetine with other antidepressants. They found differences in tolerability and efficacy but did not feel able to conclude anything clinically meaningful from the findings. This was due to the size of the trials (small) and the differences in outcome measures. They recommend larger, better quality studies, but in the meantime suggest treatment should be based on considerations of drug toxicity, patient acceptability and cost.

As this was the only systematic review, individual studies comparing fluoxetine with other antidepressants after 2005 were sought. There were 40 clinical trials containing fluoxetine in the title between 2006 and 2007. Seven pertained to its use in depression. Nemeroff et al (2007) compared fluoxetine with venlafaxine and found both to be of comparable efficacy, with modest indications that venlafaxine had better outcome at six weeks. Schatzberg and Roose (2006) found no difference between venlafaxine, fluoxetine and placebo in their study of treatment of depression in older adults. All 300 improved over the 8 week period with venlafaxine showing most adverse events (27%) followed by fluoxetine (19%) and then placebo (9%). In an attempt more overtly to include economic factors in day-to-day clinical decision making Serrano-Blanco et al (2006) compared fluoxetine to imipramine for clinical effectiveness and cost of treatment. They concluded that imipramine may represent a more cost-effective method of treatment for major depressive disorder and dysthymic disorder, as there was little difference in efficacy.

Choi-Kwon et al (2006) found fluoxetine to be ineffective in treating post-stroke depression. It was more effective in reducing symptoms of anger and emotional disturbance however. They noted that more people dropped out of the fluoxetine group than the placebo group because of adverse events, but all safely tolerated fluoxetine. McGrath et al (2006) examined relapse in a prospective study designed to identify risk factors in relapse. In the process they randomly assigned people with major depressive disorder to either placebo or fluoxetine for 52 weeks, following initial response to fluoxetine. Chronicity, symptom severity, a neurovegetative symptom pattern, and female gender were all associated with a significantly greater risk of relapse, with no difference observed between fluoxetine and placebo. That is, these high risk people relapsed whether they had treatment or not. However, fluoxetine was significantly more effective than placebo across the whole study population during this treatment phase.

Fluoxetine is not always compared with pharmaceutical agents but is sometimes used as a baseline upon which to examine the efficacy of other treatments. For example, in an 8 week randomised double blind trial of 40 patients treated for mild to moderate depression Akhondzadeh Basti et al (2007) found similar efficacy and side effects between fluoxetine and petal of *Crocus sativus L*. The study is too small to base global predictions on the efficacy of *Crocus sativus*, and also goes against NICE advice not to prescribe in mild depression. However, it reveals the authors' underlying assumption that fluoxetine is effective and therefore a reliable method of comparison. This is a widely held view, and the clearest conclusion from this literature is that fluoxetine works. Some of its wider claims have yet to be demonstrated. For example in an older study Bech et al (2000) systematically reviewed published and unpublished randomised controlled trials comparing fluoxetine with tricyclic antidepressants, and found a trend in favour of fluoxetine in studies conducted in the USA, and a trend favouring tricyclic antidepressants in studies conducted outside the USA. This illustrates one of the challenges in collating international data.

Citalopram and depression

Imperadore et al (2007) are in the process of compiling a systematic review regarding the efficacy of citalopram, using the same strategy as Cipriani et al

(2005) for fluoxetine as above. Both groups are part of the Meta-Analyses of New Generation Antidepressants (MANGA) Study Group which will finish its remit with a 'mega-review' of all their meta-analyses; a kind of meta-analysis meta-analysis. This should be complete in 2008.

The only other review included in Cochrane was by Keller (2000). Cochrane criticised Keller on the grounds of limiting his literature search and for not being explicit in his inclusion criteria. However, Keller only included high quality randomised controlled trials and Cochrane concluded that his conclusions follow from the evidence presented. His conclusions were that citalopram:

- is superior to placebo in the treatment of depression;
- has efficacy similar to that of the tricyclic and tetracyclic antidepressants and to other SSRIs; and
- is safe and well tolerated in the therapeutic dose range of 20–60 mg/day.

Distinct from some other agents in its class, citalopram exhibits linear pharmacokinetics and minimal drug interaction potential (Keller, 2000).

Citalopram hydrobromide is a potent and highly selective SSRI. That is, it has minimal effect on the neuronal reuptake of norepinephrine and dopamine (Imperadore et al, 2007), unlike fluoxetine. This leads the manufacturers to claim unique clinical benefit, and may in part underpin Keller's conclusions.

As well as systematic reviews the Cochrane library contained 332 individual clinical trials studying or comparing citalopram. Ninety-three of these pertained to depression, 22 of which took place since 2003. In order to further reduce these only trials testing citalopram alone or comparing citalopram directly with another treatment are reported. This left six trials which will be discussed very briefly here.

As with fluoxetine, not all comparitors are pharmaceuticals. Gastpar et al (2006) compared citalopram with hypericum (St John's wort) and found similar efficacy when treating outpatients with moderate depression. Hypericum had better tolerability. Again, the underlying implicit assumption is that citalopram works and is therefore a worthy comparator, which is demonstrated in its superiority to the placebo group in this trial.

In comparing sertraline with citalopram Rocca et al (2005) concluded that both were effective at improving minor depressive disorder in non-demented elderly patients over a one year period. Both drugs were equally well tolerated and both induced a significant, sustained, and comparable improvement in depressive symptoms and social functioning. Again it is interesting to note that mild depression is not recommended to be treated pharmacologically in the UK (NICE, 2004).

A small Chinese study ($N = 44$) concluded that citalopram and amitriptyline were equally effective in treating depression in elderly patients (Li et al, 2004). Miao and Shi (2004) found citalopram to be an effective treatment in post-stoke depression. Citalopram also appears to be well tolerated and effective in treating children with depression according to Wagner et al (2004). They used a randomised, controlled, double blind method to confirm the previous findings from open label trials that citalopram was safe and effective in children and adolescents with major depression.

Allard et al (2004) compared venlafaxine with citalopram in 151 older adults and found similar efficacy. They were particularly interested in adverse events as pharmacological treatment in old age is associated with an increased risk of adverse pharmacokinetic and pharmacodynamic drug interactions. They found citalopram caused more tremor and venlafaxine more nausea; otherwise side effect profiles were similar. Venlafaxine has subsequently been found to correlate with cardiac complications (Medicine and Healthcare Regulations Agency, 2006).

Lofepramine and depression

Lofepramine is a tricyclic antidepressant (TCA). It works by blocking the norepinephrine reuptake pump, which presumably increases noradrenergic neurotransmission (Stahl, 2006). It can increase dopamine transmission as dopamine is inactivated by norepinephrine reuptake in the frontal cortex, which largely lacks dopamine transporters. At high doses it may also boost serotonin hence presumably serotonergic neurotransmission.

There are no systematic reviews of lofepramine in the Cochrane library. There are 55 clinical trials in all, and only six of these relate directly to the treatment of depression. All of these are more than 10 years old. For example most recently Moon and Vince (1996) found lofepramine to be as effective as paroxetine in treating 138 people in general practice. Paroxetine (Seroxat) has since become embroiled in controversy, with accusations of information withholding directed at its patent holder GlaxoSmithKline. While irrelevant to this discussion it illustrates why more up-to-date trials are necessary to make meaningful conclusions. This is difficult in the case of lofepramine as interest waned in it with the introduction of the SSRIs. However, for the purpose of this literature review the search was broadened to include other databases. PubMed was searched which revealed one trial (and two articles) in the last five years. PsychInfo returned no new data. Peveler et al (2005) conducted a randomised controlled trial ($N = 357$) comparing SSRIs with TCAs and lofepramine to assess cost-effectiveness. They found SSRIs were likely to be the most cost-effective option. Lofepramine was likely to lead to a greater proportion of patients switching treatment in the first few weeks.

An older meta-analysis by Anderson (2001) also commented on the paucity of data on lofepramine. However, Anderson highlighted a meta-analysis by Kerihuel and Dreyfuss (1991) which he felt was of a high enough quality to consider. Kerihuel and Dreyfus went back to original data in 34% of the 2040 original case report forms and found no major deviation from the published data. As such, their conclusion that more patients improved on lofepramine as opposed to other TCAs is credible. Tolerability was similar, with fewer people experiencing side effects on lofepramine. Individual studies revealed less dizziness, dry mouth and sedation. Anderson (2001) felt able to conclude from his analysis that lofepramine is at least as effective as TCAs and that it is probably better tolerated than older TCAs (ibid: 175).

It is scrutiny of evidence such as this which underpins NICE guidance on treatment of moderate to severe depression:

> *When an antidepressant is to be prescribed in routine care, it should be a selective serotonin reuptake inhibitor (SSRI), because SSRIs are as effective as tricyclic antidepressants and are less likely to be discontinued because of side effects.*

> (NICE 2007: 4)

The rationale for supporting lofepramine as a secondary option is based upon a similar rationale. That is, it appears to be just as effective but less toxic. It is also cheap.

What is the worst that can happen?

Generally side effects are tolerable, and many diminish quickly. *Table 5.2* illustrates broad incidence percentages of common side effects of the SSRIs and TCAs. However, as with all drugs some side effects are more serious, and others life-threatening. There is also the added complication of prescribing for a high suicide risk group. This will be discussed separately. Otherwise the most serious adverse effect is serotonin syndrome.

Serotonin syndrome

The first known death from serotonin syndrome was reported in 1955 (Gilman and Whyte, 2004). Fifty have since been described, yet toxicity is generally a result of combination therapy and therefore predictable. Serotonin toxicity and death can be caused by a single therapeutic dose. It is best viewed as a spectrum of events which range from mild symptoms controllable with dose reduction through to severe symptoms which require early recognition. By definition serotonin toxicity is an iatrogenic reaction mediated by excess serotonin in the synapse. An important fact to remember is that it can be suppressed with chlorpromazine, a 5-HT2A antagonist. Serotonin syndrome usually refers to a toxicity which is clinically significant, and is reported in around 15% of overdoses using SSRIs. It usually occurs with combinations of serotonergic drugs. Most severe cases involve monoamine oxidase inhibitors (MAOIs) in combination with any drug having the property of a serotonin reuptake inhibitor, e.g. SSRIs, tramadol, amphetamine, St John's wort.

The clinical picture appears as a triad of neuroexcitatory features which range from mild to life-threatening (Dunkley et al, 2003). The triad comprises altered mental state, neuromuscular hyperactivity and autonomic activity. More specifically key symptoms include agitation, anxiety, hypomania and confusion. Neuromuscular symptoms include tremor, clonus (involuntary muscular spasm), myoclonus (involuntary muscular twitch), hyper-reflexia (over-responsive reflex) and in the advanced stages, rigidity. Autonomic hyperactivity presents as diaphoresis (sweating), fever, tachycardia and tachypnoea. *Table 5.3* illustrates serotonin-related signs stratified by severity.

Investigation is through history and examination, particularly neurological examination for clonus, hyper-reflexia and rigidity. Treatment is to stop causal agents and administer chlorpromazine or cyproheptadine. Control of agitation with benzodiazepines is essential according to Boyer and Shannon (2005). Boyer and Shannon's (2005) illustration of a person presenting with moderate signs is shown in *Figure 5.3*.

Suicide

One of the greatest worries in prescribing pills for people with depression is the concern that you may be giving them the tools to kill themselves at the very time when they are most likely to attempt it. This is one of the major attractions of the SSRIs, given that they are much less toxic in overdose than TCAs and particularly MAOIs. However, every year one million people worldwide commit suicide, more than die in homicide and war combined (Krastev, 2006). Between 59% and 87% of these people are thought to have or have had a depressive disorder (Rihmer et al, 2002). In diagnosing someone with depression you have also identified a person who is at far greater risk than the norm of committing suicide. There are two ways of significantly reducing this risk

- understand the level of risk, and
- ensure the tools are not available.

The second measure is effective only to the extent that the individual is unmotivated to seek another method. Paradoxically, increased motivation

Table 5.3. Serotonin-related signs stratified by severity (Gilman and Whyte, 2004)

Severity	Examples of causal drugs	Signs		
		Mental	Neuromuscular	Autonomic
Mild	SSRI plus lithium or buspirone	No abnormality	Shivering, occasional myoclonus, tremor, hyper-reflexia	Fever (37.5–38.5°C)
Moderate	Overdose of SSRI	Confusion or agitation	Regular myoclonus, inducible ankle clonus, hyper-reflexia	Fever (38.5–39.5°C)
Severe	MAOI or RIMA plus SRI	Marked confusion	Generalised myoclonus, sustained ankle clonus, hypertonia/rigidity, marked hyper-reflexia	Fever (>39.5°C)

MAOI: monoamine oxidase inhibitor; RIMA: reversible inhibitor of monoamine oxidase type A; SRI: serotonin reuptake inhibitor; SSRI: selective serotonin reuptake inhibitor

may be a factor underpinning evidence suggesting increased suicidal ideation among some SSRI users (Osterwell, 2007). That is, suicidal ideation, where there was none before, could suggest that the medication is working. It has long been suspected that increased motivation played a part in increased suicide rates seen in people responding in the early stages of electroconvulsive therapy (Barraclough et al, 1974). That is, people's motivation had apparently improved to the extent that they were now in a position to consider suicide where previously they could not even be bothered to kill themselves. This 'activating hypothesis' (Osterwell, 2007) remains the subject of much debate. However, from a purely practical perspective there is evidence that reducing paracetamol pack sizes and restricting their sales has had an impact on 'impulsive' self-harm. Therefore prescribing the less harmful drug in smaller doses (NICE, 2007) makes sense in the prevention of impulsive attempts, and is notable as such. But this will

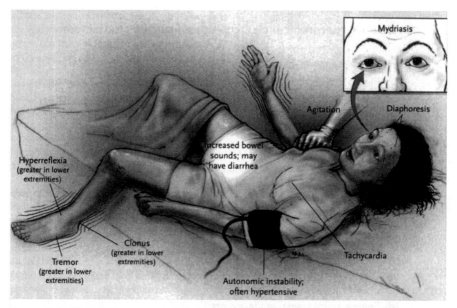

Figure 5.3. Clinical signs in moderate serotonin syndrome (Reproduced with permission from Boyer and Shannon, 2005).

only prevent attempts where the person is both impulsive and/or ignorant of the inefficacy of the method.

Of far greater benefit is accurate assessment of suicidal intent as part of a therapeutic relationship. This is a deeper and more sophisticated method which incorporates the debate above and individualises risk. For example, individual belief in whether or not a particular suicide method would work is far more indicative of suicidal intent than the apparent severity of a suggestion. Eliciting and acting on this information requires great skill based on a rich therapeutic relationship (Kroll, 2007). This aspect of the risk assessment is mentioned in 1c in *Box 5.1*. I would argue this is the most important aspect. *Box 5.1* shows a hierarchy of risk factors as identified by Rihmer et al (2002).

In a study of 48277 people treated for depression participating in clinical trials Khan et al (2003) found no difference in rates of completed suicides between people treated with SSRIs, TCAs or placebo. Seventy-seven people commited suicide. The above risk factors would therefore appear more pertinent than the type of medication taken, although the debate on association between SSRIs and suicide seems unlikely to be resolved quickly.

Other adverse events

Although generally considered the safer option serotonergic antidepressants have been associated with the following medical complications: syndrome of inappropriate antidiuretic hormone secretion, bleeding, serotonin-

---

Box 5.1 Hierarchical classification of suicide risk factors

1. Primary (psychiatric-medical) suicide risk factors
   (a) Major psychiatric illness (depression, schizophrenia, substance use disorders) ± co-morbid anxiety or personality disorder, serious medical illness; ± feeling of hopelessness and insomnia, concomitant anxiety
   (b) Previous suicide attempt(s)
   (c) Communication of wish to die/suicide intent (direct or indirect)
   (d) Suicide among family members (biological or social 'inheritance')
   (e) Disregulated serotonergic system, low total serum cholesterol, abnormal dexamethasone suppression test during depression
2. Secondary (psycho-social) risk factors
   (a) Childhood negative life-events (separation, parental loss, etc.)
   (b) Isolation, living alone (divorce, separation, widowhood, etc.)
   (c) Loss of job, unemployment
   (d) Severe acute negative life-events
   (e) Smoking
3. Tertiary (demographic) suicide risk factors
   (a) Male sex
   (b) Adolescent and young men, old age (both sexes)
   (c) Vulnerable intervals (spring/early summer, pre-menstrual period, etc.)
   (d) Minority groups (relatives of suicide victims, victims of disasters, bisexuality, same-sex orientation, etc.)

---

discontinuation syndrome, and adverse pregnancy and neonatal effects (Looper, 2007). They also generate the same side effects as the TCAs but to a greater or lesser degree (*Table 5.2*). As already mentioned, the antimuscarinic effects are improved, but unpleasant excitatory effects remain, and in some instances increase.

Idiosyncrasies and uncorroborated evidence

Citalopram is metabolised in the liver and the biotransformation of citalopram to its demethyl metabolites depends on both CYP2C19 and CYP3A4, with a small contribution from CYP2D6 (Imperadore et al, 2007). Lofepramine is metabolised more by 2D6, and as such the 5–10% (Stahl, 1999) of the population who have a phenotypic variant of this may thus be susceptible to severe side effects at low dosages (Stahl, 2006). Fluoxetine is also metabolised by 2D6 and by 3A4. As such it may reduce the clearance of other drugs metabolised by these enzymes such as diazepam and codeine (2D6) or buspirone and triazolam (3A4) thus increasing their levels.

Fluoxetine also has antagonist properties at 5-HT2C receptors which could increase norepinephrine and dopamine neurotransmission. Some people may experience increased agitation or energy as a result. Fluoxetine's active metabolite is norfluoxetine and it has a long half-life of 2–3 days. As such, tapering is not necessary as fluoxetine tapers itself. The downside of this is that switching to another antidepressant needs caution as serotonin syndrome is a real possibility. Caution is recommended during the first five weeks. Fluoxetine would be a good first choice for atypical depression, for example hypersomnia, low energy and mood reactivity. Conversely, it should be avoided in people experiencing agitation and insomnia.

Citalopram's inactive R enantiomer may block the therapeutic action of the S enantiomer, hence the launch of escitalopram, which is only the S enantiomer. It is considerably more expensive, and the claim for escitalopram's clinical superiority has not yet been independently corroborated. Citalopram has mild antagonist properties at H1 histamine receptors. This may be the cause of sedation and fatigue in some individuals, which may be a potential advantage in patients excessively activated by other SSRIs. Citalopram may be tolerated better than most antidepressants.

Lofepramine boosts norepinephrine. Since dopamine is inactivated by norepinephrine reuptake in the frontal cortex, which largely lacks dopamine receptors, lofepramine can increase dopamine neurotransmission in this part of the brain. At high doses it can also boost serotonin and hence presumably increase serotonergic neurotransmission. It can treat insomnia and anxiety immediately. Many depressed patients have a partial response where some symptoms improve but others persist, paradoxically insomnia, fatigue and concentration problems. It has been shown to prolong QTc and raise seizure threshold. QTc interval can be prolonged in overdose and also in combination with other drugs which inhibit its metabolism via 2D6. Caution must therefore be observed, and the risk/benefit ratio may not justify the use of TCAs in cardiac impairment (Stahl, 2006: 105). Its potential advantages are in patients with insomnia, severe or treatment resistant depression or anxious depression. Lofepramine may also be useful for patients experiencing chronic pain. It has fewer anticholinergic side effects than some other TCAs.

Summary

This chapter has shown that antidepressants are effective. It has discussed prescribing decisions against a backdrop of the NICE guideline for depression. As in treatment of psychosis in the previous chapter if pharmacological intervention is warranted then accurate, replicable, structured and systematic

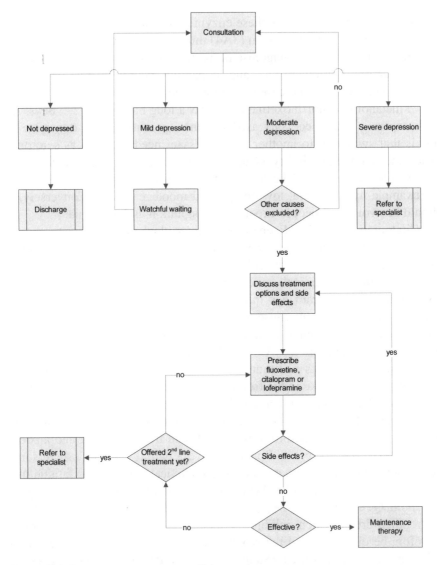

Figure 5.4. Decisions in treatment of depression.

diagnosis is the key to supporting this decision. Concordance is best achieved through mutual understanding and this takes skilled communication based upon the current principles of partnership and recovery in mental health nursing (Scottish Executive, 2006). Prescribing decisions will therefore be clear, evidence based and agreed. Monitoring should encompass extensive knowledge of potential adverse events as discussed at length in this chapter. In this way the person seeking help can be assured of safe, competent and caring help. The flowchart in *Figure 5.4* illustrates how these factors inter-relate.

Further reading

Barondes SH (2003) *Better than Prozac*. Oxford: Oxford University Press

Solomon Snyder states: 'I have devoted the last 40 years of my life to psychopharmacology, yet Barondes' book conveys much that I did not know. For an educated lay reader, this volume serves as a Scientific American-level presentation of drugs and the brain as well as a comforting, edifying guide for the emotionally perplexed. This is likely the finest book I have ever read on psychopharmacology.'

Healy D (2004) *Let Them Eat Prozac*. New York: New York University Press

Healy argues that the cure for depression may be worse than the disease. This perspective emerges from his investigation into the pharmaceutical industry, a project started in his two previous books. It is a thought-provoking book, and again centres on criticism of the politics of the randomised controlled trial and the propensity of power to maintain power at all costs.

Stahl S (2006) *Essential Psychopharmacology. The Prescriber's Guide: Antidepressants*. Cambridge: Cambridge University Press

This guidebook is an easy-to-read source of information on antidepressants. It is well laid out and illustrated in the style of Stahl's other books. Again, his 'clinical pearls' are useful clinical additions which add a sense of practicality which can be missing in other publications on practical psychopharmacology.

References

Allard P, Gram L, Timdahl K, Behnke K, Hanson M, Søgaard J (2004) Efficacy and tolerability of venlafaxine in geriatric outpatients with major depression: A double-blind, randomised 6-month comparative trial with citalopram. *Int J Clin Psychiatry* **19**(12): 1123–9

Anderson IM (2001) Meta analytical studies on new antidepressants. *Brit Med Bull* **57**(1): 161–78

Ausejo M, Glennie JL (1997) *A Clinical and Economic Evaluation of Selective Serotonin Reuptake Inhibitors in Major Depression*. Ottawa: Canadian Coordinating Office for Health Technology Assessment

Barondes SH (2003) *Better than Prozac*. Oxford: Oxford University Press

Bech P, Cialdella P, Haugh MC, Birkett MA, Hours A, Boissel JP, et al (2000) Meta-analysis of randomised controlled trials of fluoxetine versus placebo and tricyclic antidepressants in the short-term treatment of major depression. *Brit J Psychiatry* **176**: 421–8

Boyer EW, Shannon M (2005) The serotonin syndrome. *New Engl J Med* **352**(11): 1112–23

Choi-Kwon S, Han SW, Kwon SU, Kang DW, Choi JM, Kim JS (2006) Fluoxetine treatment in poststroke depression, emotional incontinence, and anger proneness: A double-blind, placebo-controlled study. *Stroke* **37**(1): 156–61

Cipriani A, Brambilla P, Furukawa T, Geddes J, Gregis M, Hotopf M, Malvini L, Barbui C (2005) Fluoxetine versus other types of pharmacotherapy for depression. *Cochrane Database of Systematic Reviews*, Issue 4. Art. No.: CD004185. DOI: 10.1002/14651858.CD004185.pub2

De Beer M (2002) *Medical Mnemonics*. Available from: http://www.medicalmnemonics. com/cgi-bin/return_browse.cfm?browse=1&discipline=Psychiatry [Accessed 12 April 2008]

Dunkley E, Isbister G, Sibbritt D, Dawson AH, Whyte IM (2003) Hunter serotonin toxicity criteria: A simple and accurate diagnostic decision rule for serotonin toxicity. *Q J Med* **96**(9): 635–42

Gastpar M, Singer A, Zeller K (2006) Comparative efficacy and safety of a once-daily dosage of hypericum extract STW3-VI and citalopram in patients with moderate depression: A double-blind, randomised, multicentre, placebo-controlled study *Pharmacopsychiatry* **39**(2): 66–75

Gilman K, Whyte IM (2004) Serotonin syndrome. In Haddad P, Dursun S, Deakin B (eds) *Adverse Syndromes and Psychiatric Drugs. A Clinical Guide*. Oxford: Oxford University Press

Healy D (2002) *The Creation of Psychopharmacology*. Cambridge, MA: Harvard University Press

Healy D (2004) *Let Them Eat Prozac*. New York and London: New York University Press

Imperadore G, Cipriani A, Signoretti A, Furukawa TA, Watanabe N, Churchill R, McGuire HF, Barbui C for the Meta-Analysis of New Generation Antidepressants (MANGA) Study Group (2007) Citalopram versus other anti-depressive agents for depression. (Protocol) *Cochrane Database of Systematic Reviews*, Issue 2. Art. No.: CD006534. DOI: 10.1002/14651858.CD006534

Information and Statistics Division (2007) *Antidepressants*. Available from: http:// www.isdscotland.org/isd/information-and statistics.jsp?pContentID=3671&p_ applic=CCC&p_service=Content.show& [Accessed 10 January 2008]

Isacsson G (2000) Suicide prevention – a medical breakthrough? *Acta Psychiatr Scand* **102**: 113–7

Keller MB (2000) Citalopram therapy for depression: A review of 10 years of European experience and data from US clinical trials. *J Clin Psychiatry* **61**(12): 896–908

Kerihuel JC, Dreyfus JF (1991) Meta analyses of the efficacy and tolerability of the tricyclic antidepressant lofepramine. *J Int Med Res* **19**: 183–201

Khan A, Khan S, Kolts R, Brown WA (2003) Suicide rates in clinical trials of SSRIs, other antidepressants, and placebo: Analysis of FDA reports. *Am J Psychiatry* **160**: 790–2

Krastev N (2006) *CIS: UN Body Takes On Rising Suicide Rates*. Available from: http:// www.rferl.org/featuresarticle/2006/09/ab4b19da-5e47-471f-a26a-3b861a0395d8.html [Accessed 6 August 2007]

Kroll J (2007) No-suicide contracts as a suicide prevention strategy. *Psychiatric Times* **24**(8): 1–2

Looper KJ (2007) Potential medical and surgical complications of serotonergic antidepressant medications. *Psychosomatics* **48**: 1–9

McGrath PJ, Stewart JW, Quitkin FM, Chen Y, Alpert JE, Nierenberg AA, Fava M, Cheng J, Petkova E (2006) Predictors of relapse in a prospective study of fluoxetine treatment of major depression. *Am J Psychiatry* **163**(9): 1542–8

Medicines and Healthcare Regulation Agency (2006) *Press release: Updated product information for Efexor (venlafaxine).* Available from: http://www.mhra.gov.uk/home/idcplg?IdcService=SS_GET_PAGE&useSecondary=true&ssDocName=CON2023843&ssTargetNodeId=389 [Accessed August 6 2007]

Miao S-Y, Shi Y-J (2004) Related factors of post-stroke depression and therapeutical effect of citalopram. *Zhongguo Linchuang Kangfu* **8**(19): 3718–19

Moon CA, Vince M (1996) Treatment of major depression in general practice: A double-blind comparison of paroxetine and lofepramine. *Brit J Clin Practice* **50**(5): 240–5

Nemeroff CB, Thase ME, EPIC 014 Study Group (2007) A double-blind, placebo-controlled comparison of venlafaxine and fluoxetine treatment in depressed outpatients. *J Psychiatric Res* **41**(3): 351–9

NICE (2004) *Depression: Management of Depression in Primary and Secondary Care. NICE Guideline 23.* Available from: http://www.nice.org.uk/pdf/CG023quickrefguide.pdf [Accessed 6 June 2007]

NICE (2007) *Depression (amended) Management of Depression in Primary and Secondary Care. NICE Guideline 23 amended.* Available from: http://www.nice.org.uk/download.aspx?o=CG023NICEguideline&popup=no#page=41 [Accessed 6 August 2007]

Osterwell N (2007) APA: SSRIs more likely in suicides than in other young deaths. *Psychiatric Times.* Available from: http://psychiatrictimes.com/showArticle.jhtml?articleID=199702140 [Accessed 27 August 2007]

Peveler R, Kendrick T, Buxton M, Longworth L, Baldwin D, Moore M, Chatwin J, Goddard J, Thornett A, Smith H, Campbell M, Thompson C (2005) A randomised controlled trial to compare the cost-effectiveness of tricyclic antidepressants, selective serotonin reuptake inhibitors and lofepramine. *Health Technol Assess* **9**(16): 1–134

Prescribing Pricing Division (2006) *Prescribing Review: Drugs used in Mental Health.* Available from: http://www.ppa.org.uk//news/pact-092005.htm [Accessed 1 August 2007]

Rihmer N, Belso N, Kiss K (2002) Strategies for suicide prevention. *Curr Opin Psychiatry* **15**: 83–7

Rocca P, Calvarese P, Faggiano F, Marchiaro L, Mathis F, Rivoira E, Taricco B, Bogetto F (2005) Citalopram versus sertraline in late-life nonmajor clinically significant depression: A 1-year follow-up clinical trial. *J Clin Psychiatry* **66**(3): 360–69

Schatzberg A, Roose S (2006) A double-blind, placebo-controlled study of venlafaxine and fluoxetine in geriatric outpatients with major depression. *Am J Geriatric Psychiatry* **14**(4): 361–70

Scottish Executive (2006) *Rights Relationships and Recovery.* Available from: http://www.scotland.gov.uk/Resource/Doc/112046/0027278.pdf [Accessed 14 December 2006]

Serrano-Blanco A, Gabarron E, Garcia-Bayo I, Soler-Vila M, Caramés E, Peñarrubia-Maria MT, Pinto-Meza A, Haro JM, Depressió en Atenció Primària de Gavà Group (DAPGA) (2006) Effectiveness and cost-effectiveness of antidepressant treatment in primary health care: A six-month randomised study comparing fluoxetine to imipramine. *J Affective Disorders* **2**(3): 153–63

Sheikh JI, Yesavage JA (1986) *Geriatric Depression Scale (GDS): Recent evidence and development of a shorter version. Clinical Gerontology: A Guide to Assessment and Intervention* (pp 165–173) New York: The Haworth Press,

Stahl S (1999) Psychopharmacology of Antipsychotics. London: Martin Dunitz

Stahl S (2006) Essential Psychopharmacology. The Prescriber's Guide: Antidepressants. Cambridge: Cambridge University Press

Wagner KD, Robb AS, Findling RL, Jin J, Gutierrez MM, Heydorn WE (2004) A randomized, placebo-controlled trial of citalopram for the treatment of major depression in children and adolescents. *Am J Psychiatry* **161**(6): 1079–83

WHO (2007) *ICD-10 Chapter V. Mental and Behavioural Disorders (F00–F99).* Available from: http://www.who.int/classifications/apps/icd/icd10online/ [Accessed 15 August 2007]

CHAPTER 6

Anxiety and insomnia

Anxiety is a normal emotion. An optimal amount underpins motivation and encourages higher level performance (Salzman, 2006). Too much or too little has the opposite effect. In 1908 Yerkes and Dodson formulated a hypothesis correlating arousal with performance, producing the famous Yerkes Dodson Law (*Figure 6.1*). This suggests that some arousal is necessary for peak performance but beyond this performance wanes with further arousal. It therefore implies an optimal level of arousal for a particular task. It offers a simple visual explanation of why performance and function appear to increase with appropriate arousal and diminish with intense anxiety.

It is important to recognise that the reality is unlikely to be as simple as this. For example Hanoch and Vitouch (2004) reject the one-dimensional conceptualisation of arousal. Experiments have failed to replicate Yerkes and Dodson's original conclusions (Gunther, 1994), and Winton (1987) claims the law was not invented by Yerkes and Dodson at all. However, despite this and other evidence to the contrary, the law is generally accepted as at least intuitively useful, certainly as a starting point for discussion, as it represents the concept of anxiety within a 'normal' continuum.

Abnormal anxiety is highly prevalent and problematic. In a literature review of 46 epidemiological studies of the adult population (age 18–64 years) Somers et al (2006) found a lifetime prevalence rate of 16.6%. They concluded that if all these people sought help they would overrun the capacity

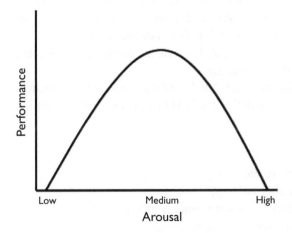

Figure 6.1. Yerkes Dodson Law (1908).

of specialised mental health services. Prevalence rates differed markedly within the studies however, particularly in regard to specific categories of anxiety disorder. For example, the lifetime prevalence of social anxiety disorder was 2.7% in one large survey in the US (Robins and Regier, 1991) and 13.3% in another (Kessler et al, 1994). Criteria for inclusion are different between studies, with DSM-III diagnostic criteria generating the lowest prevalence according to Starcevic (2006). Starcevic suggests using 'clinical significance criteria' as developed by Narrow et al (2002) to approach a more meaningful estimate when aggregating differently generated prevalence estimates. Nevertheless, it is clear that even the more conservative figures indicate a significant and serious public health problem.

Anxiety disorders are currently described in ICD-10 in the categories F40–F48 which include the neurotic, stress-related, somatoform disorders (WHO, 2007). F40 describes phobias and F42–F48 describe obsessive, stress-related, dissociative, somatoform and other neurotic disorders. This chapter focuses on generalised anxiety disorder (GAD) and panic disorder as categorised in F41, where manifestation of anxiety is the major symptom and is not restricted to any particular environmental situation. By taking this approach prescribing decisions can be framed in terms of anxiety alone. The principles for wider prescribing for anxiety-related disorders can then be connected to this basic discussion.

One of the main criticisms that could be levelled at this approach is that generalised anxiety disorder rarely stands alone. For example a US National Comorbidity Survey found that over 90% of people diagnosed with GAD had a comorbid diagnosis, including dysthymia (22%), depression (39–69%), somatisation, other anxiety disorders, bipolar disorder, or substance abuse (Stein, 2002). Personality disorder is also widely correlated (Dyck et al, 2001). However, for the purpose of discussing pharmacological intervention the strategy of conceptualising it as a standalone entity will be adopted here. This is both theoretically useful and practically relevant as the same differentiation is followed in NICE Guideline 22 (amended) as illustrated in the algorithm in *Figure 6.2*. Prescribers should adhere to this guideline if prescribing for these conditions.

As with depression in Guideline 23, NICE (2004a) goes on to advocate a stepped care approach in their guideline for GAD and panic disorder, which should be familiar now:

- Step 1: recognition,
- Step 2: treatment in primary care,
- Step 3: review and treat alternatively,
- Step 4: review and refer to specialist mental health service,
- Step 5: treat in specialised mental health services.

Diagnosis

NICE (2004a) conclude that there is insufficient evidence on which to recommend a well-validated, self-reporting screening instrument to use in the diagnostic process, and so consultation skills should be relied upon to elicit all necessary information (1.2.2.2). This should always be the case, and consultation skills are discussed at the beginning of this section. However,

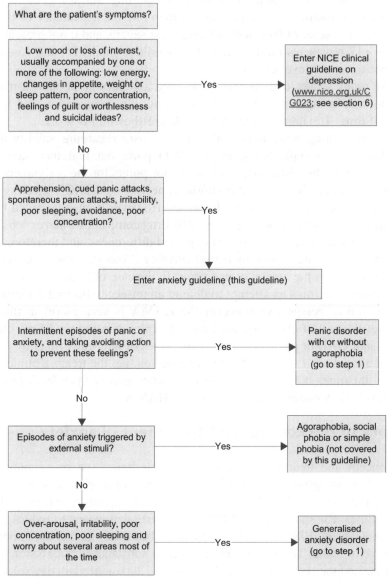

Figure 6.2. Decision flowchart on when and how to use NICE Guideline 22.

it would be helpful to discuss the best known tool for assessing anxiety in order to frame some of the diagnostic issues.

The Hamilton Anxiety Rating Scale (HAMA; Hamilton, 1959) is used in the majority of clinical trials as an assessment tool of treatment efficacy. This is because it is widely recognised and considered broadly effective; hence results can be meaningfully pooled and aggregated. HAMA is a 14-item rating scale, further subdivided into a series of symptoms. For example the item on 'tension' is further clarified as subsuming 'startles, cries easily, restless and trembling'. The clinician can then rate the appearance of these symptoms on a scale of 0–4, with 4 being most severe, and 0 not present. A score of <17 represents mild anxiety, 18–24 mild to moderate, and 15–30 a moderate to severe level of anxiety.

Like many scales, once it was established and became popular it made sense to keep using it as data can be meaningfully compared over a long period of time. The items in the rating scale are shown in *Box 6.1*.

Like any rating scale it is subject to criticism regarding validity and reliability. For example Shear et al (2001) point out that there are no instructions for administration, or clear anchor points for the assignment of the severity ratings. It is likely that similar concerns led to NICE rejecting all screening instruments for anxiety diagnosis. However it must be noted that criticisms such as this are often generated by drug companies when expensive multi-centre drug trials do not detect expected differences, and therefore the measuring tool comes under increased scrutiny. 'Shooting the messenger' often accompanies the receipt of bad news. In the case of Shear et al's study the criticism underpins an attempt to defend an unsuccessful trial for Pfizer. From a clinical perspective however the HAMA is very useful in that it illustrates the sort of questions and areas of exploration required for a clear diagnosis of GAD or panic disorder. Also, issues of inter-rater reliability are avoided altogether if the rater is the same person, i.e. the treating clinician. *Box 6.2* illustrates ICD-10 criteria for F41 'other anxiety disorders'. Notice how closely they compare to the content of HAMA.

History of the concept and treatment of anxiety

The concept and treatment of anxiety are interlinked, so one cannot be discussed meaningfully without the other. There is historical evidence that people have always used anxiolytics to control fear, therefore fear existed in ancient times. Russian soldiers 2000BC used chemical means to reduce fear in battle (Gabriel, 1987). Koyak and Wiros tribes used amanita mushrooms on the eve of battle. The Vikings used a similar substance in 900AD stored in deer urine and the Hashshashin used hashish in 1200AD. Modern day soldiers continue to medicate themselves to combat fear. Outside of battle opium

Box 6.1. Hamilton Anxiety Rating Scale

Anxious mood
- worries
- anticipates worst

Tension
- startles
- cries easily
- restless
- trembling

Fears
- fear of the dark
- fear of strangers
- fear of being alone
- fear of animals

Insomnia
- difficulty falling asleep or staying asleep
- difficulty with nightmares

Intellectual
- poor concentration
- memory impairment

Depressed mood
- decreased interest in activities
- anhedonia
- insomnia

Somatic complaints – Muscular
- muscle aches or pains
- bruxism

Somatic complaints – Sensory
- tinnitus
- blurred vision

Cardiovascular symptoms
- tachycardia
- palpitations,
- chest pain
- sensory or feeling faint

Respiratory symptoms
- chest pressure
- choking sensation
- shortness of breath

Gastrointestinal symptoms
- dysphagia
- nausea or vomiting
- constipation
- weight loss

Genitourinary symptoms
- urinary frequency or urgency
- dysmenorrhoea
- impotence

Autonomic symptoms
- dry mouth
- flushing
- pallor
- sweating

Behaviour at interview
- fidgets
- tremor
- paces

has a lengthy history as a sedative for more mundane fears. Anxiety is not limited to humans, so it is often studied through comparative biology, with the caveat that anxiety is probably more complex in humans. In other words, animal tests are useful to a degree as anxiety appears universal. Drugs which work by calming humans have a similar effect in animals and vice versa.

The earliest interpretations of anxiety appear to be spiritual, which is not surprising considering the history of madness as discussed in *Chapter 2*. That is, mental states were seen as the result of external forces. For example, the word panic is derived from the Greek god Pan, who could

---

Box 6.2. F41 'Other anxiety disorders' ICD-10 (WHO, 2007)

F41

Disorders in which manifestation of anxiety is the major symptom and is not restricted to any particular environmental situation. Depressive and obsessional symptoms, and even some elements of phobic anxiety, may also be present, provided that they are clearly secondary or less severe.

F41.0

The essential feature is recurrent attacks of severe anxiety (panic), which are not restricted to any particular situation or set of circumstances and are therefore unpredictable. As with other anxiety disorders, the dominant symptoms include sudden onset of palpitations, chest pain, choking sensations, dizziness, and feelings of unreality (depersonalisation or derealisation). There is often also a secondary fear of dying, losing control, or going mad. Panic disorder should not be given as the main diagnosis if the patient has a depressive disorder at the time the attacks start; in these circumstances the panic attacks are probably secondary to depression.

Panic:
● attack
● state

Excludes: panic disorder with agoraphobia (F40.0)

F41.1

Anxiety that is generalised and persistent but not restricted to, or even strongly predominating in, any particular environmental circumstances (i.e. it is 'free-floating'). The dominant symptoms are variable but include complaints of persistent nervousness, trembling, muscular tensions, sweating, lightheadedness, palpitations, dizziness, and epigastric discomfort. Fears that the patient or a relative will shortly become ill or have an accident are often expressed.

Anxiety:
● neurosis
● reaction
● state

Excludes: neurasthenia (F48.0)

---

inspire irrational fear especially when woken from his sleep. The Greeks believed that performance in battle was indicative of character. Heroes controlled their fears and cowards did not (Gabriel, 1987). This was clearly an important distinction. The Greeks rejected weapons which distanced them from the enemy for over 400 years in order to maintain the clarity between heroes and cowards in battle. There is also evidence that it remains an important distinction. The American Army used tattooing and branding as a punishment for cowardice in the 1870s. Many British men were shot by their own officers for cowardice in the First World War. Bravery is still publicly lauded with awards ceremonies.

Freud

Around 400BC Hippocrates believed that only women were affected by anxiety. This is difficult to understand when heroism and cowardice were clearly related to what would now be considered anxiety, yet associated solely with males at this time. It would seem fear and anxieties were seen as qualitatively separate. Nevertheless anxiety was explained by Hippocrates as the result of the womb (hyster) travelling periodically to the brain. The remedy was early marriage. The notion of a connection between sexual frustration and hysteria has persisted. It appears again in the time of Pinel, who also advocated early marriage as a cure in the 1790s (Stone, 1997). The link between sex and anxiety was reinforced by Freud.

The term hysteria was widely applied to anxiety and related disorders around the turn of the 16th century (Shorter, 1997). Charles LePois (1563–1633) stated that hysteria had nothing to do with the uterus and that it could affect men as well as women, but the prevailing view remained for 250 years. For example Freud's teachers denied that men could suffer from hysteria.

The important notion of hysterical conversion originated with John Ferriar (1761–1815). It referred to the observation that a distant bodily organ can somehow act in sympathy with the organ which appears to be primarily affected. Eduard Beneke (1798–1854) and then Freud took this a step further by suggesting that an unbearable idea can somehow be converted into a bodily symptom. This concept of an unbearable idea appears to persist through many understandings of anxiety, regardless of what the unbearable idea may be. However the unbearable idea often appears moral in some manner.

For example ancient Egyptian and Hebrew notions of anxiety were seen as a function of individual sin. This idea also appears later in the Christian faith, particularly in considering the readings of Kierkegaard (1980), who relates anxiety with the concept of original sin. That is, anxiety exists as a consequence of original sin and could not exist without it. This is important from a historical perspective as threads of these ideas permeated Freud's psychodynamic understanding of anxiety, which dominated the early 20th century and continue to exert influence.

Freud himself suffered from anxiety (Sheehan, 1986), and published his first paper on psychoanalytic treatment of hysteria in 1893. He described 'anxiety neurosis' in 1895, which was a broad term covering panic states and milder anxiety. Kraepelin refined this category in his 6th edition of *Psychiatrie* in 1899, which formed the foundation for current diagnostic understandings of anxiety-related disorders.

Pharmacology

Healy (2004) argues that the vast majority of nervous states in the first 80 years of the 20th century were seen as anxiety disorders. He believes it was only with the advent of the selective serotonin reuptake inhibitors (SSRIs) that a large proportion of these disorders came to be conceptualised as secondary to the primary problem of depression. In fact, this conceptual shift probably has a slightly longer history than this. The term nostalgia was used as a diagnostic category back in 1678 to describe a combination of depression and anxiety seen in homesick Swiss soldiers (Gabriel, 1987). One of the first empirical indications of a biochemical relationship between modern understandings of anxiety and depression came with Klein and Fink's now ethically impossible experiment in 1957 (Barondes, 2003). They gave imipramine to 200 patients on the psychiatric ward of Hillside Hospital, Long Island, regardless of diagnosis, for a period of three weeks. Fourteen patients responded with a reduction in certain types of episodic anxiety. This finding was subsequently repeated in placebo controlled trials. By the 1980s imipramine was being widely used for panic disorder, a category of disorder which did not exist until a drug was found to cure it. Imipramine is also an effective antidepressant.

As a consequence it has become standard practice to test new antidepressants on people with panic disorder. The SSRIs are considered to be effective and interchangeable by the American Psychiatric Association and are now more widely prescribed than imipramine in the USA. A logical step was therefore to test their efficacy in other areas of anxiety disorder. This was happening rapidly in the 1980s to fill the gap left by the benzodiazepines, whose fortunes were in decline.

Benzodiazepines

The rise of the benzodiazepines began with the launch of meprobamate in 1955. Marketed as Miltown in the USA it was discovered by Frank Berger who noted his laboratory animals were calm but not unduly sedated. He adopted the new term tranquilliser to describe the effect, a term originally coined by Yonkman to describe the effects of reserpine (Bein, 1970).

Miltown made people feel 'better than well' (Healy, 2004: 5), which in retrospect should probably have triggered earlier scepticism and caution. However, librium and valium quickly followed, and were even more successful as they caused still less sedation. Hoffman La Roche encouraged doctors to prescribe them for any potentially psychosomatic disorder such as hypertension, asthma and ulcers, as all these were potentially related to 'stress'. In 1979 diazepam was the second most widely prescribed drug (after cimetidine) in the world (Salzman, 2006).

Fortunes changed with the threat of dependence. In the UK the tabloid media portrayed benzodiazepines as addictive. This is not supported by the majority of clinical evidence. Mellinger et al (1984) determined only 1.65% of the US population was regularly taking a benzodiazepine even at the height of its prescribing popularity. There has never been a benzodiazepine addiction problem in Japan. Animal tests show they do not have the abuse liability of heroin or cocaine, yet these comparisons were being made by television consumer programmes such as *'That's Life'*. Most patients are able to discontinue benzodiazepines without incident. Also, benzodiazepines have a clear therapeutic niche. That is, they are highly effective anxiolytics.

However, some people did appear to be dependent at normal dosage, and benzodiazepine 'addicts' came to be seen as victims of the medico-pharmaceutical establishment. Health professionals subsequently became wary of anything promoted to instantly 'cure' anxiety, on the grounds that this too may later turn out to be addictive. Buspirone failed to sell around this time despite a very expensive launch founded on its non-addictive properties. Paradoxically this left anxiety uncurable as it was understood at the time. The only recourse for the purpose of pharmacological intervention was therefore to reframe the concept of anxiety. The market needed a demonstrably non-addictive treatment, and anxiety treatment was reframed as secondary to underlying depression. This is why the SSRIs are currently both popular and closely monitored for addictive qualities.

A less cynical perspective suggests that anxiety and depression actually are different expressions of a similar disorder with a common neurobiological substrate. In other words the reframing was correct. Alternatively anxiety and depression may be discrete diagnostic entities that respond to independent pharmacological effects of the same drugs. They may otherwise be a combination of both. Again, the solution is pragmatic. The most relevant clinical finding is that some antidepressants appear effective in the acute treatment of generalised anxiety disorder (Casacalenda and Boulenger, 1998).

NICE (2004) advocate a wide range of treatments for anxiety including psychological therapies and self-help founded on shared decision making.

This chapter focuses on the practicalities of their recommendations for pharmaceutical intervention. Benzodiazepines are not recommended in the treatment of panic disorder, as they are associated with a poor long-term outcome. Antidepressants are the drug of choice, and unless otherwise indicated the antidepressant should be an SSRI licensed for panic disorder (NICE, 2004a). If there is no improvement after 12 weeks NICE recommend switching to an approved tricyclic antidepressant.

Benzodiazepines are recommended for short term (2–4 weeks) use in generalised anxiety disorder. Sedating antihistamines are also recommended for immediate management. Longer-term management is again suggested to consist of antidepressant medication, again, preferably an SSRI. If this does not work after 12 weeks another SSRI is recommended as second line treatment. The next section examines the clinical evidence regarding the use of diazepam and SSRIs in GAD, and SSRIs in panic disorder.

Diazepam and generalised anxiety disorder

The Cochrane library was searched for studies on diazepam in generalised anxiety disorder. Four systematic reviews were found. Chessick et al (2006) conducted a systematic review of azapirones, including buspirone for generalised anxiety disorder. These drugs were compared with diazepam. In summarising their findings of the 36 trials ($N = 5908$) they concluded that azapirones may not be as effective as benzodiazepines. Also, fewer people stopped taking benzodiazepines throughout the trials, suggesting they are also more tolerable. The conclusion is that benzodiazepines are effective in treating GAD, given that Chessick et al found azapirones more effective than placebo.

Three other reviews on the database were criticised by Cochrane for potential errors in their reporting and are therefore not included here. A total of 36 clinical trials were then identified, but only three examined the effects of diazepam alone or compared diazepam directly with another intervention in the last 10 years. The main findings were as follows.

Pomara et al (2005) found chronic diazepam treatment reduced plasma cortisol levels, particularly in the elderly. This is consistent with the implication of the hypothalamic-pituitary-adrenal axis in stress and depression (Holsboer, 2000) giving further support to the hypothesis that anxiety and depression may be linked at some biological level. Rickels et al (2000) found evidence for discontinuation symptoms, but only in patients treated for more than 12 weeks with diazepam. They had earlier compared gepirone with diazepam (Rickels et al, 1997) and again found diazepam very effective and tolerable in treating GAD, but also responsible for mild rebound symptoms after 8 weeks. It may be that these findings are linked. They all lend support for the short-term use of diazepam, as it is clearly effective and well tolerated in GAD but can quickly cause rebound symptoms. The problem of dependence will be discussed later.

SSRIs and generalised anxiety disorder

The Cochrane library revealed one Cochrane systematic review of antidepressants for GAD (Kapczinski et al, 2003). It concluded that imipramine, venlafaxine and paroxetine were superior to placebo in treating GAD. One of the included trials suggested a similar efficacy between imipramine and paroxetine. Overall, the authors concluded that about five people needed to be treated in order for one person with GAD to benefit from antidepressant treatment.

Despite the long-term evidence of the efficacy of imipramine, SSRIs are currently the recommended first-line treatment for the long-term management of GAD (NICE, 2004a; 2007). NICE leaves the decision to the clinician, but makes a particular effort in clarifying cautions in prescribing venlafaxine. Implicitly therefore NICE appears to consider this a suitable choice. Evidence pertaining to venlafaxine in GAD was therefore sought from the Cochrane library.

Forty one clinical trials have been undertaken in the last 10 years and all support the efficacy of venlafaxine in GAD. Rynn et al (2007) concluded that extended-release venlafaxine may be an effective, well-tolerated short-term treatment for paediatric generalised anxiety disorder. This was a large double blind randomised controlled trial. In an open trial Kim et al (2006) found the extended release venlafaxine to be as effective and well tolerated as paroxetine.

Lenox-Smith and Reynolds (2003) conducted a double-blind, randomised, placebo controlled, and parallel-group 24 week trial with 244 patients. They found venlafaxine to be more effective than placebo in treating anxiety in patients both with and without depressive symptoms. Likewise, Montgomery et al (2002a) found venlafaxine to be effective in both short-term and long-term treatment of GAD. They followed this up with a study examining long-term treatment of GAD with venlafaxine in more detail. Montgomery et al (2002b) concluded remission was more likely to be maintained in those continuing to take venlafaxine following recovery.

In summary, each of the studies could be criticised. For example. Rynn has received research support from AstraZeneca, Eli Lilly, Forest Laboratories, Pfizer, and Wyeth Pharmaceuticals and has served as a consultant and on speaker's bureaus for Eli Lilly, Pfizer, and Wyeth Pharmaceuticals (Rynn et al, 2007). She therefore has to defend herself against accusations of bias. However, despite their overall size, quality or affiliations, it is fair to say there are no clinical trials in the Cochrane database which do not support the efficacy of venlafaxine in the short-term or long-term treatment of GAD, with or without depressive symptoms.

SSRIs and panic disorder

The Cochrane Library was searched for 'SSRI' and 'panic disorder' in the title and revealed only one study. Individual SSRIs were therefore substituted for the general term 'SSRI' and a total of 90 clinical trials were returned when fluoxetine, citalopram, venlafaxine and paroxetine were combined. Paroxetine generated the most information with 42 trials (the tricyclic antidepressant imipramine had most trials overall with 67). A summary of the salient findings for the SSRIs follows.

Ferguson et al (2007) found that time to relapse was significantly longer with venlafaxine ER (extended release) than placebo in their trial comparing relapse rates in panic disorder. All secondary measures of quality of life were also significantly better in the treatment group ($n = 169$) over a 2-year period. They concluded venlafaxine was safe, well tolerated, and effective in preventing relapse in outpatients with panic disorder. The short-term efficacy of venlafaxine was demonstrated by Bradwejn et al (2005) in a study of 361 outpatients. They found it to be well tolerated but at final evaluation it was not associated with a greater proportion of patients being free from full-symptom panic attacks. However, their positive conclusion was justified as other measures of symptom improvement (e.g. anticipatory anxiety, fear and avoidance) were demonstrated.

Sheehan et al (2005) compared paroxetine controlled release ($n = 444$) with placebo ($n = 445$) in three identical, 10-week, double blind trials. They found paroxetine superior on the primary measure. That is, 63% people on paroxetine were free of panic attacks 2 weeks prior to endpoint as opposed to 53% on placebo. There were no unexpected adverse events and severe adverse events were rare and only marginally higher than placebo (2.3% paroxetine, 1.8% placebo). Bandelow et al (2004) compared the efficacy of paroxetine with sertraline, and found both to be equally effective in the treatment of panic disorder. However, sertraline was better tolerated and caused less clinical worsening when tapering off the medication.

Perna et al (2001) compared paroxetine with citalopram, and again found comparable efficacy. They also found them to be comparable in tolerability. In a controlled, prospective, 1-year trial of citalopram Lepola et al (1998) found citalopram to be both an effective and tolerable long-term treatment of panic disorder, as long as the dose was not less than 20mg daily. Michelson et al (2001) found fluoxetine also to be effective at higher doses, and a long-term evaluation of fluoxetine compared with imipramine found fluoxetine to be quicker in symptom relief but otherwise equally effective (Amore et al, 1999a). Long-term evaluation has demonstrated high rates of persistent full remission with both fluoxetine and citalopram (Amore et al, 1999b).

In other words, an examination of the high quality literature suggests a comparable efficacy and tolerability of all the SSRIs reviewed in the treatment of panic disorder.

Diazepam and dependence

Diazepam has long been associated with dependence. For example, studies in the 1980s suggested a third of people taking it became dependent on it (Vinarova et al, 1982). Although these numbers have been questioned it indisputably produces dependence in some people. More recent articles have therefore focused on the possible biological mechanisms underpinning dependence. For example, Ohkuma et al (2001) suggest that different individual expressions of diazepam binding inhibitor (DBI), a peptide consisting of 87 amino acids, may be a factor in eliciting drug dependence in mice. This research is ongoing. However, a major clinical feature of dependence is anxiety, which is what the drug is used for in the first place, making it extremely difficult in some instances to separate the concepts of 'illness' and 'dependence'. This continues to be a significant factor in discussions on dependence, which often end up more emotive than rational. This is important as effective treatment may well be being withheld on the basis of conceptual misunderstanding as opposed to evidence.

For example Strelzer and Johansen (2006) presented a case of a patient with chronic pain who developed an addiction to multiple drugs and tragically overdosed. They go on to develop a position against chronic opioid analgesic therapy, which they describe as a 'medical subculture. Fishbain et al (2006) counter this position by providing an alternative interpretation of the evidence citing three meta-analyses supporting the therapeutic benefit of long-term usage of opioids in chronic pain relief. They suggest that 10–15% of the US general population suffer addiction disorders. This is the same number as suffer addiction disorders in the chronic pain population. The conclusion is that pain should be treated according to the best available evidence and not according to over-generalisations from single emotive case studies. Naturally Strelzer and Johansen disagree with Fishbain's interpretation of the data.

With specific regard to benzodiazepine dependence Hall et al (1999) estimated the 12-month prevalence of benzodiazepine dependence in the Australian population to be no more than 0.4%. Abuse of high benzodiazepine doses is more common among people with alcohol-related problems (Ciraulo et al, 1998). Anxiety disorders in turn may be more likely to precede substance use disorders (Merikangas et al, 1998). Again, this is hardly surprising when the symptoms of anxiety are successfully treated by anxiolytics and anxiety avoidance may well be the goal of the substance abuser. By contrast lower doses of benzodiazepines and no previous withdrawal experience predicted successful discontinuation of benzodiazepines (Vorma et al, 2005).

The concepts of addiction disorder, abuse and dependence are often used interchangeably, which adds to the confusion. ICD-10 (WHO, 2007) records the following criteria for 'dependence syndrome', a subsection of categories of behavioural and mental disorders associated with various substances (F11–F19):

A cluster of behavioural, cognitive, and physiological phenomena that develop after repeated substance use and that typically include a strong desire to take the drug, difficulties in controlling its use, persisting in its use despite harmful consequences, a higher priority given to drug use than to other activities and obligations, increased tolerance, and sometimes a physical withdrawal state.

The dependence syndrome may be present for a specific psychoactive substance (e.g. tobacco, alcohol, or diazepam), for a class of substances (e.g. opioid drugs), or for a wider range of pharmacologically different psychoactive substances.

This is similar to the substance abuse category in DSM-IV which equates with older notions of addiction. F13 is the ISD-10 category of mental and behavioural disorders due to the use of sedatives or hypnotics. F13.2 is the above symptoms specifically secondary to diazepam abuse.

Treatment is complex. When I first qualified as a registred mental nurse public concern was at a peak (Ashton, 1984) and withdrawal from long-term benzodiazepine use was a major goal of many patients and GPs as a consequence. Tapering schedules were used along with a lot of nursing support. Treatment involved titration of all prescribed benzodiazepines to an equivalent diazepam dose and then gradually reducing the dose, sometimes over a year or more, eventually administering the tiniest of liquid doses before stopping altogether. This was successful in those motivated and well supported, and less so in others.

Current management guidelines are based on consideration of all the above, hence the recommendation of strictly short-term prescribing, and caution in those at high risk of dependence. There is little evidence of dependence syndromes in treatment under 8–12 weeks (Rickels et al, 1997, 2000). In an international study of expert opinion Uhlenhuth et al (1999) concluded that benzodiazepines 'pose a higher risk of dependence and abuse than most potential substitutes but a lower risk than older sedatives and recognised drugs of abuse'. This suggests Uhlenhuth et al believe dependence is not the inevitable consequence of diazepam prescription. Anxious patients may be currently under-treated as a consequence of erroneous opinions comparable to those that preclude appropriate narcotic prescription for terminally ill cancer patients in order to avoid dependence (Salzman, 2006: 8).

The main predictors of benzodiazepine dependence severity, as measured by the ICD-10, DSM-IIIR scales, and Bendep-SRQ Rasch scales, are, in decreasing order:

- being a self-help patient;
- higher benzodiazepine dose, longer duration of benzodiazepine use, younger age; and
- non-native cultural origin, lower level of education, being in outpatient treatment for alcohol and/or drug dependence, and the interaction of benzodiazepine dose with duration of benzodiazepine use.

It is concluded that a limited number of recognisable risk factors appear to predict the severity of benzodiazepine dependence (Kan et al, 2004)

Kan et al (2004) note that within the literature only severe somatisation and insomnia have consistently been found to constitute risk factors for dependence. The findings surrounding other potential risk factors are inconsistent. They could not explain a substantial part of benzodiazepine dependence severity. However, the risk factors identified above constitute their major findings. In other words, if a patient is not in this group of higher risk individuals there is no coherent rationale to withhold treatment based on the fear of dependence.

Insomnia

Beginning with the discovery of fermentation and alcohol, drugs have been used to treat insomnia for at least 8000 years (Lader, 1993). The search for a 'cleaner', dependence-free substitute has been ongoing. It has included opium, chloral hydrate (Micky Finn), barbiturates, bromides, nitrous oxide, chloroform, paraldehyde and more recently chlorpromazine, reserpine, meprobamate, diazepam, antidepressants, antipsychotics and other antihistamines. It is interesting to note that chloral hydrate, a popular hypnotic in my experience of the older adult wards of the 1980s, was often given with sherry and is itself metabolised to an alcohol derivative. In some ways it could be argued we have not come very far in 8000 years. Chloral hydrate is now mainly used as preoperative sedation in children as it is considered very dangerous in overdose (Frankland and Robinson, 2001) and therefore rarely prescribed for people at potential risk of self-harm. This trend towards increasing safety and regulation of hypnotics is a mirror of the development and utility of the antipsychotics, antidepressants and anxiolytics as seen in *Section 1.*

Throughout history medicines given to induce sleep have also been used during the day to reduce anxiety, thus conceptually correlating anxiety and insomnia. For example diazepam and lorazepam are licensed for both insomnia and anxiety and are listed in the anxiolytic section of the *British National Formulary* (Section 4.1.2). Current guidance on treatment of insomnia in UK is provided by NICE (2004b: 1.1.1):

When, after due consideration of the use of non-pharmacological measures, hypnotic drug therapy is considered appropriate for the management of severe insomnia interfering with normal daily life, it is recommended that hypnotics should be prescribed for short periods of time only, in strict accordance with their licensed indications.

In order to prescribe safely it is important to understand what the terms in this statement mean. For example what are the non-pharmacological measures and why should they take precedence? What is 'severe insomnia interfering with normal daily life'? What is the 'short period of time' referred to and what are the 'licensed indications'? These questions will be answered in turn.

What is insomnia?

According to NICE (2004b: 2.2.1) insomnia is:

a disturbance of normal sleep patterns commonly characterised by difficulty in initiating sleep (sleep onset latency) and/or difficulty maintaining sleep (sleep maintenance). However, insomnia is highly subjective and although most healthy adults typically sleep between 7 and 9 hours per night, patterns vary greatly between people, and in any given person there are variations from night to night.

ICD-10 categorises insomnias as part of the behavioural syndromes associated with physiological disturbances and physical factors (F50–F59). This category also includes eating disorders and sexual dysfunction for example. Non-organic insomnia (F51) is equivalent to the DSM-IV category of primary insomnia (307.42), which is classed as a 'problem' only if

...over a period of at least one month, a person has difficulty falling asleep or maintaining their sleep. To be diagnosed as primary insomnia, the sleep problem must cause difficulty in the person's social, school, work, or other significant area of life. Most often, people with insomnia complain of problems in falling asleep, or they complain of fitful sleeping or frequent awakening. Some report that the quality of their sleep is poor, that they are restless during sleep. This condition may turn into an aggravating cycle in that the more a person focuses on their sleep problems, they may be less likely to get good quality sleep. Insomnia can also lead to difficulties with a person's concentration, energy level, or mood. The main characteristics of primary insomnia are:

- *For at least a month the person's main complaint has been trouble going to sleep, staying asleep or feeling unrested.*
- *The insomnia, or resulting daytime fatigue, causes clinically important distress or impairs work, social or personal functioning.*
- *It does not occur solely in the course of breathing-related or circadian rhythm sleep disorder, narcolepsy or a parasomnia.*
- *It does not occur solely in the course of another mental disorder (such as a delirium, generalised anxiety disorder, major depressive disorder).*
- *These symptoms are not directly caused by a general medical condition or substance use, including medications and drugs of abuse.*

It will be obvious that depression and anxiety can have very similar presentations as acknowledged in the fourth bullet point above. That is, depression and anxiety can also correlate with difficulty in concentration, low energy levels and rumination on negative possibilities (e.g. 'I will not get to sleep'). It is for this reason that insomnia is rarely seen as primary. Treatment is related to cause, so if the cause is for example high caffeine consumption, alcohol abuse or depression then this would be the focus of treatment in the first instance. ICD-10 classification is broadly similar but not as specific. However a diagnosis of sleep disorder is likewise only made when the problem is perceived as a condition in itself or one of the major complaints. Non-organic insomnia (F51.0) is defined as:

A condition of unsatisfactory quantity and/or quality of sleep, which persists for a considerable period of time, including difficulty falling asleep, difficulty staying asleep, or early final wakening. Insomnia is a common symptom of many mental and physical disorders, and should be classified here in addition to the basic disorder only if it dominates the clinical picture.

To take these definitions back to the original NICE guidance (1.1.1) it can be seen that there is no clear corollary of 'severe' insomnia to align with the guidance. Although the DSM criteria specify one month duration for a diagnosis of primary insomnia there is no such specificity in ICD-10. What is clearer is that insomnia is almost universally seen as a symptom of another issue, although there is debate as to which comes first. Not all hold this view; Atalay (2004) suggests that instead of considering insomnia as a secondary symptom of a psychiatric or medical condition, insomnia itself should be accepted as an unrelated clinical entity or disorder. Others see insomnia as a predictor of anxiety (Necklemann et al, 2007), as opposed to the more commonly held view that insomnia is secondary to it. Even if viewed in this manner it remains up to the clinician to establish the current primary presenting complaint. That is, diagnosis of primary insomnia is differential, and is therefore currently excluded by the presence of anxiety or depression. This does not prevent treatment however.

More specific detail exists in the International Classification of Sleep Disorders (ICSD, 2001), the current diagnostic system used by most sleep disorder specialists. However, the essential features of the equivalent category of psychophysiological insomnia (307.42.0) are familiar. The disorder is described as 'somatised tension and learned sleep-preventing associations that result in a complaint of insomnia and associated decreased functioning during wakefulness' (ICSD, 2001: 22). In other words it is seen as objectively verifiable through recognition of the mutual reinforcement of learned sleep preventing associations and somatised tension. It is therefore conceptualised largely as a behavioural problem. That is, problematic causative associations are learned during the insomnia.

The assumption is that these associations then persist beyond the resolution of the actual (primary) cause of the insomnia. This view naturally supports non-pharmacological interventions aimed at addressing this incongruence, such as cognitive-behavioural therapy and relaxation techniques. The ICSD manual runs to 208 pages. In some ways these different views can be difficult to reconcile. However, there is significant crossover of definition and categorisation, and an appreciation of each system enhances overall understanding. The three systems relate to each other as shown in *Table 6.1* (Estivil et al, 2003).

What are the non-pharmacological measures and why should they take precedence?

Non-pharmacological methods for the management of insomnia have been given a high priority in the NICE guidance, and will therefore be briefly discussed here. That is, non-pharmacological measures are given equivalent

Table 6.1. ICSD, ICD-10 and DSM-IV classifications of sleep disorders

ICSD		ICD-10		DSM-IV	
Name	Code	Name	Code	Name	Code
1a. Adjustment sleep disorder	307.41-0	Non-organic insomnia	F51.0		
1b. Psycho-physiological insomnia	307.42-0	Non-organic insomnia	F51.0	Primary insomnia	307.4
Disorder of initiating or maintaining sleep	G47.0				
5b. Central sleep apnoea syndrome	780.51-0	Sleep apnoea	G47.3	Breathing-related sleep disorder	780.5
5c. Central alveolar hypoventilation syndrome	780.51-1				
5f. Altitude insomnia	289	Other altitude effects	T20.2		
7a. Short sleeper	307.49-0				
8e. Fatal familial insomnia	337.9	Other degenerative diseases	G31	Insomnia due to ...indicate medical pathology	780.X
11. Idiopathic insomnia	780.52-7	Disorder of initiating or maintaining sleep	G47.0	Primary insomnia	307.4

status in guidelines on depression and anxiety whereas pharmacological measures are distinctly secondary in the case of insomnia treatment. Yet despite awareness of the guideline and the high priority of the non-pharmacological suggestions there is evidence clinicians do not appear to be following it. For example Donaldson and Muzaffar (2005) found zopiclone to be the most regularly prescribed hypnotic in their survey of Scottish GPs and psychiatrists. NICE recommend the drug with the lowest purchase cost (currently temazepam) where a hypnotic is indicated. Nearly all (96%, *n* = 46) gave advice on sleep hygiene, but only 17% (*n* = 8) regularly offered non-pharmacological interventions, which is suggested as first-line treatment (NICE 1.1.1). This may simply be a matter of provision. For example it is widely accepted that cognitive-behavioural therapy is an effective therapy for depression, anxiety and insomnia. As yet demand outweighs supply. However, it is worth briefly examining the evidence regarding non-pharmacological interventions in insomnia, as in this case they are recommended as first-line treatment.

Biancosino et al (2006) conducted a small pilot study of psychoeducational intervention in helping 36 patients with chronic insomnia. Results seemed promising. It reduced the incidence of *pro re nata* (PRN) medication administration over the study period. Irwin et al (2006) conducted a meta-analysis of 23 trials comparing three different behavioural treatments: cognitive-behavioural therapy, behavioural therapy only and relaxation techniques. They found significant overall moderate to large effects of these treatments on subjective sleep outcomes, and found no difference between them. In other words they were all equally effective. Moderate intensity exercise combined with not napping in the evening has been associated with improved length of sleep in older adults (Tanaka et al, 2001). Sleep restriction during the day in general has proven to be effective (Collier and Skitt, 2003). This is why modafinil claims a therapeutic niche. This drug has been marketed, licenced and designed to aid sleep by keeping people with sleeping difficulties awake during the day.

However, NICE clearly support non-pharmacological interventions in the first instance. In support of this position is some high quality evidence of some of the risks inherent in prescribing hypnotics. For example Glass et al (2005) conducted a meta-analysis of risks and benefits of hypnotics in older people and found evidence supporting their efficacy in aiding sleep. However this benefit was offset by the subsequent increased risk of falls and cognitive deficits. They therefore concluded that the use of hypnotics could not be justified in this population. Paediatric insomnia is poorly studied and described (Glaze et al, 2002), and so efficacy of subsequent treatment is not clear.

What is normal sleep?

Normal sleeping patterns can be divided into two states, rapid eye movement (REM) and non-rapid eye movement (NREM). NREM can be further divided into four stages with each progressive stage referring to a

---

Box 6.3. Sleep cycle

Stage 1

Stage 1 sleep, or drowsiness, is often described as first in the sequence, especially in models where waking is not included. The eyes are closed during Stage 1 sleep, but if aroused from it, a person may feel as if he or she has not slept. Stage 1 may last for five to 10 minutes.

Stage 2

Stage 2 is a period of light sleep. The heart rate slows and body temperature decreases. At this point, the body prepares to enter deep sleep.

Stages 3 and 4

These are deep sleep stages, with Stage 4 being more intense than Stage 3. These stages are known as slow-wave, or delta, sleep.

Non-REM sleep

The period of non-REM sleep (NREM) is comprised of Stages 1–4 and lasts from 90 to 120 minutes, each stage lasting anywhere from 5 to 15 minutes. Stages 2 and 3 repeat backwards before REM sleep is attained. So, a normal sleep cycle has this pattern: waking, stage 1, 2, 3, 4, 3, 2, REM. Usually, REM sleep occurs 90 minutes after sleep onset

Stage 5, REM

REM sleep is distinguishable from NREM sleep by changes in physiological states, including its characteristic rapid eye movements. However, polysomnograms show wave patterns in REM to be similar to Stage 1 sleep. The first period of REM typically lasts 10 minutes, with each recurring REM stage lengthening, and the final one lasting an hour.

---

deeper level of sleep, with stage 4 being the deepest (Antai-Otong, 2005). The five stages of sleep, including their repetition, occur cyclically. The first cycle, which ends after the completion of the first REM stage, usually lasts for 100 minutes. Each subsequent cycle lasts longer, as its respective REM stage extends. A typical night's sleep consists of five cycles (see *Box 6.3*). It is interference with this 'norm' which initiates complaints of sleep disturbance. The hypnotics also interfere with this natural rhythm, which is possibly why people do not feel refreshed after a drug-induced sleep. It is generally stage 3 and 4 NREM sleep which is reduced in older adults and this is thought to be the cause of the sensation of feeling unrefreshed (Ohayon et al, 2004).

All benzodiazepines modify the sleep cycle. They decrease the period of time required to fall asleep as well as altering the time spent in the individual sleep cycles. In general, all benzodiazepines will decrease the period of time required to fall asleep, the number of awakenings during the night, and the time spent awake. More specifically they increase Stage 2 sleep, and cause a small decrease in Stages 3 and 4 and REM sleep. The total sleep time is usually increased (Matthews, 2006).

Both REM and NREM states are qualitatively different from waking states which supports the idea that a person can exhibit pathology during sleep regardless of their state of health when awake (Roehrs and Roth, 2004).

How big is the problem?

It is clear that insomnia is a problem for a significant proportion of the population, however defined or understood. It has been estimated that 10–40% of adults presenting in primary care complain of sleeping difficulties, and about 15% of the adult population suffer from some form of chronic (six months and longer) (ICSD, 2001) insomnia (Kiley, 1999; Roth, 2001). In sleep disorder centres 15% of the population are diagnosed with psychophysiological insomnia, but the prevalence in the general population is unknown (ICSD, 2001) due to the differences in diagnostic criteria (Roehrs and Roth, 2004). Using the DSM-IV classification system, several European studies found that primary insomnia accounted for 16%; insomnia associated with mental disorders, 44%; insomnia associated with general medical disorders, 7%; other sleep disorders, 5%; and insomnia due to substance use, 2%. For the remaining 26% of cases, no differential could be determined (Ohayon, 2002). Medications that can cause insomnia are shown in *Box 6.4*.

When the 'z drugs' were first marketed it was as a safer alternative to the dependence-causing benzodiazepines. However, this claim has not been substantiated. For example Huang et al (2007) found zolpidem to cause dependence at ultra high levels. It is fair to say that 'ultra high levels' are not therapeutic, but it does show the abuse potential has not been entirely eliminated. As there is no solid evidence supporting the clinical superiority of the 'z drugs' NICE recommend prescribing the cheapest hypnotic. This is currently temazepam. Other medications that may be used for insomnia include sedating antidepressants such as tricyclic antidepressants or trazodone, as well as antihistamines (e.g. diphenhydramine).

Summary

This chapter has shown that anxiolytics are effective. It has discussed prescribing decisions against a backdrop of the NICE guideline for anxiety and insomnia. As in treatment of psychosis and depression in the previous chapters, if pharmacological intervention is warranted then accurate, replicable, structured and systematic diagnosis is the key to supporting

---

Box 6.4. Medications that can cause insomnia

Anticonvulsants	Phenytoin
Antihypertensives	Furosemide, methyldopa, hydrochlorothiazide, metoprolol, nadolol, propranolol
Calcium-channel blockers	Diltiazem, verapamil
Corticosteroids	Cortisone, dexamethasone, prednisone
Decongestants	Pseudoephedrine, phenylephrine
Dopamine agonists	Amantadine, bromocriptine, levodopa
Weight loss medications /appetite suppressants	Phentermine, sibutramine
SSRIs	Citalopram, fluoxetine, fluvoxamine, paroxetine, sertraline
Other antidepressants	Bupropion
MAOIs	Phenylzine, tranylcypromine
Theophylline	
Thyroid replacements	
Oral contraceptives	(various)
Other agents	Cimetidine, alcohol, caffeine, nicotine
Ma huang (ephedrine)	
Nicotine gum and patches	
Phenylpropanolamine	
Herbs/supplements with stimulant properties	

---

this decision. Concordance is best achieved through mutual understanding and this takes skilled communication based upon the current principles of partnership and recovery in mental health nursing (Scottish Executive, 2006). Prescribing decisions will therefore be clear, evidence based and agreed. Monitoring should encompass extensive knowledge of potential adverse events and risk factors as discussed at length in this chapter. In this way the person seeking help can be assured of safe, competent and caring help. The flowchart in *Figure 6.3* illustrates how these factors interrelate.

Further reading

Storr A (2001) *Freud. A Very Short Introduction.* Oxford: Oxford University Press

It is arguably unrealistic to understand anxiety without engaging with Freud. Whether you disagree with him or not a great deal of our current language of anxiety can be traced back to his ideas. This book is a very

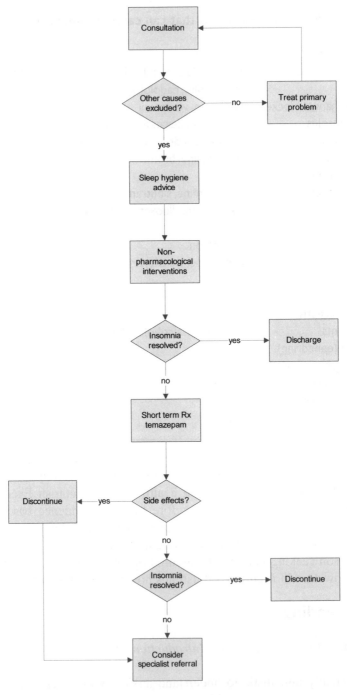

Figure 6.3. Summary flowchart: treatment of insomnia.

accessible, easy-to-read and balanced introduction with pointers to further readings throughout.

Kierkegaard S (1980) T*he Concept of Anxiety. A simple Psychologically Oriented Deliberation on the Dogmatic Issue of Hereditary* (Sin. R Thomte transl and ed). Princeton University Press, New Jersey

This is a difficult book but notable as the origin of contemporary notions of existential angst. It draws heavily on Christian philosophy in that Kierkegaard examines the relationship between angst and the concept of original sin, a sense of guilt that for him appears unrelated to moral behaviour.

Appignanesi L (2008) *Mad, Bad and Sad; A History of Women and the Mind Doctors From 1800 to the Present.* London: Virago Press

This book is not specifically about anxiety. In fact it charts the relationship between many psychiatric diagnoses and society. What is different is that it charts this history through many case studies of women labelled mad, bad or sad since 1796. This feminist voice is missing in much of the other literature which is the poorer for it. Appignanesi charts many of the wider issues discussed in this book and others besides from a unique and balanced perspective.

Gabriel RA (1987) *No More Heros; Madness and Psychiatry in War.* New Yor: Hill and Wang

Gabriel's focus is the psychological costs of war on its soldiers. Professor Gabriel shows that psychiatric casualties are the most prevelent type of injury on the battlefield. Except for the truly insane he believes anybody would break down on the battlefield no matter how brave. Taken together with Appignanesi's book one gets a very broad perspective of anxiety as understood in gender terms.

References

Amore M, Magnani K, Cerisoli M, Casagrande C, Ferrari G (1999a) Panic disorder. A long-term treatment study: Fluoxetine vs imipramine. *Human Psychopharmacol* **14**(6): 429–34

Amore M, Magnani K, Cerisoli M, Ferrari G (1999b) Short-term and long-term evaluation of selective serotonin reuptake inhibitors in the treatment of panic disorder: Fluoxetine vs citalopram. *Human Psychopharmacol* **14**(6): 435–40

Antai-Otong D (2005) Risks and benefits of non-benzodiazepine receptor agonists in the treatment of acute primary insomnia in older adults. *Perspectives in Psychiatric Care* **42**(3): 196–200

Ashton H (1984) Benzodiazepine withdrawal: An unfinished story. *Brit Med J (Clin Res*

Ed) **288**(6424): 1135–40

Atalay H (2006) Insomnia: Recent developments in definition and treatment. *Primary Care and Community Psychiatry* **11**(2): 81–91

Bandelow B, Behnke K, Lenoir S, Hendriks GJ, Alkin T, Goebel C, Clary CM (2004) Sertraline versus paroxetine in the treatment of panic disorder: An acute, double-blind noninferiority comparison. *J Clin Psychiatry* **65**(3): 405–13

Barondes SH (2003) *Better than Prozac.* Oxford: Oxford University Press

Bein H (1970) Biological research in the pharmaceutical industry with reserpine. In Ayd FJ, Blackwell B (eds) *Discoveries in Biological Psychiatry.* Philadelphia: Lippincott

Biancosino B, Rocchi D, Donà S (2006) Efficacy of a short-term psychoeducational intervention for persistent non-organic insomnia in severely mentally ill patients. A pilot study. *Euro Psychiatry* **21**(7): 460–2

Bradwejn J, Ahokas A, Stein DJ, Salinas E, Emilien G, Whitaker T (2005) Venlafaxine extended-release capsules in panic disorder: Flexible-dose, double-blind, placebo-controlled study. *Brit J Psychiatry* **187**: 352–9

Casacalenda N, Boulenger JP (1998) Pharmacologic treatments effective in both generalized anxiety disorder and major depressive disorder: Clinical and theoretical implications. *Can J Psychiatry* **43**(7): 722–30

Chessick CA, Allen MH, Thase ME, Batista Miralha da Cunha ABC, Kapczinski FFK, de Lima MSML, dos Santos Souza JJSS (2006) Azapirones for generalized anxiety disorder. *Cochrane Database of Systematic Reviews*, Issue 3. Art. No.: CD006115. DOI: 10.1002/14651858.CD006115.

Ciraulo DA, Sands BF, Shader R (1998) Critical review of liability for benzodiazepine abuse among alcoholics. *Amer J Psychiatry* **145**(12): 1501–6

Collier E, Skitt G (2003) Non pharmaceutical interventions for insomnia. *Ment Health Practice* **6**(6): 29–32

Donaldson A, Muzaffar N (2005) A survey of current practice in the management of insomnia. *Int J Family Pract Amer Family Physicians*. Available from: http://www.priory.com/fam/insomniabulletin.htm [Accessed 15 August 2007]

Dyck IR, Phillips KA, Warshaw MG, Dolan RT, Shea MT, Stou RL, Massion AO, Zlotnick C, Keller MB (2001) Patterns of personality pathology in patients with generalized anxiety disorder, panic disorder with and without agoraphobia, and social phobia. *J Personality Disord* **15**: 60–71

Estivill E, Bov A, Garca-Borreguero D, Gibert J, Paniagua J, Pin G, Puertas FJ, Cilveti R and members of the Consensus Group (2003) Consensus on drug treatment, definition and diagnosis for insomnia. *Clin Drug Invest* **23**(6): 351–85

Ferguson JM, Khan A, Mangano R, Entsuah R, Tzanis E (2007) Relapse prevention of panic disorder in adult outpatient responders to treatment with venlafaxine extended release. *J Clin Psychiatry* **68**(1): 58–68

Fishbain DA, Gallagher RM, Strelzer J, Johansen J (2006) Comments on "Prescription drug dependence and evolving beliefs about chronic pain management"/Drs. Streltzer and Johansen Reply. *Amer J Psychiatry* **163**(12): 2194

Frankland A, Robinson MJ (2001) Fatal chloral hydrate overdoses: Unnecessary tragedies. *Can J Psychiatry/La Revue Canadienne de Psychiatrie* **46**(8): 763–4

Gabriel RA (1987) *No More Heros; Madness and Psychiatry in War.* New York: Hill and Wang

Glass J, Lanctôt KL, Hermann N, Sproule BA, Busto UE (2005) Sedative hypnotics in older people with insomnia: Meta-analysis of risks and benefits. *Brit Med J* **331**: 1169

Glaze DG, Rosen CL, Owens JA (2002) Towards a practical definition of pediatric insomnia. *Curr Therapeutic Res* **63**(Suppl B): B4–17

Gunther B (1994) On the validity of the Yerkes Dodson Law. *Studia Psychologica* **36**(3): 205–9

Hall W, Teesson M, Lynskey M, Degenhardt L (1999) The 12-month prevalence of substance use and ICD-10 substance use disorders in Australian adults: Findings from the National Survey of Mental Health and Well-Being. *Addiction* **94**(10): 1541–50

Hamilton M (1959) The assessment of anxiety states by rating. *Brit J Med Psychol* 32: 50–5

Healy D (2004) *Let Them Eat Prozac*. New York and London: New York University Press

Holsboer F (2000) The corticosteroid receptor hypothesis of depression. *Neuropsychopharmacology* **23**(5): 477–97

Huang M, Lin H, Chen C (2007) Dependence on Zolpidem. *Psychiatry ClinNeurosci* **61**(2): 207–8

International Classification of Sleep Disorders (2001) *Revised Diagnostic and Coding Manual*. Available from: http://www.absm.org/PDF/ICSD.pdf [Accessed 15 August 2007]

Irwin MR, Cole JC, Nicassio PM (2006) Comparative meta-analysis of behavioral interventions for insomnia and their efficacy in middle-aged adults and in older adults 55+ years of age. *Health Psychol* **25**(1): 3–14

Kan CC, Hilberink SR, Breteler MHM (2004) Determination of the main risk factors for benzodiazepine dependence using a multivariate and multidimensional approach. *Comp Psychiatry* **45**(2): 88–94

Kapczinski F, Lima MS, Souza JS, Cunha A, Schmitt R (2003) Antidepressants for generalized anxiety disorder. *Cochrane Database of Systematic Reviews*, Issue 2. Art. No.: CD003592. DOI: 10.1002/14651858.CD003592

Kessler RC, McGonagle KA, Zhao S, Nelson CB, Hughes M, Eshleman S, Wittchen HU, Kendler KS (1994) Lifetime and 12-month prevalence of DSM-III-R psychiatric disorders in the United States: Results from the National Comorbidity Survey. *Arch Gen Psychiatry* **51**: 8–19

Kierkegaard S (1980) T*he Concept of Anxiety. A simple psychologically oriented deliberation on the dogmatic issue of hereditary sin*. Edited and translated by Thomte R. Princeton, NJ: Princeton University Press

Kiley J (1999) Insomnia research and future opportunities. *Sleep* **22**(Suppl 1): S344–5

Kim TS, Pae CU, Yoon SJ, Bahk WM, Jun TY, Rhee WI, Chae JH (2006) Comparison of venlafaxine extended release versus paroxetine for treatment of patients with generalized anxiety disorder. *Psychiatry Clinical Neurosci* **60**(3): 347–53

Lader M (1993) Historical development of the concept of tranquiliser dependence. In Hallstrom C (ed) *Benzodiazepine Dependence*. Oxford: Oxford University Press

Lenox-Smith AJ, Reynolds A (2003) A double-blind, randomised, placebo controlled study of venlafaxine XL in patients with generalised anxiety disorder in primary care. *Brit J Gen Pract* **53**(495): 772–7

Lepola UM, Wade AG, Leinonen EV, Koponen HJ, Frazer J, Sjödin I, Penttinen JT, Pedersen T, Lehto HJ (1998) A controlled, prospective, 1-year trial of citalopram in the treatment of panic disorder. *J Clin Psychiatry* **59**(10): 528–34

Matthews D (2006) Review of insomnia: The sleep cycle and treatment options. P*harmacy Times.* Available from: https://secure.pharmacytimes.com/lessons/200306-01.asp# [Accessed 15 August 2007]

Mellinger GD, Balter MB, Uhlenhuth EH (1984) Prevalence and correlates of the long term regular use of anxiolytics. *J Amer Med Assoc* **251**(3): 375–9

Merikangas KR, Mehta RL, Molnar BE, Walters EE, Swendsen JD, Aguilar-Gaziola S, Bijl R., Borges G, Caraveo-Anduaga JJ, DeWit DJ, Kolody B, Vega WA, Wittchen HU, Kessler RC (1998) Comorbidity of substance use disorders with mood and anxiety disorders: Results of the International Consortium in Psychiatric Epidemiology. *Addictive Behaviors* **23**(6): 893–907

Michelson D, Allgulander C, Dantendorfer K, Knezevic A, Maierhofer D, Micev V, Paunovic VR, Timotijevic I, Sarkar N, Skoglund L, Pemberton SC (2001) Efficacy of usual antidepressant dosing regimens of fluoxetine in panic disorder: Randomised, placebo-controlled trial. *Brit J Psychiatry* **179**: 514–8

Montgomery SA, Mahé V, Haudiquet V, Hackett D (2002a) Effectiveness of venlafaxine, extended release formulation, in the short-term and long-term treatment of generalized anxiety disorder: Results of a survival analysis. *J Clinical Psychopharmacol* **22**(6): 561–7

Montgomery SA, Sheehan DV, Meoni P, Haudiquet V, Hackett D (2002b) Characterization of the longitudinal course of improvement in generalized anxiety disorder during long-term treatment with venlafaxine. *J Psychiatric Res* **36**(4): 209–17

Narrow WE, Rae DS, Robins LN, Regier DA (2002) Revised prevalence estimates of mental disorders in the United States: Using a clinical significance criterion to reconcile two surveys' estimates. *Arch Gen Psychiatry* **59**: 115–23

Necklemann D, Amstein M, Alv AD (2007) Chronic insomnia as a risk factor for developing anxiety and depression. *Sleep* **30**(7): 873–80

NICE (2004a) *Anxiety Management of Anxiety (Panic Disorder, With or Without Agoraphobia, and Generalised Anxiety Disorder) in Adults in Primary, Secondary and Community Care.* Available from: http://www.nice.org.uk/pdf/CG022NICEguideline. pdf [Accessed 8 August 2007]

NICE (2004b) *Guidance on the Use of Zaleplon, Zolpidem and Zopiclone for the Short-Term Management of Insomnia.* Available from: http://www.nice.org.uk/pdf/ TA077fullguidance.pdf [Accessed 14 August 2007]

NICE (2007) *NICE Clinical Guideline 22 Anxiety Management of Anxiety (Panic Disorder, With or Without Agoraphobia, and Generalised Anxiety Disorder) in Adults in Primary, Secondary and Community Care.* Draft for consideration. Available from: http://guidance.nice.org.uk/page.aspx?o=397856 [Accessed 9 August 2007]

Ohayon MM, Carskadon MA, Guilleminault C, Vitiello MV (2004) Meta analysis of quantitative sleep parameters from childhood to old age in healthy individuals: Developing normative sleep values across the human lifespan. *Sleep* **27**: 1255–73

Ohkuma S, Katsura M, Tsujimura A (2001) Alterations in cerebral diazepam binding inhibitor expression in drug dependence. A possible biochemical alteration common to drug dependence. *Life Sci* **68**(111): 215–2

Perna G, Bertani A, Caldirola D, Smeraldi E, Bellodi L (2001) A comparison of citalopram and paroxetine in the treatment of panic disorder: A randomized, single-blind study.

Pharmacopsychiatry **34**(3): 84–90

Pomara N, Willoughby LM, Sidtis JJ, Cooper TB, Greenblatt DJ (2005) Cortisol response to diazepam: Its relationship to age, dose, duration of treatment, and presence of generalized anxiety disorder. *Psychopharmacol* **178**(1): 1–8

Rickels K, DeMartinis N, Aufdembrinke B (2000) A double-blind, placebo-controlled trial of abecarnil and diazepam in the treatment of patients with generalized anxiety disorder. *J Clinical Psychopharmacol* **20**(1): 12–8

Rickels K, Schweizer E, DeMartinis N, Mandos L, Mercer C (1997) Gepirone and diazepam in generalized anxiety disorder: A placebo-controlled trial. *J Clin Psychopharmacol* **17**(4): 272–7

Robins LN, Regier DA (1991) Psychiatric Disorders in America. New York: Macmillan

Roehrs T, Roth T (2004) Sleep disorders. An overview. *Clin Cornerstone* **6**(Suppl 1C): S6–16

Roth T (2001) New developments for treating sleep disorders. *J Clin Psychiatry* **62**(Suppl 10): 3–4

Rynn MA, Riddle MA, Yeung PP, Kunz NR (2007) Efficacy and safety of extended-release venlafaxine in the treatment of generalized anxiety disorder in children and adolescents: Two placebo-controlled trials. *Amer J Psychiatry* **164**(2): 290–300

Salzman C (2006) Older drugs to treat anxiety and disordered sleep. *Primary Psychiatry* **13**(12): 59–64

Scottish Executive (2006) *Rights Relationships and Recovery*. Available from: http://www.scotland.gov.uk/Resource/Doc/112046/0027278.pdf [Accessed 14 December 2006]

Shear KM, Bilt JV, Rucci P, Endicott J, Lydiard B, Otto MW, Pollack MH, Chandler L, Williams J, Ali A, Frank DM (2001) Reliability and validity of a structured interview guide for the Hamilton Anxiety Rating Scale (SIGH-A). *Depression and Anxiety* **13**(4): 166–78

Sheehan DV (1986) *The Anxiety Disease*. New York: Bantam Books

Sheehan DV, Burnham DB, Iyengar MK, Perera P, Paxil CR (Panic Disorder Study Group) (2005) Efficacy and tolerability of controlled-release paroxetine in the treatment of panic disorder. *J Clin Psychiatry* **66**(1): 34–40

Shorter E (1997) *A History of Psychiatry; From the Era of the Asylum to the Age of Prozac*. New York: John Wiley and Sons

Somers J, Goldner EM, Waraich P, Hsu L (2006) Prevalence and incidence studies of anxiety disorders: A systematic review of the literature. *Can J Psychiatry* **51**: 100–13

Starcevic V (2006) Commentary on review: Worldwide lifetime prevalence of anxiety disorders is 16.6%, with considerable heterogeneity between studies. *Evidence-Based Mental Health* **9**: 115

Stein D (2002) Comorbidity in generalised anxiety disorder: Impact and implications. *J Clin Psychiatry* **62**: 29–34

Stone MH (1997) *Healing the Mind; A History of Psychiatry from Antiquity to the Present*. New York: WW Norton and Co

Streltzer J, Jonansen L (2006) Prescription drug dependence and evolving beliefs about chronic pain management. *Am J Psychiatry* **163**:594–8

Tanaka H, Taira K, Arakawa M, Toguti H, Urasaki C, Yamamoto Y, Uezu E, Hori T, Shirakawa S (2001) Effects of short nap and exercise on elderly people having difficulty in sleeping. *Psychiatry Clin Neurosci* **55**(3): 173–4

Uhlenhuth EH, Balter MB, Ban TA (1999) International study of expert judgment on therapeutic use of benzodiazepines and other psychotherapeutic medications: IV. Therapeutic dose dependence and abuse liability of benzodiazepines in the long-term treatment of anxiety disorders. *J Clin Psychopharmacol* **19**(6, Suppl 2): 23S–29S.

Vinarová E, Vinar O, Štika L (1982) Diazepam and drug dependence. *Activitas Nervosa Superior* **24**(4): 261–2

Vorma H, Naukkarinen H, Sarna S, Kuoppasalmi K (2005) Predictors of benzodiazepine discontinuation in subjects manifesting complicated dependence. *Substance Use and Misuse* **40**: 499–510

WHO (2007) *ICD-10 Chapter V. Mental and Behavioural Disorders (F00-F99)*. Available from: http://www.who.int/classifications/apps/icd/icd10online/ [Accessed 15 August 2007]

Winton WM (1987) Do introductory textbooks present the Yerkes-Dodson Law correctly? *Amer Psychologist* **42**(2): 202–3

CHAPTER 7

Safety

Introduction

Safe prescribing of the drugs presented in this book requires engagement with all the issues raised. Safe prescribing for more complex conditions or in more complex combinations requires a deep understanding of clinical psychopharmacology not presented here. It also requires extensive clinical experience. This book offers enough information for clinicians to start practising within their sphere of clinical competence. In other words, the requisite clinical experience needs to start somewhere. There is evidence to suggest that prescribing becomes less daunting with experience, in that many anxieties expressed by newly qualified prescribers are not experienced by the same prescribers after a year of prescribing practice (Latter et al, 2007a). However there is also evidence that the wider clinical environment remains ambivalent about mental health nurse prescribing (Scottish Executive, 2006; Department of Health, 2006a; Barker, 2006). Many remain convinced prescribing is not the right thing for mental health nurses to do.

This final chapter takes a last look at some of these issues which continue to bubble under the surface of the non-medical prescribing agenda. It will specifically criticise some of the enduring arguments opposing mental health nurse prescribing. The chapter starts by summarising common concerns raised by opponents of prescribing in mental health nursing. The scene is then set for a contextual examination of these positions. By synthesising material discussed in earlier chapters a coherent analysis is presented of two apparently enduring and specific criticisms of mental health nurse prescribing:

- Nurses should not prescribe because they should be doing something else.
- Nurses do not need to prescribe.

It is argued that these positions are misguided and evidence is offered to support an alternative.

The chapter then focuses on governance issues which all agree must be addressed for safe prescribing practice. This is done by examining the evidence regarding nurse prescribing safety in general. It is concluded from this that the framework to prescribe safely is now specific and coherent. It just needs to be followed and applied.

The chapter finishes by outlining many of the areas the book has necessarily not covered. Integrated throughout is emerging primary evidence regarding the efficacy of mental health nurse prescribing in practice.

Opposition to mental health nurse prescribing

None of the issues raised throughout this book has straightforward conclusions, and most are emotive. Combining them only adds to complexity and consequently impacts further on safety. For example the concept of schizophrenia generates accusations of oppression and misunderstanding of the beauty and uniqueness of experience (Shean, 2004). Depression raises serious questions of the profits to be made out of the medicalisation of unhappiness (Healy, 2002), and anxiety provokes anxiety (Kierkegaard, 1980). Combinations of these disorders become exponentially problematic. No other branch of care elicits these responses. Diabetes, Parkinson's disease, cancer, stroke and heart failure are all massive public health issues, yet pharmacological intervention can take place against a backdrop of public and professional support.

The only time the public gets visibly stirred is when demonstrably effective drugs are withheld on the basis of cost. Non-mental health nurse specialists can prescribe complex medication regimes for medical conditions without encountering the question of whether they should. Prescribing is therefore a logical extension of the general nurse and allied health professional role. Not so mental health nursing and this is why mental health nurse prescribing is unique. Mental health nurses not only have to understand the finer aspects of psychopharmacology but also explore the recipients' view of their illness in unmatched detail in order to promote recovery-based concordance. The language accompanying these discussions is much more complex than the language of purely physical ill health.

For example, consider the concept of panic disorder. The fact that imipramine was successful in treating various symptoms of anxiety led these symptoms to be grouped together under a new classification (panic disorder). This classification did not exist before a drug was found to cure it. Again, this is clearly not so with aetiologically distinct medical disorders such as stroke and cancer. Imipramine is still one of the most widely prescribed drugs for panic disorder. Cynics have an easy target here as the generation of new markets for drug companies goes hand in hand with instant medical legitimacy, which in turn is justified by the efficacy of the drug treatment.

However, this perspective ignores the most salient aspect. That is, medication brings relief to individuals in distress. In this example, imipramine brings relief to people suffering from panic disorder. Should they be denied the opportunity to feel better because the concept of panic disorder is logically dependent on itself? It would be difficult to argue this from a purely pragmatic position, and as has been seen, mental health nurses are pragmatic.

Nurses should not prescribe

However, despite this pragmatic outlook, a main area of contention remains that prescribing does not sit conceptually with current concepts of mental health nursing (Barker, 2006). The argument persists that:

- Prescribing is not what mental health nurses should be doing, because
- They should be doing something else.

    These issues will be discussed in turn.

Prescribing is not what mental health nurses should be doing

The fact that prescribing does not easily correlate with the philosophy of recovery can be illustrated with an examination of the language used to define prescribing and recovery. That is, the language of prescribing does not correlate with the language of mental health nursing if mental health nursing is defined purely in terms of a recovery model. For example, prescribing decisions are based on diagnoses. Mental health nursing decisions are based on negotiations. In advocating the person-centred recovery approach (Barker, 2002) inherent in the latest reviews of mental health nursing in Scotland (Scottish Executive, 2006) and England (Department of Health, 2006b) mental health nursing language is deliberately distancing itself from the language of prescribing. This is further clouded by the fact that mental health diagnostic language is in itself unclear, and prescribing concordance is described in terms of negotiation, thereby reinforcing the illusion that the language of mental health nursing is very similar to the language of prescribing.

The first point about diagnostic language has already been discussed. That is, diagnostic language has been widely criticised for its ambiguity (Kutchins and Kirk, 1997). Words such as 'more', 'change ' and 'loss' are widely employed to describe categories which are subject to different interpretations. The language of mental health diagnostics is therefore unclear. Consequently there is no guarantee that one person's description of the symptoms of depression will be the same as another person's interpretation of that description (Keller, 1995).

The second point seems paradoxically to address the first. That is, if the language of mental illness is unclear then perhaps a clearer picture can be achieved through negotiation. Through negotiation an individual view of mental illness can be explored with a professional in order to agree jointly on what is most suitable for that individual. However, although this is clearly what is meant by concordance within the spirit of the recovery model (Scottish Executive, 2006), this is not what prescribing concordance means in practice, hence the paradox.

That is, concordance is currently seen as the best way of managing medication (Weiss and Britten, 2003; Medicines Partnership, 2003; Latter et al, 2007b). The term literally means 'together-heart' and suggests complete agreement on a contract. This renders the concepts of non-compliance and non-adherence nonsensical as there should be no problems complying or adhering to a regimen you personally generated and agreed. If someone does not adhere to a regimen that arose from a concordant discussion then it is the discussion that was at fault, not the 'non-adherer'.

The problem is that prescribing concordance is professionally directed and follows consultation and diagnostic guidelines as described throughout this section. Certainly the patients' views are sought and respected but only to the end of prescribing adherence (Cribb and Barber, 2005). A prescription is an instruction that surely alludes to an unequal (non-concordant) relationship. A patient has to be told about the script and given directions. It could certainly be argued that implicitly, if not explicitly, the patient and the prescriber therefore come to an agreement, a concord (Snowden, 2008). It is clear, however, that this justification is tautological. That is, if concordance can be made into an all encompassing good it loses coherence as a concept and therefore cannot be tested empirically.

For example, Latter et al (2000) studied mental health nurses managing medication. They found the nurses were quite happy to go along with their patients' beliefs about medication, even to the extent that they colluded with their hallucinations as long as the end result was that people took their medication. When patients' beliefs suggested they would not be taking their medication nurses tried to amend these beliefs. A more recent study by Latter et al (2007b) further confirmed that nurses were not as good at practising concordance as they thought they were. This may well be because it is not possible (Cribb and Barber, 2005; Snowden, 2008). In other words the patient does not really control this discussion at all.

This is against the spirit of recovery and should therefore be rejected if equality cannot be realistically facilitated or approached. An unequal specialist relationship subsumes paternalism and compliance, which is ultimately about following instructions. One apparently reasonable conclusion to this is that mental health nurses may simply reject the (more difficult) task of accurately describing signs and symptoms for the genuinely concordant humanistic approach favoured by the language of the recovery model. Prescribing is

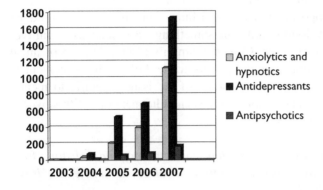

Figure 7.1.
Psychotropic drugs
prescribed by
nurses in Scotland
(Information and
Statistics Division,
2007).

conceptually inconsistent with the recovery model and therefore not what mental health nurses should be doing.

However, this argument rests on a clear concept of what a mental health nurse should be doing. As has been demonstrated in *Chapter 3* this concept does not exist in the pure form necessary to reject prescribing from a philosophical perspective. Consider Hopton's view in *Chapter 2*. He bemoans the lack of a coherent philosophy of mental health nursing but does not provide one. The reality is that philosophical purity has never gone hand in hand with mental health nursing and is highly unlikely to in the future. There is no rational argument which suggests the ability to apply up-to-date knowledge of diagnostics and psychopharmacology opposes the principle of recovery in practice. It cannot. A total of 92% of people with mental health needs took prescribed medication in 2006 (Healthcare Commission, 2007) and 91% of mental health inpatients take two or more drugs. Therefore disengagement with it is not currently an option. Barker's (2006) main opposition is to pharmacological intervention generally and therefore his opposition to nurse prescribing is secondary to this. This is a different argument.

As a further complication it is not just nurses and patients who are involved in this debate. Doctors, politicians, economists, administrators, regulators and private business also have vested interests in prescribing, which in many cases do not align with one another. As a consequence, the argument that nurses should not prescribe is ultimately just a personal view, completely dependent on a personal view of what a nurse does. Bemoaning the fact that nurses can now prescribe is to disengage with reality (*Figure 7.1*).

Mental health nurses should be doing something else

The problem with the opinion that nurses should be doing something else is that it is also based on the faulty logic as described above. However, it is worth examining the argument in itself, as it is often presented as a discrete argument opposing nurse prescribing. That is, nurses should be concentrating on developing skills in something else, such as cognitive-behaviour therapy for example. Consider Smith's (2007) defence of nurse prescribing in the general practitioner magazine *Pulse*. This statement is simply used as a vehicle to discuss some of the issues specific to mental health nurse prescribing and is not meant as an indictment of Smith's overall views, which are clearly thoughtful:

> *I would prefer that we focus on what makes nursing more distinct from medicine and improves care for the users involved, not a role that draws us nearer the medical model.*

This raises most of the issues common to the debate that mental health nurses should be doing something other than prescribing. They are that nurses somehow need to make themselves distinct, that nurse prescribing is not improving care for users and that the medical model is somehow inherently worth drawing away from. The speculation that nurse prescribing is not improving care for users will be examined through the clinical evidence, but what of the other two points?

The drive to make mental health nursing distinct and unique is defensive. Nottingham (2006) makes a strong case to suggest that the political activities of established professions tend to be defensive while those of insecure professions tend to be promotional. In other words in making a defensive stance the message delivered is that of an established profession. At a more overt level however, the question is more basic: are mental health nurses under any particularly new threat? It would appear that since the 1959 Mental Health Act that the role has been constantly challenged by social workers, psychologists, occupational therapists and general nurses as it becomes less custodial. It is currently threatened by substantial cuts in preregistration training numbers in Scotland, probably as a long-term strategic move towards post-registration specialisation in mental health nursing. However, long-term strategic plans come and go, and as *Chapter 3* showed mental health nurses have a long history of development despite such disconnected political decisions. Leaving aside the issue of whether or not they would want to, does anybody else actually have the skills to do the job of a mental health nurse?

I recently spent five years working as a community psychiatric nurse in an older adult community mental health team in Greenock. In that time we implemented single shared assessment, a process of joint working between health and social care (Joint Future Group, 2000). Role anxieties were expressed by all and it appeared everybody felt equally threatened by the process. There appeared to be no desire for takeovers at the operational level. This evidence is purely anecdotal and should be treated as such. Nevertheless, there is evidence that occupational therapists find role clarity difficult within mental health teams (Harrison, 2005) and some feel particularly threatened (Cohen, 2003). Parallels can be drawn with any new merger or partnership. The balance between maintaining individual identity and obtaining the benefits of partnership can be seen in the European Union for example. It is difficult, but most wish to engage in the process without usurping one another. I would argue that a genuine defence of mental health nursing will only be necessary in the presence of a real alternative to it, and as yet nothing has transpired. This is not stated to engender complacency but to give thought to mental health services without mental health nurses. It is not currently realistic. Mental health nursing is therefore distinct and unique.

This leads on to Smith's other point that the medical model somehow needs to be avoided. Why? Would the medical model be so disparaged if it were better understood? The evidence for the effectiveness of the medical model is overwhelming. Ignoring it by rejecting it without question is naive. Offering an alternative is undoubtedly the best course of action to support a wider choice for patients, but this does not have to include artificial delineation between ideologies. A genuine alternative to the medical model based on informed critique of its methodology is highly credible, but only possible through direct engagement with it. The same is surely true of prescribing. Put the other way around, in what way would a deeper knowledge of prescribing make a mental health nurse worse?

Smith's statement alludes to a possible answer. That is, one interpretation of the theme of Smith's statement is that if nurses spend time on learning how to prescribe then it will change them into prescribers first and foremost. The nurse will favour prescribing over other therapeutic options. Again this begs the question: Would it? Bradley et al (2007) suggest not. People need multi-skilled clinicians (Scottish Executive, 2006), so surely the more skills the better? Why reject an opportunity to become more skilled for fear it may teach the wrong skills? This does not make sense. It relies on an understanding of learning devoid of critical analysis and defends a concept of nursing which does not exist.

The more rational argument is that if nurses have any time at all to focus on further education then perhaps they should focus on specific skills relevant to their individual needs. This is absolutely fair and should be based on population as well as individual need. The argument that this should not include nurse prescribing is not logical. Mental health nurses have been historically creative with resources as seen in *Section 1*. Using all available opportunities to enhance patient care is not only sensible; it is the right thing to do.

Nurses do not need to prescribe

Of probably greater practical significance to the immediate uptake of prescribing is the opinion that nurses do not need to prescribe. This is a widely held view, certainly among some nurse directors. This opinion probably underpinned Watterson et al's (in press) finding that the strategic development of nurse prescribing in Scotland was patchy. They found 'a lack of coherent, integrated and stable board-level infrastructure for prescribers and, in some instances, there have been slow responses of boards to the prescribing agenda.' (Scottish Government, 2007: 5).

Some of the thinking behind this is nicely illustrated by Ramsden (2005) who questions the need to extend prescribing at all when the skill mix already exists to provide easier alternatives. The argument follows that there is already provision to manage emergency care, and that therefore the status quo is fine. This argument therefore depends very heavily on the assumption that the status quo is in fact fine. This is quite clearly not the case. Recent reviews of health services in Scotland (Joint Futures Group, 2000; Scottish Executive, 2005) and England (NHS Employers, 2007) advocate radical change based on the assumption that existing services cannot cope with the predicted changing demands on it.

Intermediate care and single shared assessment have already emerged as solutions to these predicted changes in demand. *Our NHS, Our Future* adds a primary care focus, particularly regarding equitable access to general practitioner services. What these solutions have in common is that they are proactive and encourage 'fairer, more personalised and more effective' (NHS Employers, 2007) systems. What this has meant in practice so far is increased responsibility for a wider group of multi-disciplinary professionals. Wider prescribing rights are coherent with this way of thinking. Nurses do need to prescribe.

Nurses prescribing is unsafe

Even if it is accepted that a greater number of competent prescribers can only be good, anxiety remains about just how competent these new prescribers are likely to be. Each recent extension of prescribing powers has been accompanied by cautionary and inflammatory comments from the medical press. One of the more recent soundbites has been that nurses' diagnostic skills were 'pathetically poor' (Hoey, 2007). This is the article Smith (2007) was responding to above. The article was entitled *Huge explosion in nurse prescribing*, which would not have been out of place in the tabloid press. The poll which accompanied this issue of *Pulse* suggested 60% of readers believed nurses were prescribing beyond their competence. There was no suggestion of how many people this sample entailed. It would have been interesting to see a comparative poll of how many readers thought doctors were prescribing beyond their competence. There appears to be an unspoken assumption that their prescribing activity is beyond reproach. Yet in an extremely candid letter to the *British Medical Journal* general practitioner Masters (2003) admitted to reading the *British National Formulary* on 'quite a few occasions' in order to discover the clinical indication of some of the medicines he was responsible for prescribing. It would be useful to know how familiar this is to all prescribers. Perhaps a more rational debate would follow.

In the longer term the evidence will speak for itself. However, there is a good chance that opinions such as Hoey's will survive in the short-term. For example just before the consultation which resulted in full prescribing rights for non-medical practitioners, a flurry of opinion appeared in the *British Medical Journal*. Under the heading 'absolute idiocy' many opinions were voiced in opposition to nurse prescribing, some more reasonable than others. Montgomery (2005) for example did not believe that the patient benefit had been demonstrated, and Sumner (2005) felt the Government was deliberately attacking medical authority without considering the wider clinical consequences of removing this power. There was opinion that the Government position was financially and politically driven given that non-medical prescribing is cheaper than medical prescribing and nurses are allegedly easier to dictate to (Blakemore-Brown, 2005). Sumner (2005) illustrated the level of emotion felt by some by making a metaphorical comparison to the UK occupation of Iraq, whereby the Government destroy a system (general practice in Sumner's view) with little thought to what goes in its place.

Shaw (2007) writes an interesting article on the role of the media in this debate and concludes unsurprisingly that the media favour the medical perspective. This is seen as an artefact of tradition (Ragan et al, 1995):

Particularly in Western medicine, patients have been socialised to view their medical caregivers as omniscient dispensers of both medication and medical wisdom.

Presumably Shaw's point is that the media are as well trained as Ragan's patients. However not all views of non-medical prescribing have been negative. Many welcomed the initiative (Avery and Pringle, 2005), and Portman (2005) even took the alternative argument to its logical end point, eliminating all health professionals from the prescribing process. As can be seen from *Chapter 3* this position has been the case throughout the vast majority of history, and is not particularly radical when viewed in this context. What all these disparate views arguably have in common however is a genuine concern for patient safety and hence appropriate governance. Sharma (2005) sums this up, believing that it does not matter who is prescribing as long as he or she is accountable and therefore safe. The next section of this chapter therefore discusses issue of governance in prescribing.

Evidence for the safety of nurse prescribing

The issue of safety is clearly uppermost on the Government agenda. When nurse prescribing was expanded in May 2006 the following stated aims accompanied the venture (Department of Health, 2006b: 4):

- Improve patient care without compromising patient safety.
- Make it easier for patients to get the medicines they need.
- Increase patient choice in accessing medicines.
- Make better use of the skills of health professionals.
- Contribute to the introduction of more flexible team working across the NHS.

A review carried out by the University of Stirling (Watterson et al, in press) has found that many of these claims have been borne out. It found that (Scottish Government 2007: 4):

- The public had considerable confidence in nurse prescribing.
- Nurse prescribers believed their prescribing roles made them more effective nurses.
- General practitioners' workloads had been reduced as a result of nurse prescribing.
- Nurses were regarded as 'safe prescribers' by patients and professionals.

It is important to acknowledge that the evidence presented by Watterson et al relates to nurse prescribing as a whole. I acknowledge that this may be considered as inconsistent given that the vast majority of this book has sought to clarify why prescribing is different for mental health nurses. However, the issue of safety is a cross-disciplinary one. Registered mental nurses apply and follow the same code of conduct as all other UK registered nurses and are subject to the same concerns regarding clinical governance. I recently held a workshop at a conference on nurse prescribing at Hampden, Glasgow, organised by NHS Greater Glasgow and Clyde (Snowden, 2007). One of the questions I asked participants was how we could ensure the safety of mental health nurse prescribing. Most respondents felt the question irrelevant to the workshop. That is, mental health nurse prescribing should be subject to the same systems of scrutiny and support as other methods of prescribing. The following evidence therefore represents this view.

Literature on issues of safety in nurse prescribing

Bradley et al (2007) conducted a small qualitative study on how newly qualified prescribers describe and rate their prescribing. Their purpose was to ascertain the conditions which foster the highest levels of safety, and how to support nurse prescribers in practice. Thirty-one nurses completed an in depth interview and all were acutely aware of the responsibility prescribing entails. Although a predictor of safe prescribing the authors note that this caution may underpin the finding that eight of them had not prescribed since qualifying. Safety issues therefore need to be balanced with competence, and adequate support is vital. For example the nurses in this study felt that multidisciplinary working was vital to supporting practice. This study therefore supports the idea that nurse prescribing will contribute to more flexible team working (Department of Health, 2006a: 4), and further states that the nurses in this study were very cautious when it came to prescribing, and were therefore highly unlikely to prescribe beyond their competence. These nurses felt an enhanced sense of responsibility and accountability. There is still a fear that with experience nurse prescribers might become over confident and start making mistakes (Mayo and Duncan, 2004), but this has not been evidenced so far. As mentioned above it is unlikely this fear will dissipate, as it is unrelated to the evidence, but is rather an exemplar of how anxiety surrounding extended prescribing is likely to evolve as independent prescribing itself evolves.

In an older but highly relevant article Brooks et al (2001) asked what patients thought of nurse prescribing. Although the study could be criticised for its sampling methods (respondents were 'chosen' by their prescribing nurses) it asks a fundamental question of the most important group of people. Brooks et al concluded that the nurse prescribers were meeting the needs of their patients through enhancement of the nurse–patient relationship and the convenience of prescribing. Concerns expressed by patients appeared to reflect Government concerns of the time, particularly in regard to public safety and the competence of the prescribers.

Competence appears as a safety concern in many studies. A major anxiety expressed by practically all nurses on starting the prescribing course was their inadequate knowledge of pharmacology (Bradley et al, 2006). Some lecturers believed this may actually be a more general expression of their lack of confidence and competence to prescribe at this stage. In the West Midlands, mental health nurse prescribers requested a 'top up' course on neuropharmacology consisting of an additional module. A module was developed and proved very successful.

Latter et al (2007a) also commented that pharmacology was the area most likely to cause concern for nurses in the early literature on the safety of nurse prescribing. However, there is emerging evidence that this may be offset post-qualification. Latter et al (ibid: 694) found that the vast majority (>95%) of prescribers (N = 246) who had been qualified between 6 and 12 months felt competent, confident and up to date with their pharmacology knowledge. This study is the first national survey of the education and professional development experiences of independent nurse prescribers in England. The findings would suggest that the lecturers' point raised in Bradley et al's study appears supported.

Courtenay et al (2006) conducted a study of 868 independent nurse prescribers to ascertain their prescribing practice and confidence to educate and assess future prescribing students. They concluded that more highly qualified nurses and those who had access to continuing professional development were statistically more likely to feel confident to adopt this role.

These three studies focused on nurse prescribing training and broadly found it of appropriate quality and content. While they all acknowledge limitations there is evidence the courses are producing safe practitioners.

With specific regard to nurse prescribing being unsafe, the vast majority of the evidence so far negates this. Reasons for this are likely to be many. For example, one line of reasoning suggests that the first nurses qualified to prescribe are likely to be more senior, more experienced and more cautious. This is in fact the case. However using this as a rationale to oppose the expansion of nurse prescribing merely perpetuates the fear that nurse prescribing may be dangerous at some hypothetical point in the future, when subsequently trained nurse prescribers would not be as good as they are now. This is merely free floating anxiety. Nurse prescribing has been demonstrated to be safe so far.

This would suggest that systems of support and evaluation are effective. In other words the rationale for past and present safe nurse prescribing has been the combination of working within one's scope of practice and good clinical governance based on appropriate negotiation within one's employing authority (*Drug and Therapeutics Bulletin*, 2006). The scope of competence was discussed in detail at the end of *Section 1*. Therefore it is worth looking at practical aspects of governance which entail appropriate negotiation within one's employing authority.

Clinical governance

Negotiation with one's employing authority in this instance means clarifying what the employer will permit you to do. That is, it is unlikely your employer will support any activity not covered by policy. Nurse prescribing is a policy 'grey area' and prescribers are advised by the Nursing and Midwifery Council to join a nursing union to help support them should any malpractice allegation be raised. That is, nurse prescribing malpractice has not yet been tested in the courts and so employers are naturally wary of incurring massive compensation claims.

However, in a way this is just another level of insurance. Most organisations have local governance policies which include standard operating procedures for non-medical prescribing. By way of illustration the standard operating procedure for non-medical prescribing for NHS Greater Glasgow and Clyde is included in full in the appendix.

The Nursing and Midwifery Council (2006) standards for nurse prescribers indicate the qualifications required before an applicant can be accepted on the course. One of the major prerequisites is competence in history taking, diagnosis and clinical assessment. It is hoped this book has provided the framework for competence with regard to mental health nurse prescribers.

Following qualification continuing professional development needs to be formally addressed. This can be through clinical supervision, further education or specific support forums. It is the prescriber's responsibility to access this support and the employers to provide it. These governance structures are mandatory (Scottish Executive Health Department, 2006: 19).

A systematic way to approach continuing professional development is through examining and reflecting on the competencies as specified by the Nursing and Midwifery Council (2006). The Nursing and Midwifery Council competencies are expected of all nurse prescribers. Therefore in addressing these competencies both format and structure relate to local and national policy guidelines as well as professional ones. The content can and should be driven by individual clinical need. For example, consider some of the competencies illustrated in *Box 7.1*. Examining any one of these areas would be appropriate. Examining the area you find most difficult in an environment where this examination is structured and encouraged is good clinical governance.

It is important to remember that it is the signature on the prescription that matters in law (Fellows, 1999). The signature implies that the prescriber understands what the prescribed drug is likely to do and what side effects and adverse reactions it may cause. This potentially litigious bottom line will be less daunting for those nurses prescribing against a background of supportive policy. This is what 'appropriate negotiation within one's employing authority' means. It is important to ensure that these systems are in place.

In summary, there has now been enough exploration of dead ends to inform a coherent action plan for nurse prescribing. There should be no more

---

Box 7.1. Principle areas, knowledge, skills and competencies required to underpin prescribing practice (Nursing and Midwifery Council, 2006)

- Able to work with patients/clients as partners in treatment
- Able to assess when to prescribe or make appropriate referral
- Able to refer back to a medical practitioner when appropriate
- Aware of policies that have an impact on public health and influence prescribing practice
- Able to articulate the boundaries of prescribing practice in relation to the duty of care to patients/clients and society
- Able to apply the principles of accountability to prescribing practice
- Able to account for the cost and effects of prescribing practice
- Regularly reviews evidence behind therapeutic strategies
- Able to assess risk to the public of inappropriate use of prescribed substances
- Understand where and how to access and use patient/client records
- Able to write and maintain coherent records of prescribing practice
- Able to communicate effectively with patients/clients and professional colleagues
- Able to advise and guide peers in the practice of prescribing

---

jumping through hoops (Kaplan and Brown, 2007) but rather synthesis of all these experiences to inform clear leadership. For example, clear guidelines already exist for admission to the prescribing course at all higher education institutes offering non-medical prescribing in Scotland. These simply need to be applied.

Speculation

In looking to the future, more advanced prescribing is a logical next step for mental health nurses. For example some trials appear to support the combination of fluoxetine and olanzapine in treatment resistant depression (Thase et al, 2007; Corya et al, 2006), and this combination has also been tried in generalised anxiety disorder (Pollack et al, 2006). A single pill is available (Stahl, 2006: 82) for treatment of bipolar depression, psychotic depression and treatment resistant unipolar depression. It could be the action at 5-HT2C receptors which underpins this finding as both exert an effect here. In a separate combination study Rampello et al (2004) found a combination of citalopram and amitryptyline effective in relieving chronic tension headache, often associated with depression, where monotherapy had failed. However, engaging with advanced decisions like these is likely to be a long way off for the majority of mental health nurses. Many remain unconvinced it is the right thing to do.

The history of psychopharmacology, prescribing and mental health nursing has converged for the first time. This is a unique opportunity which other professions will happily take if mental health nurses do not. For example why should a pharmacist with a special interest in mental health not prescribe the drugs described in this book? Why should a district nurse or physiotherapist not feel capable of it? If their diagnoses are clear and their treatment safe what more could a mental health nurse add? To finish off I shall conclude that paradoxically all the criticism just rejected in relation to why mental health nurses should not prescribe becomes a major factor underpinning why they should.

Operationalising mental health nurse prescribing has proved difficult, as there are currently not many successful examples of practice. They are developing though, and innovative areas exist. In Lanarkshire mental health nurses work in primary care in a way similar to that illustrated in the flowchart in *Chapter 5*. A well-evaluated pilot has just been completed in the addictions services in NHS Greater Glasgow and Clyde. In Staffordshire the local trust has actively and strategically supported mental health nurse prescribing. There is early evidence that care standards have improved as a result (Nolan, 2007, personal communication). There have been 50% fewer errors since the introduction of nurse prescribing. Getting the right medicine to the right patient in the right way has improved. This is thought to be because:

- More attention is given to prescribing and medicines generally within the trust.
- More nurses are concerned about administration.
- Increased accountability is devolved to nurses.
- Service users are encouraged to ask more questions.

There are therefore clear secondary gains to be had from a workforce more engaged with medication management in general. For example, given that the process of drug discovery for mental illness relies on identifying mood-altering side-effects, new classes of psychoactive compounds are unlikely to be discovered outside the clinical setting. It is therefore essential to monitor all effects systematically. In 1990, Gelenberg noted that a schizophrenic patient responded dramatically to famotidine, a histamine H2 receptor antagonist that the patient was receiving as treatment for a peptic ulcer. Nurses should get more involved in this empiricism by recording their observations in yellow cards whether they are prescribers or not. The observation skills are already there, and these observations could potentially be as enlightening as Gelenberg's. Surely the most important effect is the one felt by the patient? This is what needs to be systematised, and the tools to do so are already here.

As a mental health nurse prescriber I used supplementary prescribing as it was the only option open to me at the time. This is no longer the case, but there is a security in supplementary prescribing which may be very useful not just to the novice prescriber but to other partners as well. A colleague of mine regularly changes medication for his patients in local nursing homes. He has set up clinical management plans with local supportive general practitioners and has found an enhanced working relationship has resulted. The general practitioners do not get called to the homes as often and he knows the patients probably better than the general practitioners.

Supplementary prescribing has been suggested as a 'stepping stone' to independent prescribing and there is logic and safety in this apprenticeship approach. However it is acknowledged that nursing skills must prevail as these are clearly valued by patients, and prescribing should not necessarily be seen as the solution to every ill. How can this be ensured?

I would argue that paradoxically that assurance lies in the pragmatic application of the principles of the recovery approach. Mental health nurses are trained to engage in partnership with people with mental health problems in a way no other professionals are. Now consider the conclusions of all the nurse researchers, scientists, biochemists, geneticists and psychiatrists who investigate the psychobiology of mental health in relation to the efficacy of psychotropics. They all conclude the best approach involves an individualised interconnection of biological, psychological, social and spiritual care. No one is currently better placed to deliver this approach than mental health nurses. No one is more used to the pragmatic application of these competing agendas.

Further reading

Cribb A, Barber N (2005) Unpicking the philosophical and ethical issues in medicines prescribing and taking. In *Concordance Adherence and Compliance in Medicine Taking* (Chapter 6). London: National Co-ordinating Centre for NHS Service Delivery and Organisation Research and Development.

This is an excellent discussion on the philosophical and ethical implications of the concept of concordance. In brief the authors argue that concordance is too wide a concept for the purpose of research and evaluation (p. 115). Instead they identify aspects of medication management which have demonstrable effects and can therefore be assessed, including public health and economic considerations.

References

Avery AJ, Pringle M (2005) Extending prescribing by UK nurses and pharmacists. *Brit Med J* **331**: 1154–5

Barker P (2006) Mental health nursing: The craft of the impossible? *J Psychiatric Ment Health Nursing* **13**(4): 385–7

Blakemore-Brown LC (2005) Re: Absolute Idiocy. *Brit Med J*. Available from: http://bmj. bmjjournals.com/cgi/eletters/331/7526/1154 [Accessed 31 August 2007]

Bradley E, Blackshaw C, Nolan P (2006) Nurse lecturers' observations on aspects of nurse prescribing training. *Nurse Education Today* **26**: 538–44

Bradley E, Hynam B, Nolan P (2007) Nurse prescribing. Reflections on safety in practice. *Soc Sci Med* **65**(3): 599–609

Brooks N, Otway C, Rashid C, Kilty L, Maggs C (2001) Nurse prescribing. What do patients think? *Nurs Standard* **15**(17): 33–8

Cohen ZA (2003) The Single Assessment Process: An opportunity for collaboration or a threat to the profession of occupational therapy? *Br J Occup Ther* **66**(5): 201–8

Corya SA, Perlis RH, Keck PE, Lin DY, Case MG, Williamson DJ, Tohen MF (2006) A 24-week open-label extension study of olanzapine-fluoxetine combination and olanzapine monotherapy in the treatment of bipolar depression. *J Clin Psychiatry* **67**(5): 798–806

Courtenay M, Carey C, Burke J (2006) Independent extended supplementary nurse prescribers, their prescribing practice and confidence to educate and assess prescribing students. *Nurse Education Today* **27**: 739–47

Cribb A, Barber N (2005) Unpicking the philosophical and ethical issues in medicines prescribing and taking (Chapter 6) In *Concordance Adherence and Compliance in Medicine Taking*. London: National Co-ordinating Centre for NHS Service Delivery and Organisation Research and Development

Department of Health (2006a) *From Values to Action. The Chief Nursing Officer's Review of Mental Health Nursing*. Available from: http://www.dh.gov.uk/en/ Publicationsandstatistics/Publications/PublicationsPolicyAndGuidance/DH_4133839 [Accessed 7th June 2007]

Department of Health (2006b) *Improving Patients' Access to Medicines: A Guide to Implementing Nurse and Pharmacist Independent Prescribing Within the NHS in England*. Available from: http://www.dh.gov.uk/assetRoot/04/13/37/47/04133747.pdf [Accessed 24 April 2006]

Drug and Therapeutics Bulletin (2006) Non-medical prescribing. *Drug and Therapeutics Bulletin* **44**(5): 33–7

Fellows P (1999) Nurse prescribing. The medical opinion. In Jones M (ed) *Nurse Prescribing. Politics to Practice*. London: Bailliere Tindall, RCN

Harrison D (2005) Context of change in community mental health occupational therapy: Part two. *Int J Ther Rehabil* **12**(10): 444–8

Healthcare Commission (2007) *Talking about Medicines: The Management of Medicines in Trusts Providing Mental Health Services*. London: Commission for Healthcare Audit and Inspection

Healy D (2002) *The Creation of Psychopharmacology*. Cambridge, MA: Harvard University Press

Hoey R (2007) Huge explosion in nurse prescribing. *Pulse*. Available from: http://www. pulsetoday.co.uk/story.asp?storyCode=4114218&sectioncode=23#commentForm last [Accessed 3 September 2007]

Information and Statistics Division (ISD) (2007) *Antidepressants*. Available from: http://www.isdscotland.org/isd/information-and statistics.jsp?pContentID=3671&p_ applic=CCC&p_service=Content.show& [Accessed 10 January 2008]

Joint Future Group (2000) *Report of the Joint Future Group*. Available from: http://www. scotland.gov.uk/library3/social/ccjf.pdf [Accessed 27 December 2007]

Kaplan L, Brown MA (2007) The transition of nurse practitioners to changes in prescriptive authority. *J Nurs Scholarship* **39**(2): 184–90

Keller R (1995) *Zeicentheorie: zu einer theorie semiotischen Wissens*. Tubingen und Basel, Francke Verlag

Kierkegaard S (1980) *The Concept of Anxiety. A Simple Psychologically Oriented Deliberation on the Dogmatic Issue of Hereditary Sin*. (Thomte R transl and ed) Princeton University Press, New Jersey

Kutchins H, Kirk H (1997) *Making us Crazy. DSM: The Psychiatric Bible and the Creation of Mental Disorders*. New York: Simon and Shuster

Latter S, Maben J, Myall M, Young A (2007a) Evaluating nurse prescribers' education and continuing professional development for independent prescribing practice: Findings from a national survey in England. *Nurse Education Today* **27**: 685–96

Latter S, Maben J, Myall M,Young A (2007b) Perceptions and practice of concordance in nurses' prescribing consultations: Findings from a national questionnaire survey and case studies of practice in England. *Int J Nurs Studies* **44**(1): 9–18

Latter S, Yerrell P, Rycroft-Malone J, Shaw D (2000) Nursing, medication education and the new policy agenda: The evidence base. *Int J Nursing Studies* **37**(6): 469–79

Masters NJ (2003) Compliance enhanced by drug indication on every repeat script. *Brit Med J*. Available from: http://www.bmj.com/cgi/eletters/327/7419/819 [Accessed 28 November 2007]

Mayo A, Duncan D (2004) Nurse perceptions of medication errors: What we need to know for patient safety. *J Nurs Care Quality* **19**(3): 209–17

Medicines Partnership (2003) *Project Evaluation Toolkit*. London: Medicines Partnership

Montgomery AG (2005) Absolute idiocy. *Brit Med J*. Available from: http://bmj. bmjjournals.com/cgi/eletters/331/7526/1154 [Accessed 31 August 2007]

NHS Employers (2007) *Our NHS, Our Future: Key Points*. Available from: http://www. nhsemployers.org/workforce/workforce-2979.cfm [Accessed 20 December 2007]

Nottingham C (2006) *Insecure Professionals in Theory and Practice Sixth European Social Science History Conference*. Available from: http://www2.iisg.nl/esshc/ programme9606.asp?selyear=8&pap=3308 [Accessed 4 September 2007]

Nursing and Midwifery Council (2006) *Standards of Proficiency for Nurse Prescribers Without a Specialist Practice Qualification to Prescribe from the Community Practitioner Formulary*. Available from: http://www.nmc-uk.org/aDisplayDocument. aspx?DocumentID=2477 [Accessed 27 August 2007]

Pollack MH, Simon NM, Zalta AK, Worthington JJ, Hoge EA, Mick E, Kinrys G,

Oppenheimer J (2006) Olanzapine augmentation of fluoxetine for refractory generalized anxiety disorder: A placebo controlled study. *Biol Psychiatry* **59**(3): 211–5

Portman N (2005) A useful step in the right direction. *Brit Med J*. Available from: http://bmj.bmjjournals.com/cgi/eletters/331/7526/1154 [Accessed 31 August 2007]

Ragan SI, Beck CS, White MD (1995) Educating the patient: Interactive learning in an OB-GYN context. In GH Morris, R Chenail (eds) *The Talk of the Clinic* (pp. 185–207). Hillsdale, NJ: Lawrence Erlbaum

Rampello L, Alvano A, Chiechio S, Malaguarnera M, Raffaele R, Vecchio I, Nicoletti F (2004) Evaluation of the prophylactic efficacy of amitriptyline and citalopram, alone or in combination, in patients with comorbidity of depression, migraine, and tension-type headache. *Neuropsychobiol* **50**(4): 322–8

Ramsden AR (2005) Is it really necessary? *Brit Med J*. Available from: http://bmj.bmjjournals.com/cgi/eletters/331/7526/1154 [Accessed 31 August 2007]

Scottish Executive (2005) *A Report on the Future of the NHS in Scotland*. Available from: http://www.scotland.gov.uk/Publications/2005/05/23141307/13104 [Accessed 18 December 2007]

Scottish Executive (2006) *Rights Relationships and Recovery*. Available from: http://www.scotland.gov.uk/Resource/Doc/112046/0027278.pdf [Accessed 14 December 2006]

Scottish Executive Health Department (2006) *Non-Medical Prescribing in Scotland Guidance for Nurse Independent Prescribers and for Community Practitioner Nurse Prescribers in Scotland: A Guide for Implementation*. Available from: http://www.scotland.gov.uk/Publications/2006/08/23133351/29 [Accessed 11 September 2007]

Scottish Government (2007) *Consultation on A Safe Prescription: Developing Nurse, Midwife and Allied Health Profession (NMAHP) Prescribing in NHS Scotland*. Available from: http://www.scotland.gov.uk/Publications/2007/11/08120246/18 [Accessed 18 December 2007]

Sharma R (2005) Whoever prescribes should be accountable. *Brit Med J*. Available from: http://bmj.bmjjournals.com/cgi/eletters/331/7526/1154 [Accessed 31 August 2007]

Shaw S (2007) Constructing media images of nursing: How does the media represent nurses when reporting on nurse prescribing? Do doctors dominate the discourse? One nurse observer thinks so. *Nursing New Zealand* **13**(1): 16

Shean GD (2004) *What is Schizophrenia and How Can We Fix It?* Oxford: University Press America

Smith P (2007) huge explosion in nurse prescribing – comments. *Pulse*. Available from: http://www.pulsetoday.co.uk/comments.asp?storycode=4114218 [Accessed 8 November 2007]

Snowden A (2007) Mental health prescribing in Scotland. Time for change. *Nurse Prescribing* **5**(11): 493–500

Snowden A (2008) Medication management in older adults: A critique of concordance. *Brit J Nursing* **17**(2) 114–9

Stahl S (2006) *Essential Psychopharmacology. The Prescriber's Guide: Antidepressants*. Cambridge: Cambridge University Press

Sumner KR (2005) The final death throes of general practice? *Brit Med J*. Available from: http://bmj.bmjjournals.com/cgi/eletters/331/7526/1154

Thase ME, Corya SA, Osuntokun O, Case M, Henley DB, Sanger TM, Watson SB, Dubé S (2007) A randomized, double-blind comparison of olanzapine/fluoxetine combination, olanzapine, and fluoxetine in treatment-resistant major depressive disorder. *J Clin Psychiatry* **68**(2): 224–36

Watterson A, Turner F, Boreham N, at al. (in press) *Report on the Evaluation of the Extension of Independent Nurse Prescribing in Scotland.*

Weiss M, Britten N (2003) What is concordance? *Pharmaceutical Journal* **271**(7270): 493

Appendix

Standard operating procedure for nurse/pharmacist supplementary and nurse independent prescribing

NHS Greater Glasgow and Clyde
(This document is in the process of revision)

Introduction

This standard operating procedure (SOP) sets out the process and steps required from enrolment to practice as non-medical independent and supplementary prescribers. Nursing staff should read this document in conjunction with Scottish Executive Health Department publication *Prescribing by Nurse Independent Prescribers in Scotland; A Guide for Implementation* (2006).

Background

There are clear benefits to non-medical prescribing including an improvement in patient care, and better use of health professional's and patient's time. The Higher Education Institute courses for education and training to become a prescriber, equip nurses and pharmacists with the principles of prescribing to enable them to be safe, effective and cost-efficient prescribers. Qualified nurses will be able to prescribe as supplementary and independent prescribers and pharmacists currently as supplementary prescribers.

Supplementary prescribing will continue to have a place in the care of patients, for the newly qualified prescriber and where certain drugs cannot be prescribed by the nurse independent prescriber. The clinical management plan (CMP) is the cornerstone of supplementary prescribing which is defined as: 'As a voluntary partnership between an independent prescriber (doctor/dentist) and a supplementary prescriber, to implement an agreed patient/client-specific CMP with the patient's agreement.' The working definition of independent prescribing is 'a practitioner responsible and accountable for the assessment of patients with undiagnosed or diagnosed conditions and for decisions about the clinical management required, including prescribing.'

Implementation of non-medical prescribing

Non-medical prescribing lead

Within NHS Greater Glasgow and Clyde (NHSGGC) one person has been appointed as the non-medical prescribing lead. This person will work within the Pharmacy and Prescribing Support Unit (PPSU). They will lead on the implementation of non-medical prescribing within the health board area. This will enable a single database and point of contact for all non-medical prescribers. It will provide a valuable information resource and opportunity for dissemination of information in a timely manner. All applications and registrations for non-medical prescribers will be logged through their office. The non-medical prescribing lead will work within the medicines management team to review prescribing information and provide support to non-medical prescribers.

Identifying a need for non-medical prescribers

If a patient/client group requires quicker and more efficient access to medicine, this prescribing need can be addressed by training a nurse or pharmacist to become an independent/supplementary non-medical prescriber. If a need for non-medical prescribing is identified by a nurse or pharmacist, s/he should discuss this issue with the appropriate line manager and the clinical staff responsible for the care of the patient group involved. A request for review of the service for the implementation of non-medical prescribing should be submitted to the non-medical prescribing lead at PPSU. The review will be conducted and if favourable will be approved by the non-medical prescribing sub-committee of the Area Drugs and Therapeutics Committee (ADTC).

Non-medical prescribing was piloted and found to be beneficial in the following NHSGGC areas and evidence from some of the pilot areas has shown that it is safe and effective:

- Specialist services
  - Cardiology and heart failure
  - Oncology
  - Community addictions
  - Elderly services
  - Diabetes
  - Palliative care
  - Rheumatology
  - Learning disabilities
  - Homeless services

- Sexual health
- Mental health
- Dermatology
- Neonatology
- Anti-coagulation therapy
■ Nurse and pharmacist led clinics
  - Specialist services
  - Chronic diseases
  - Polypharmacy
■ Accident and emergency
■ Practice nurses
■ Out of hours services
■ Inpatient services
  - Mental health
  - Learning disabilities
  - Palliative care
■ Prescribing management
■ Frail elderly
■ New Community Pharmacy Contract
  - Minor Ailment Scheme (MAS)
  - Chronic Medication Service (CMS)

Educational requirements

Nurses must be first level registered nurses, midwives or specialist community nurses with the ability to study at level 3 (degree level) and have at least 3 years post-registration clinical nursing experience (or part-time equivalent), with the preceding year in the clinical field in which the prescribing is to relate to, e.g. mental health. Pharmacists must be registered with the Royal Pharmaceutical Society of Great Britain (RPSGB) and have a minimum of 2 years post-registration experience. In addition, all suitable candidates must have:

■ A medical supervisor, recognised by the supporting organisation, willing to contribute to and supervise learning in practice (who has signed part 2 of the application form)
■ The support of their employer to confirm
  - Support in undertaking the prescribing programme (study leave form)
  - The need and opportunity to prescribe
  - Access to a prescribing budget
  - Assessment against competency framework within speciality area

as competent to undertake the prescribing course (signed part 4 of application form)

- Access to continuing professional development opportunities

NHS National Education Scotland (NES) is responsible for quality assuring and approving training programmes for extended and supplementary prescribing in conjunction with the respective professional bodies.

Registration of prescribing qualification within NHSGGC

Following completion of the course, the successful candidate should register with the appropriate professional body as independent and/or supplementary prescriber.

On receipt of registration, it is individuals' responsibility to register their status with the non-medical prescribing lead for NHSGGC, using the Prescribing Registration form. This form, along with a copy of their professional registration and permission to prescribe from their practice (community prescribers who use GP practices), should be sent to the non-medical prescribing lead at PPSU. Non-medical prescribers within hospitals will be sent a form confirming their status as a prescriber for delivery to the clinical pharmacy where the individual prescriber will provide a specimen signature for the clinical pharmacy records.

The prescribers' details will be maintained in a database within PPSU and made available to the ADTC on an annual basis. It may also be used to provide confirmation of prescribing authority to community pharmacists and service leads.

What can be prescribed

Independent prescribing
All prescription only medicines (POMs) for all medical conditions, with the exception of some controlled drugs which are authorised for certain list conditions, and which the nurse is competent to prescribe within his or her own area of expertise. Unlicensed medicines cannot be prescribed as a nurse independent prescriber and can only be prescribed under a CMP.

Supplementary prescribing
Supplementary prescribers prescribe in partnership with the doctor or dentist (the independent prescriber). They are able to prescribe all medicines and for the full range of medical conditions, provided they do so under the terms of a patient-specific CMP. The plan will be drawn up with the patient's agreement and following agreement between the IP and SP.

Clinical management plans

CMPs may still be an appropriate method for prescribing in some cases, e.g. where a nurse/pharmacist is newly qualified as a prescriber, or a team approach to patient/client care is clearly appropriate. Supplementary prescribing under a CMP is also appropriate where the patient's CMP includes certain controlled drugs. In such circumstances nurse prescribers should refer to Practice Standard 8 in the 2006 NMC Standards. Pharmacist prescribers should refer to RPSGB Standards and Clinical Governance Framework for Pharmacy Prescribers.

Professional responsibility and accountability

Where nurses/pharmacists are appropriately trained and qualified as independent and supplementary prescribers and prescribe with the organisation's consent and within the agreed parameters and their sphere of competence, the organisation is vicariously liable for the practitioners' actions.

It is the responsibility of the prescribers to ensure that they have professional indemnity insurance, as they deem necessary, for instance by means of a professional organisation membership.

Pharmacist's role

Pharmacy staff should keep a list of all prescribers with their specimen signatures and check prescriptions against this list. The Non-Medical Prescribing lead within PPSU will provide individual nurse and pharmacist prescribers with a form confirming their authority to prescribe to be presented to pharmacy departments and signed to provide the specimen signature. Notification of prescribers will also be sent directly to hospital pharmacies to ensure the list is correct and up to date. All community pharmacists and certain GPs are also required to have details of lost or stolen prescriptions and the method of identifying genuine prescriptions that are to be used by the non-medical prescriber for an agreed period.

Clinical governance and effectiveness

Clinical governance provides a framework for enabling non-medical prescribers to practice safely, within their competency, and in the interest of patient safety. A review of independent non-medical prescribing should be carried out as part of the overall prescribing monitoring framework as currently in place in service areas within NHSGGC, which will include monitoring of prescribing practice and cost data.

Non-medical sub-committee of the ADTC

The non-medical sub-committee of the ADTC will take a strategic view of the implementation of non-medical prescribing in NHSGGC. The sub-committee will support the non-medical prescribing lead in the implementation of non-medical prescribing, and it will regularly report to the ADTC on the numbers of staff qualified as independent and supplementary prescribers. It will be accountable to the ADTC for its activities and actions.

Record keeping

All nurses and pharmacists are required to keep contemporaneous records, which are unambiguous, accurate, comprehensive and legible. The principles underlying record keeping, for nurses, are detailed in national guidelines for record and record-keeping. Specifically in relation to prescribing, nurses should refer to NMC, Practice Standard 7.1 and 7.2, and for supplementary prescribing Practice Standard 7.3, which states that the doctor/dentist and the supplementary prescriber should have access to the same common record.

Adverse drug reaction (ADR) incident reporting

If a patient suffers a clinically significant suspected ADR to a prescribed, over-the-counter (General Sales List) or herbal medicine, the ADR should be reported. (An explanation of Yellow Card system is given in the *British National Formulary*). Prescribers should also record known sensitivities in the patient/client's notes, advise patients of possible ADRs prior to prescribing and ensure that, if an ADR incident occurs, that it is recorded on the patient/client's notes and that the incident is reported to any appropriate clinical colleagues.

Continuing professional development (CPD)

All nurses and pharmacists have a professional responsibility to maintain their competence and keep themselves abreast of clinical and professional developments. Prescribers will be expected to keep up to date with best practice in the management of conditions for which they may prescribe, and in the use of the drugs, dressings and appliances from the *British National Formulary* and/or *Scottish Drug Tariff*. Details of additional training and updating will need to be incorporated by individuals into their personal professional profile/CPD record.

Prescribers are encouraged to contact the PPSU and link into local groups whether in speciality area or geographic area, where best practice can be shared and to provide an opportunity for practitioners to reflect on prescribing practice. Registering of these groups through the PPSU is encouraged and meetings can be promoted to other prescribers through circulars to members of the prescribing database. The non-medical prescribing lead will ensure that non-medical prescribers receive up-to-date copies of the *British National Formulary* and/or *Scottish Drug Tariff.*

Communication

The non-medical prescribing lead will communicate with prescribers held on the database to inform prescribers of any legislative changes, alerts and medicine withdrawals, meetings and available updates.

A quarterly newsletter will be circulated to members of the database.

Risk management

Adverse incidents should to be reported irrespective of the prescriber through the local systems currently in place. These incidents are currently reviewed and the learning opportunities shared with the clinical community.

Prescribing in the community will be monitored through the prescription information system (PRISM) and feedback provided to prescribers either with practice reviews or through teams as appropriate.

Prescription rejections will continue to be reviewed as they currently are for all community prescribers. Individual prescribers will be notified of these rejections.

Index